Revision
and
Self-Editing
for
Publication SECOND EDITION

Revision and Self-Editing for Publication SECOND EDITION

Techniques for
Transforming
Your First Draft
Into a Novel
That Sells

James Scott Bell

WRITER'S DIGEST BOOKS

WRITER'S DIGEST BOOKS

An imprint of Penguin Random House LLC
penguinrandomhouse.com

ISBN 978-1-59963-706-8

Printed in the United States of America

Edited by Rachel Scheller
Designed by Claudean Wheeler
Cover photograph by luckylight/Fotolia.com

Dedication
To my writing friends of ChiLibris.

Table of Contents

Introduction
to the 2nd Edition

In one of my favorite movies, *The Hustler*, Paul Newman plays Fast Eddie Felson, a pool shark from Oakland who wants to be the best in the world. To do that he'll have to beat Minnesota Fats (Jackie Gleason), who hasn't lost a match in fifteen years.

At the beginning of the film Eddie does play Fats, and is winning. But he gets a little cocky and drinks a bit too much. At this point Fats's manager, Bert Gordon (played with Faustian precision by George C. Scott), tells Fats, "Stay with this kid. He's a loser."

Well, Eddie does lose, and he's back to the bottom of the heap. In a bus station he meets a woman named Sarah (Piper Laurie), who is also at the bottom. She's pretty, but obviously has had a hard time of it. She drinks. She's been abused. Yet she and Eddie forge a relationship and he moves in with her.

One day he asks her, "Do you think I'm a loser?" He tells her about Bert Gordon's remark. Sarah asks if Gordon is a "winner." Eddie says, "Well, he owns things."

"Is that what makes a winner?" Sarah asks.

Then Eddie tells her how it feels to play pool. How anything can be great, even bricklaying, if a guy knows what he's doing and can pull it off. "When I'm goin', I mean when I'm really goin', I feel like a jockey must feel. He's

1

sitting on his horse, he's got all that speed and that power underneath him, he's coming into the stretch, the pressure's on him, and he *knows*. He just *feels* when to let it go and how much. 'Cause he's got everything working for him—timing, touch. It's a great feeling, boy, it's a really great feeling when you're right and you know you're right. It's like all of a sudden I've got oil in my arm. The pool cue's part of me. You feel the roll of those balls and you don't have to look, you just know. You make shots nobody's ever made before. I can play that game the way nobody's ever played it before."

Sarah looks at him and says, "You're not a loser, Eddie, you're a winner. Some men never get to feel that way about anything."

When you write fiction, and you know what you're doing and how to pull it off, when you know what's wrong and how to fix it, it's a great feeling, boy.

Since the publication of the first edition of *Revision and Self-Editing*, I've been most gratified to have writers come up to me with their tattered, dog-eared copies and say things like, "This book has been a lifesaver for me." One writer told me it was "her bible," and that she used it with every book she wrote.

Another showed me his copy that had color-coded sticky tabs all over it. "I wouldn't write a novel without this," he said.

All of which warms those ever-loving cockles of a teacher's heart.

It's why I wrote the book. I saw a need for writers to have a comprehensive and systematic way to approach the editing and revision tasks. Most writers I knew (and I was one of them) just dove into revisions without a plan. Which is a little like a strawberry jumping into a blender.

Instead, knowing what to do and when to do it, knowing what questions to ask and when to ask them, creates a feeling of power in the writer that is invariably reflected in the finished manuscript.

And as writers, we can always go deeper.

Which is why Writer's Digest Books and I are coming out with a second edition.

In addition to the character questions asked in chapter two, I've added a chapter called "Deepening." I've found in my own writing, as well as the work of students in my workshops, that there is a perfect place between the initial read-through and the start of revisions to add layers of solid material to the book.

This is done through some of the exercises I've used in my Next Level workshops. Many of my students have told me that one or more of these exercises opened up their stories like nothing else they've done, before or after. Major character motivations and plot problems have been solved this way. New and exciting story material has popped up out of the "basement" and demanded to be noticed.

What will you do with this new material?

Like Fast Eddie says, you'll just *know*. You'll feel it, when to let it go and how much. You'll have everything working for you.

And it's a really great feeling, boy, it's a great feeling when you write and you know you're right.

On Becoming a Writer

About ten years ago, losing all rationality, I decided to take up golf.

In those first couple of years I bought books and tapes and subscribed to the magazines. I was sure with enough study and practice I'd be shooting eighty soon.

Those of you who golf are laughing now. But I wasn't laughing. I also wasn't having fun. I thought the best course might be to chuck the whole thing and take up needlepoint.

What had happened was I'd pumped my head full of techniques and tips and reminders and visuals. And I was always trying to remember every one of them as I played. You know, like the twenty-two steps to perfect putting and the thirteen most important things to remember at point of impact.

Insanity.

Just before flinging my clubs into the Dumpster, I met a golf teacher named Wally Armstrong. Wally is well known for his teaching skills, using simple household items—like brooms and coat hangers and sponges—to implant the *feel* of various aspects of the game.

If you're thinking about the swing while you're playing, Wally says, you're lost. You'll tense up. You will find yourself in a labyrinth of theory, with no way out.

But if you have the feel ingrained, you can forget about all the technical stuff and just play. Your body, trained in the feel, does its thing.

Wally was right, and I've been enjoying the game ever since. I don't shoot below eighty yet, but I have fun and don't embarrass myself.

Or rarely, that is.

Now, it seems to me that writing good fiction is a lot like playing good golf. With the same dangers, too. There is no end of books and articles teaching various aspects of the craft. But if you are trying to think of them all *as you write*, you'll tense up. You won't write, as Brenda Ueland puts it, "freely and rollickingly." Plus, it won't be any fun. You'll feel like throwing your pages in the Dumpster (okay, many writers feel this way anyway, but that's just an occupational hazard).

So what I want you to be able to do is *feel* your writing. When you sit down for a writing stint, don't think about technique. Just write. Let it flow. Later, you'll come back to it and revise. This book will show you how.

When you're not writing, keep learning the craft. Increase the storehouse of knowledge. Analyze your work with techniques in mind.

But when you're writing, write. Trust that the techniques you are learning will flow out naturally.

When they don't, you can learn to see where the problems are.

That's what self-editing and revision are all about. Learning, feeling, writing, analyzing, correcting, and making your writing better.

Over and over.

The rest of your life.

That's right. You're a *writer*, not someone who wants to write some books. You are a person of the craft, a dues-paying member of the club.

So pay your dues by doing the following:

1. READ

You can't be a great fiction writer without reading. A lot. All kinds of novels. And poetry and nonfiction.

Each time you read a book, the flow and rhythm of the writing implants itself in your brain. When it's good writing, when you respond to it, it goes in the *good* file. When it's not-so-good writing, you'll sense it and put in under *bad*.

You'll learn about plot and story construction and character building. Your storehouse will fill up and be ready for you when you're in need.

Be self-directed in your reading. In *Plot & Structure* I explained a process for learning plot so you'll begin to feel it in your marrow. Here's a brief recap:

1. Get half a dozen novels of the type you want to write.

2. Read the first book for pleasure and think about it afterward. What did you like about it?

3. Now read the second book and take some time to think about it, too.

4. Read the next four books in the same fashion.

5. Now go back to book one and, on index cards, mark each scene. Number them, then give us the setting, what the scene is about, and what, if anything, makes you want to read on.

6. Repeat this drill for all the books.

7. Beginning with any stack of cards, go through them quickly, remembering the book, giving yourself a movie in the mind.

8. Do the same with the other stacks of index cards.

What this exercise does is burn plot and structure into your mind. Keep those cards and review them periodically.

With some modification, you can do the same thing for any aspect of the fiction craft. See #4 below.

So read.

2. RECORD YOUR OBSERVATIONS

When I was first trying to figure out this writing thing, I got very excited every time I spotted something in a novel that worked. Or got a technique from a writing book that made a little lightbulb go off in my head.

Whenever I learned something, I'd jot it down. Sometimes on paper, sometimes on a napkin, whatever was handy. I still have a stack of these notes, carefully preserved in a large envelope. I look at them from time to time just to get my juices flowing again.

For example, here's one of my early notes, with the heading "READ ON TECHNIQUES!"

1. Action, peril, chase, jeopardy—then leave the scene before resolution. (See *Watchers* by Koontz, chapter one.)

2. Mention a portent, then cut to another scene. (See *The Dead Zone* by King, end of first scene.)

3. Hint—pull back.

4. The moment of decision, then leave the scene.

I still get a charge out of this. I was trying to learn how to write a novel readers couldn't put down, and these were like finding gold nuggets.

Make a habit of recording the things you learn, every time something comes through. Don't let any insight slip away.

3. ASSIMILATE

When you learn a technique from a writing book that looks promising, practice it. Write a scene that uses the technique.

Get it out of your head and onto the page.

When you do this, you're assimilating the information. It's going from information to transformation, making you into a better writer. It soaks into your memory, the way a golf technique that's *felt* soaks itself into your muscles.

You will know, absolutely, that your writing is getting better and better. It's an intoxicating feeling. As Ray Bradbury has said, stay drunk on writing so reality doesn't destroy you.

4. CONTINUE TO LEARN

Don't ever stop your growth process as a writer. Even after publication.

No, especially after publication. You want to keep publishing, and you do that by trying to make each new book a little better than the last. So improve.

In fact, be systematic about improving. Create your own "plan of attack" for strengthening your work.

Several novels into my career I stepped back and assessed where I was in my writing. I knew I was strong on plot but felt I wasn't strong enough on character. I wanted to go deeper with my story people.

So I sat down and created a plan, with these steps:

- Pick several novels with unforgettable characters.
- Locate the character sections of the best writing books on my shelf.
- Read and analyze the above over several weeks. Take notes.
- Analyze and structure the notes, and compare to my own characters.
- Create characters for my next book using the principles learned.

Even after you get to #1 on the *New York Times* best-seller list, don't stop learning. One writer I know who reached that level still went to a seminar led by a famous editor, simply because he didn't want to rest on his laurels. His level of success has increased since.

HOW TO USE THIS BOOK

In Part I: Self-Editing, we will be covering a broad range of fiction technique, with exercises—a sort of writing boot camp.

Now, whole books have been written on the subjects covered in each of the chapters. For that reason, the material here is not intended to be comprehensive. My purpose is to explain and illustrate *the most important aspects* of each, the things that must be imagined *so you don't have to think about them.*

Beginning writers will therefore find this an essential overview of the craft of novel-length fiction. It is a compendium of the items that are non-negotiable in writing a solid novel. Do these things, and the chances of your selling a novel increase enormously.

If you're a more advanced writer, you can also use this book. Think of it as a giant checklist. Use it for brushing up on certain areas, strengthening technique, rethinking an approach. Do the exercises the way you might do the morning crossword puzzle. Every little bit helps.

And all writers will benefit from Part II, which offers a systematic approach to revising the novel.

I have used both novel and film examples in this book because there is much about the elements of story that are common to both, and sometimes more people have seen the film than read the book.

My advice? Read more books and see more movies. And think about what's happening each time. That's how you get better.

Let me leave you with a credo from one of my favorite writers, the late John D. MacDonald. He was popular in the latter part of his career for the Travis McGee series. But I prefer the string of paperback originals he wrote in the 1950s. He managed to rise above the backwaters of this industry through sheer writing ability.

He was once asked what he looked for in a story, and his answer is a fitting one for all writers, in whatever genre. This is from the introduction to MacDonald's short story collection *The Good Old Stuff*:

> First, there has to be a strong sense of story. I want to be intrigued by wondering what is going to happen next. I want the people that I read about to be in difficulties—emotional, moral, spiritual, whatever, and I want to live with them while they're finding their way out of these difficulties.

Second, I want the writer to make me suspend my disbelief. ... I want to be in some other place and scene of the writer's devising.

Next, I want him to have a bit of magic in his prose style, a bit of unobtrusive poetry. I want to have words and phrases really sing. And I like an attitude of wryness, realism, the sense of inevitability. I think that writing—good writing—should be like listening to music, where you identify the themes, you see what the composer is doing with those themes, and then, just when you think you have him properly identified, and his methods identified, then he will put in a little quirk, a little twist, that will be so unexpected that you read it with a sense of glee, a sense of joy, because of its aptness, even though it may be a very dire and bloody part of the book.

So I want story, wit, music, wryness, color, and a sense of reality in what I read, and I try to get it in what I write.

Go thou and do likewise.

PART ONE

Self-Editing

. . . .

Keep working. Don't wait for inspiration.
Work inspires inspiration. Keep working.

—MICHAEL CRICHTON

CHAPTER 1

A Philosophy of Self-Editing

You may be able to write wonderful sentences. The words may sing as they ping and pong off each other.

But if that's as far as it goes, you haven't written fiction. You've written poetry. Nothing against poetry. I like it. But if you're going to write a novel, you have to know what goes into a successful full-length narrative.

Train to be your own editor. Do the exercises in this book to help you fully understand and appreciate the essentials of fiction.

As you practice, what you learn gets implanted into your writer's mind.

This is how unpublished writers become published.

There is no other way, unless you want to self-publish.

However, 99.9 percent of self-published authors need to learn how to self-edit better. If this book helps you in that regard, I will be happy. So will the people who occasionally buy self-published books.

Self-editing is the ability to *know* what makes fiction work, so when you actually write (as in a first draft) you're crafting salable fiction. You learn to be your own guide so you may, as Renni Browne and Dave King put it in *Self-Editing for Fiction Writers*, "See your manuscript the way an editor might see it—to do for yourself what a publishing house editor once might have done."

In the revision section of the book, further refinements for these topics are given as they might come up in the process of review. Revision requires a systematic approach to the whole when you have a full manuscript and have to fix it. And all manuscripts have to be fixed.

Putting it all together, by doing the self-editing exercises and writing and revising your work, you'll be operating on all cylinders. Your writing chops will sharpen, and there will be days when you'll wake up with that great feeling that you *know* what you're doing.

At the very least you will know more than you did a month or even a year before.

Never stop this process.

THE WRITING LIFE

Before we move on, let's consider a few items that recur in the writing life. These are mainly mental preparations for self-editing to keep you from deciding, a year from now, that you haven't got what it takes.

Look, if you want to be a writer, write. Don't ever stop. I mean it. Even if you can only peck out a hundred words a day (anybody can peck out a hundred words in a day—and if you say you can't then you really don't have what it takes, so quit now).

. . . .

Don't quit. It's very easy to quit during the first ten years.

—ANDRE DUBUS

Here are a few things to think about:

THE FREEZE

Once upon a time, the housekeeper for Marcel Proust, the famous novelist and author of *Remembrance of Things Past*, happened into Proust's study. Instead of finding the master at his writing table, she saw him writhing on the floor in what looked like a fit of apoplexy. Screaming, she ran to him. But he sternly told her to get out and leave him alone. It turns out he was in agony over what *single* word to write next in his manuscript.

Marcel had, perhaps, the worst case of writer's block in history.

Fortunately for literature, he found that right word, and the next, and the next. And though he often seemed in torment as he wrote, he did manage to leave behind a masterpiece.

We all have times in our writing when the words get stuck, or the story we're writing just won't get going again. Sometimes, we sit at our desks and fail even to get an idea. Time doesn't fly, but drags, like Igor shuffling across the mad scientist's laboratory. If it gets real bad, we may think we're characters in an actual horror movie called *The Block That Would Not Die*.

The most important thing to remember at this point is not to give in to despair. All creative people have moments when the flow dries up. So know this: It can, and will, be overcome. But first we have to recognize the roots.

In *The Courage to Write*, Ralph Keyes identifies three primary causes of writer's block:

1. **CAN I PULL IT OFF?** In other words, now that I've told the world I'm going to be a writer, can I deliver something people won't want to wrap fish in?

2. **PAGE FRIGHT, THE FEAR OF SITTING BEFORE A BLANK PAGE.** As John Steinbeck once said, "I suffer as always from the fear of putting down the first line."

3. **THAT NAKED FEELING.** What will others, especially my mother, really think of me once I've finished what I'm writing?

In addition to these, I sometimes find myself fighting another bugaboo, the Perfectionist Syndrome. Naturally I always want to write my best, but when putting down words I can be stopped dead in my tracks if I try to make every sentence perfect before moving on. (This, I think, is what Proust suffered from.)

There is another form of writer's block. Let's call it *the freeze*. It occurs when you look at the mess you've created and have no idea what to do next.

Here are a few things that will help:

- **WARM UP BEFORE YOU WRITE.** Say you're working on a novel, and you are about to begin your daily stint. Do some simple, free association writing drills just to get your creative juices flowing. One exercise, suggested by Natalie Goldberg, is to "keep your hand moving" for ten minutes. That is, write without stopping to edit for ten straight minutes. Start with the sentence "I remember …" and just GO. Let the writing take you on any tangents you wish. The object is not to write anything to publish (though ideas often come from this exercise). The aim is to get into a creative state of mind.

Another exercise, from Leonard Bishop's *Dare to Be a Great Writer*, is to write a page-long sentence. Take an aspect of your story—a character sketch or scene—and write a sentence that goes for a whole page without using any punctuation, employing as many techniques as you like (dialogue, flashback, description). This exercise will help free you from artificial constraints when you start your writing.

- **WRITE IN "TIGHT COMPARTMENTS."** Instead of seeing your whole novel, just see the immediate scene you're working on. Anne Lamott calls this the "one-inch frame" method. Just concentrate on the little scene within the frame, and nothing else. You'll find your revision tasks are not so daunting when viewed this way.

- **BE STRATEGIC.** Learn to identify the most important tasks for revising your manuscript, and start with the most important ones. This book will help you make those identifications.

- **GET INSPIRED.** One of my favorite movies is *Rudy*. It's the true story of Rudy Rudiger, a kid who had the dream of playing football for Notre Dame. But he was too small to make the team. So he got on the practice squad and worked his heart out. He was rewarded by getting into one game before he graduated.

  Yes, it's a familiar enough plot, the underdog who triumphs by guts and grit, but the story was well told and acted.

  Sometimes, needing a mental lift to get to my work, I'll play the football theme from *Rudy*. It's a trick, like getting a pep talk from the coach before running out on the field.

  Why not? This writing game is hard enough without brain meltdowns.

- **REPEAT THIS OFTEN: IT CAN BE FIXED.** Neil Simon was once watching a new play of his in rehearsal. It was obvious something wasn't working. The director of the play knew it, too. In the darkness Simon wrote something on a piece of paper and passed it to the director. The note said, *I can fix it.*

That's a phrase worth putting up in your writer's space. Because any writing problem can be fixed. All it takes is tools and experience, and you get both the more you write and revise.

Remember that. *Any problem can be fixed.*

Some fixes will be more painful than others, of course. You may have to tear up a lot of your book and start over.

That's all right. Because …

- **REMIND YOURSELF THAT ALL THIS WORK IS MAKING YOUR BOOK BETTER.** Imagine the look on an editor's or agent's face when they come across your manuscript. They are hoping to find that next great novel. Let it be yours. Anticipate that it will be.

STORY SELECTION

The first editing question you need to ask is, *Which story do I select to turn into a whole novel? To write from start to finish?*

You're going to be spending a long time with your novel. Months. A year. In some cases more. I don't want you to wake up twelve weeks from now and chuck all that work.

So here are a few keys to self-editing in the story selection phase:

1. **GET LOTS OF IDEAS.** The key to creativity is to get lots and lots of ideas, *ironically without any self-editing at all*, then throw out the ones you don't want.

   It's a little like how lawyers choose juries. In reality, they don't select jurors; they deselect them. The potential jurors who are seated in the box are drawn randomly. Then, through a questioning process called *voir dire*, the lawyers probe and ponder, then exercise *challenges*. They try to get rid of those jurors they believe will not be favorably disposed to their case.

   So, too, you as a writer face your box of ideas and, through probing and pondering, toss out the ones you won't be writing about.

   But first you gather, and as you do, let your imagination run free.

2. **LOOK FOR THE BIG IDEA.** A novel-length story has to have a certain size to it. Not length of words, but potential for a large canvas of emotions, incidents, and high stakes.

This is something you need to *feel* in your writer's spirit. Think about the novels that moved you most. What was it about them that got to you? If it was an unforgettable character, what made her so? If it was a turning, twisting plot, what were the stakes?

If it was a quieter novel, it had some simmering intensity about it. Think on these things as you look at ideas to nurture.

3. **WRITE YOUR BACK COVER COPY.** There are several questions to ask yourself about your idea, but at some point you need to see if it holds together, if you can get it in a form that both excites you and will excite publishers and readers.

One of the best ways to do this is to write your own back cover copy. That's the marketing copy on the back of the book (or on the dust jacket) that's intended to get readers to buy it.

When you do this, concentrate on the big picture. You'll need to write and rewrite this several times, but doing so will serve you well for the entire writing project.

Take a look at some examples and try to get the same effect for your project:

LONG LOST, BY DAVID MORRELL

Brad Denning's brother Petey is long lost. Frozen in time as a skinny nine-year-old bicycling away from his uncaring older brother, Petey haunts Brad's consciousness. To this day, within his prosperous life, Brad knows with certainty that he was responsible for the boy's disappearance. He knows how much his mother and father suffered and that nothing can ever bring Petey back again—until a stranger walks into Brad's life.

Suddenly, Brad is confronted by a man who claims to be his brother and is telling a tale of wandering, pain, and survival. As Brad gradually puts aside his suspicions, his alleged brother makes himself at home in Brad's life. Then everything is shattered. Petey is gone again. Only this time, he's taken Brad's wife and child with him.

Now Brad must struggle with a harrowing mystery. Was the man who knew all the intimate details of their childhood truly his brother or a vicious con man? Where has he taken Brad's family—and why? As the days stretch into weeks, the baffled police and the FBI are forced to end their search. Brad's only recourse is to put himself into the mind of the man who claimed to be his brother and hunt him down himself.

WHITE OLEANDER, BY JANET FITCH

Astrid is the only child of a single mother, Ingrid, a brilliant, obsessed poet who wields her luminous beauty to intimidate and manipulate men. Astrid worships her mother and cherishes their private world full of ritual and mystery—but their idyll is shattered when Astrid's mother falls apart over a lover. Deranged by rejection, Ingrid murders the man and is sentenced to life in prison.

White Oleander is the unforgettable story of Astrid's journey through a series of foster homes and her efforts to find a place for herself in impossible circumstances. Each home is its own universe, with a new set of laws and lessons to be learned. With determination and humor, Astrid confronts the challenges of loneliness and poverty, and strives to learn who a motherless child in an indifferent world can become.

BLEACHERS, BY JOHN GRISHAM

High school all-American Neely Crenshaw was probably the best quarterback ever to play for the legendary Messina Spartans. Fifteen years have gone by since those glory days, and Neely has come home to Messina to bury Coach Eddie Rake, the man who molded the Spartans into an unbeatable football dynasty.

Now, as Coach Rake's "boys" sit in the bleachers waiting for the dimming field lights to signal his passing, they replay the old games, relive the old glories, and try to decide once and for all whether they love Eddie Rake—or hate him. For Neely Crenshaw, a man who must finally forgive his coach—and himself—before he can get on with his life, the stakes are especially high.

NEVER CHANGE, BY ELIZABETH BERG

A self-anointed spinster at fifty-one, Myra Lipinski is reasonably content with her quiet life, her dog, Frank, and her career as a visiting nurse. But everything changes when Chip Reardon, the golden boy she adored in high school, is assigned as her new patient. Choosing to forgo treatment for an incurable illness, Chip has returned to his New England hometown to spend what time he has left. Now, Myra and Chip find themselves engaged in a poignant redefinition of roles and a complicated dance of memory, ambivalence, and longing.

CREATIVITY AND MARKETING

At some point, you're going to have to decide how earnest you are to sell and market your writing.

Publishing is a business. The corporations that run book companies do so to make a profit. A large profit. Which means that fiction that appeals to a large commercial audience is more likely to be published than fiction that doesn't.

This doesn't mean that quieter, more literary-style fiction—which doesn't sell as well as commercial fiction—doesn't deserve to be published and won't be.

This book deals with aspects of the fiction craft that make a story more readable and enjoyable and entertaining for the reader. Even if your bent is toward high style and more complex stories, these tools will help you realize your vision.

FICTION FORMULA

Is there a formula for fiction?

Yes. And I'm about to give it to you.

Knowing the formula alone won't guarantee your novel success. You'll still have to learn the elements of the craft in order to flesh out the whole novel. But I give it to you as an overview, something to keep in mind at all stages of writing and editing.

Here it is:

CONCEPT + CHARACTERS × CONFLICT = NOVEL

Concept is the big idea, the basic premise, the one-liner that will explain your story.

Every successful novel has a concept. It can be a "high" concept, one that has dollar signs, like many movies do: "What if a killer shark terrorizes a beach resort at the height of tourist season?"

It can be a smaller, more intimate concept, such as, "A troubled prep school kid journeys to New York to find out if life is worth living."

Characters are, of course, essential to fiction. No characters, no story.

Conflict is the blood of fiction, the heartbeat of narrative. Without conflict, the novel doesn't live and breathe. Alfred Hitchcock's axiom, which I quote often, states: "A great story is life, with the dull parts taken out."

No conflict = dull.

Now, knowing this, can you guess the formula for a great novel? Here it is:

$$\text{CONCEPT}^x + \text{CHARACTERS}^x \times \text{CONFLICT}^x = \text{GREAT NOVEL}$$

Where x represents some factor beyond the average. You take each element and make it *more*. Stronger, better.

Pause every so often and let your imagination play with each factor. Ask such questions as:

- What could make the situation worse for my Lead?
- How can I take that beyond worse and make it *worse than that*?
- What part of my concept is familiar? Has it been done before? How can I freshen it?
- What if I tried a completely different setting?
- What trait could my Lead possess that hurts her?
- How can that trait be made potentially deadly?
- How can I make the characters in conflict hate each other?
- How can I make the characters who love each other have to be on opposite sides?
- Are there relationships I can create that up the ante for each character?
- If my novel were rendered in a movie trailer, what would it look like? Would I want to see that movie? If not, what can I do to make it a *must-see*?

A FEW WORDS ABOUT THE FIRST DRAFT

So you're writing away, trying to get that first draft done, and right in the middle it has become tough slogging. Or maybe you've finished the first draft but the story just sits there, like Jabba the Hutt, mocking you.

Don't despair. All you need is a good zap to get yourself, or your book, back on track. Here's how to recharge your battery.

Sometimes writing a novel feels about as rewarding as turning a spit in the fires of hell. Worse, you may not feel you can turn the spit even one more revolution. Don't give up! There's always a way out.

Start by asking if this is writer's laziness as opposed to writer's block. Most often the parking of butt in chair, and the pounding of keys by fingers, is all you need. No mercy here. Just do it, like the ad says.

What's stopping you may be your inner editor, yelping at you *as you write*. Shut that voice off. Give yourself permission to be bad. Write first, polish later. That's the golden rule of production.

A more insidious form of blockage is loss of confidence, the feeling that everything you're putting on paper is a foolish waste of time.

This is The Wall, and it should help you to know that most novelists hit it at some point in their first drafts. For me, it's around the 30,000-word mark. I get there and suddenly think all the worst things about my novel: The idea stinks and is beyond redemption; my writing is lame, the characters uninteresting, and the plot virtually nonexistent. I can't possibly go on. Career over. The anxiety is only magnified when there's an advance already half spent.

Here's a simple prescription I've come up with:

- Take one whole day off from writing.
- Try to spend some time at a peaceful location—a park, a lakeshore, a deserted parking lot. Anywhere you can be alone.
- Spend at least thirty minutes sitting without doing anything. Don't read; don't listen to music. Breathe deeply. Hear the world around you.
- Do something for pure fun. See a movie. Shop for hours without buying. Eat ice cream.
- In the evening, drink a glass of warm milk and fall asleep reading one of your favorite writers.
- First thing the next day, write at least three hundred words on your project, no matter what. Don't edit, don't slow down. Just write. You'll start to feel excited again.
- Push on until you complete your first draft.

And know this: Your first draft is never as bad as you thought it was at The Wall.

I hope this book becomes a reference to help you break through The Wall and every other challenge you face in the writing of your novel.

CHAPTER 2

Characters

In the classic Universal horror movie *Frankenstein*, Colin Clive, overacting as Dr. Frankenstein, shouts, "IT'S ALIVE! IT'S ALIIIIIIVE!" He's thrilled to the core when his creation takes on real life.

The doc was onto something. That's how it feels when a writer creates gripping, rounded characters. Cardboard cutouts don't excite you or your readers. Living, breathing characters do.

It has been said that all fiction is "character driven." This is true. Even in a novel that is heavy on plot and action, it's only through characters that the reader connects with the story.

Fiction is the record of how a character faces a threat or challenge. It may be an outward threat, such as physical death, or an inward, psychological challenge. Whatever the danger is, readers will respond if they are connected, bonded in a way, to the Lead character.

"The first thing that makes a reader read a book," wrote novelist and teacher John Gardner, "is the characters."

Plot is important. Theme deepens the story. But without compelling characters, readers will not connect with any of it.

Character work is also the key to originality in fiction. As the great writing instructor Lajos Egri put it, "Living, vibrating human beings are still the secret and magic formula of great and enduring writing."

TYPES OF LEADS

There are three types of Lead characters:

- **THE POSITIVE LEAD.** This is what has traditionally been called the *hero*. The mark of the hero is that she represents the values of the community. She is representing the moral vision shared by most people and is someone we root for as a result.

  Most fiction uses the Positive Lead because it's the easiest to bond with and to carry an entire novel. Note that by *positive* we don't mean perfect. Leads, to be realistic, must also have flaws and foibles.

  Further, those flaws must have a basis for existing, due to something in the character's past. A flaw alone is nothing. A flaw explained is depth.

- **THE NEGATIVE LEAD.** Naturally, this is the hardest type of Lead to do, because the reader may not like him. Why read a whole book about somebody who does *not* care about the community? Who is, indeed, doing things we find reprehensible?

  There are ways to do a Negative Lead that are explained later in this chapter.

- **THE ANTI-HERO.** This is a Lead who doesn't seek to be part of the community nor actively oppose it. He is, instead, living according to his own moral code. He is the loner.

  Like the classic antihero Rick in *Casablanca*, he "sticks his head out for nobody."

  A powerful story motif occurs when the anti-hero, because of the unfolding events, is forced to join the community.

  In *Casablanca*, Rick is dragged into anti-Nazi intrigue. Will he continue to keep his neck out of trouble? He doesn't, and at the end of the film he rejoins the community by going off to fight with his new friend, Louis.

  Ethan Edwards, the character played by John Wayne in *The Searchers*, joins the common enterprise to find his niece, captured as a child by Comanches. But at the end of the film he doesn't come back into the fold. Back turned, he walks poignantly away from his family, returning to his own world.

*

For purposes of this chapter we'll concentrate on the Positive Lead. But note that many of these aspects can be incorporated for the other two types as well.

So what makes a great Lead character?

GRIT, WIT, AND IT

Lead characters must draw us in. When we think of great works of literature, we flash to the main characters: Huck Finn. Gatsby. Tom Joad. Scarlett O'Hara.

Commercial fiction works the same way. Think of the staying power of Raymond Chandler's Philip Marlowe or Janet Evanovich's Stephanie Plum.

What is it that makes these characters unforgettable? In analyzing hundreds of memorable characters, I believe three factors prevail above all. I call them *grit*, *wit*, and *it*.

Grit

Let me lead off with the one unbreakable rule for major characters in fiction: *No wimps!*

A wimp is someone who just takes it. Who reacts (barely) rather than acts. While a character may start out as a wimp, very early on he must develop real *grit*. He must do something. He must have forward motion.

Grit is guts in action. It is as described in Charles Portis's *True Grit*. Rooster Cogburn is the lawman who helps young Mattie Ross track down her father's killer. Cogburn is said by another character to be "double tough, and fear don't enter into his thinking."

All well and good, but grit in fiction must always be shown in action. Portis does this at the climax when Cogburn rides out to face Ned Pepper and his gang, reins in his mouth, firing guns with both hands.

Another gritty character is Scarlett O'Hara in Margaret Mitchell's *Gone With the Wind*. While not entirely admirable, especially early in the novel when she overplays the coquette, Scarlett faces many challenges with courage. She is the one who has to help Melanie birth her baby and later hold Tara together during Reconstruction.

In *Rose Madder*, Stephen King gives us a Lead who, in the beginning, is weak and vulnerable—a horribly abused wife. In the prologue we see Rose Daniels, pregnant, savagely beaten by her husband. The section ends, *Rose McClendon Daniels slept within her husband's madness for nine more years.*

Chapter one begins with Rose, bleeding from the nose, finally listening to the voice in her that says *leave*. She argues with herself. Her husband will kill her if she tries. Where will she go? But she works up the courage to open the front door and take *her first dozen steps into the fogbank which was her future*.

Every step she takes now requires grit. Rose is unprepared for dealing with the outside world, with simple things like getting a bus ticket or a job. And all the while she knows her husband is going to be tracking her. Still, she moves forward, and we root for her. It would have been easy for King to spend ten chapters detailing the abuse Rose took from her husband. But being a master of the craft, he knew that would have been too much "taking it."

If your novel seems to be dragging, one of the first places to look is right here, at the heart of your Lead. Is he giving up too easily? Has he been taking it for too long? Are there too many scenes where he's thinking or reacting and not *doing*?

Go back and put in some fight in an earlier scene. Get the Lead's dander up again. Make him take some action against a person or circumstance. Whether it's as simple as taking a step into the unknown or charging ahead into a dangerous battle, courage bonds us with the Lead.

To portray grit in action, you must *prepare*, then *prove*.

- Think up a scene early in your novel where your character must show inner courage. For example, he has to confront his boss over some company infraction. He can go through with it, foreshadowing a greater display of courage to come toward the end.
- Or the above character can back down, setting up the necessity for growth. In the Oliver Stone movie *Wall Street*, the young stockbroker Bud Fox is asked by financial giant Gordon Gekko to do some unethical snooping on a rival. At this crucial turning point, Fox gives in, though he knows it's wrong. Fox will have to grow through bitter experience and develop the grit to confront Gekko at the end.
- Finally, play up your character's inner battle at the time of challenge. This will add a layer of depth to the confrontation. No one except James Bond goes into battle without fear.

THE LAMBERT SECRET

When my kids were young we liked an old Disney cartoon called *Lambert the Sheepish Lion*. It was the story of a lion cub raised by sheep. As a result, he was not a roaring lion but a rather timid and cowardly creature that the others made fun of.

In other words, a wimp.

But then one day his mother was backed onto a cliff by a ravenous wolf. The wolf was going to eat her or she would fall to her death. She cries out, "Laaaaambert!"

When Lambert hears the voice he raises his head. "Mama?"

Then he sees what's happening.

And from within, the lion that was always there ROARS and leaps to her defense.

The wolf is scared right out of his fur and cowers. Too bad. Lambert bumps him right off the cliff.

From that day on, Lambert is the hero of the flock.

Know your character's inner lion. What is it that will make her roar and fight? Bring that aspect to the surface early in your story and you won't be hampered by the wimp factor.

Wit

In Kristin Billerbeck's *She's Out of Control*, lead character Ashley Stockingdale is arguing with her married and pregnant friend, Brea:

> I am seriously annoyed now. "You never dated a guy afraid of commitment. You got married young, when you weren't 'bus bait.'" Bus bait is my brother's term meaning that I have more chance of getting hit by a bus than getting married over thirty. I'm thirty-one and counting. I take crosswalks seriously.

The throwaway last line is a perfect, witty counterpoint to what could have become maudlin self-pity. Ashley's wit is what helps keep her sane in the dark world of modern dating.

Wit is something everyone warms to when it's natural, not forced. An easy way to show this is by making the wit self-deprecating. If the character has the ability to laugh at himself, wit will come naturally, as when Rhett

Butler chides Scarlett O'Hara, "Why don't you say I'm a damned rascal and no gentleman?"

Wit can also make light of an overly sentimental situation. When Scarlett dances with Rhett for the first time, she teases him to say something "pretty" to her. Rhett replies:

> "Would it please you if I said your eyes were twin goldfish bowls filled to the brim with the clearest green water and that when the fish swim to the top, as they are doing now, you are devilishly charming?"

Wit will enliven even a negative character. Thomas Harris's flesh-eating antagonist in *The Silence of the Lambs*, Hannibal Lecter, is a perfect example. Who will forget Lecter's culinary account revolving around a census taker's liver and some fava beans?

- Find an instance when your character can gently make fun of himself. Work that into a scene early in the book. This makes for a great first impression on the reader.
- Look closely at your dialogue and tweak some lines to lightly deflate moments that might be too sentimental. If you can come up with a killer *bon mot*, so much the better.

It

The novelist Elinor Glynn coined the term "It" for the Roaring Twenties generation. By *It* Glynn meant personal magnetism—sex appeal as well as a quality that invites admiration (or envy) among others. Someone who walks into a room and draws all the attention has *It*. (Clara Bow was the silent film actress who was called "The It Girl" for her portrayal of such characters.)

We've all known people like that, but getting *It* on the page can be difficult.

One way is to have the *It* character described either by the author or other characters. Margaret Mitchell does the former in the opening line of *Gone With the Wind*:

> Scarlett O'Hara was not beautiful, but men seldom realized it when caught by her charm, as the Tarleton twins were.

Here we are told by the author that Scarlett has *It*. But then Mitchell wisely provides some action to back it up:

> But she smiled when she spoke, consciously deepening her dimple and fluttering her bristly black lashes as swiftly as butterflies' wings. The boys

were enchanted, as she had intended them to be, and they hastened to apologize for boring her.

Later, at the barbecue at Twelve Oaks, Scarlett sits on an ottoman under an oak tree, surrounded by men. The scene gives us more proof of Scarlett's sex appeal. And, of course, Rhett Butler, who could have any woman, is drawn to her as well.

- Before you begin writing, hunt down a visual of your character. Go through magazines until you find a picture that seems to shout, *This is what she looks like!* Clip the picture and keep it for reference during your writing.
- Imagine a party where several people are chatting and your character walks into the room, dressed to the nines. How do the other characters react? What do they say about your character? Record these things for possible use in your novel.
- Work into your novel an early scene where another character is drawn to your Lead character. This can be because of sex appeal, power, or fascination. It can be subtle or overt. But this will set *It* in the minds of the readers.

Grit, Wit, and *It.* Work them into your main character, and you'll be on your way to creating truly unforgettable fiction.

· ·

Do not hesitate to give your hero lusts of the flesh, dark passions, impulses to evil; for these dark powers, fused with their opposites—the will to do good, the moral impulses, the powers of the spirit—will do to your character precisely what the opposite powers of fire and water do to the sword blade.

—WILLIAM FOSTER-HARRIS

ATTITUDE

Compelling characters have a way of looking at the world that's uniquely their own. This is their *attitude*, and done well it sets them apart from every other fictional creation.

If you're writing in first-person point of view, attitude should permeate the voice of the narrator. Julianna Baggott's Lead in *Girl Talk*, Lissy Jablonski, is smart, witty, and a bit cynical. She describes an old boyfriend:

> He'd been a ceramics major because he wanted to get dirty, a philosophy major because he wanted to be allowed to think dirty, a forestry major because he wanted to be one with the dirt, and a psychology major because he wanted to help people deal with their dirt. But nothing suited him.

We learn a lot about Lissy from her singular voice. One thing she's not is dull.

A third-person character shows attitude primarily through dialogue and thoughts. In *L.A. Justice*, we're given a look into the head of Nikki Hill, the deputy D.A. who is the Lead in the legal thriller by Christopher Darden and Dick Lochte. In one scene she reacts to her superior, the acting D.A. He's a man of two personalities *she had labeled "Dr. Jazz" and "Mr. Snide." In the office he was the latter, bent and dour, with an acid tongue and total lack of social grace. ... At the moment, he was definitely in his Mr. Snide mode.*

This is a quick look at Nikki's attitude toward authority, which continues to be developed in the novel.

The best way to find your character's unique views is to *listen*. You do this by creating a free-form journal in the character's voice. It's okay if you don't know what the voice is going to sound like when you start. Keep writing, fast and furious, in ten- to twenty-minute stretches. A voice will begin to emerge.

Have the character pontificate on such questions as:

- What do you care most about in the world?
- What really ticks you off?
- If you could do one thing, and succeed at it, what would it be?
- What people do you most admire, and why?
- What was your childhood like?
- What's the most embarrassing thing that ever happened to you?

Let the answers come in any form, without editing. Your goal is not to create usable copy (though you certainly will find some gems). Rather, you want to get to know, deeply, the character with whom you're going to spend an entire novel.

THE CHARACTER VOICE JOURNAL

Start a free-form document that is just the voice of your character, in stream-of-consciousness mode. Go wild with this. You're trying to let the voice of the character develop organically. You want to be able to hear the character so he doesn't sound like any of the other characters.

Personalize and make it unique. These tools help you do that.

SURPRISES

Raymond Chandler had a little advice for spicing up a plot. Whenever the story starts to drag, he counseled, "Bring in a guy with a gun." In other words, surprise.

Why not do the same thing with your characters? A character who never surprises us is dull by definition.

Surprising behavior often surfaces under conditions of excitement, stress, or inner conflict.

Archie Caswell, the fourteen-year-old protagonist of Han Nolan's *When We Were Saints*, is torn about his experience of the divine. Alone on a mountain he *dug his hands into the ground beneath him, pulling up pine needles and dirt. He threw it at the trees. He picked up some more and threw it, too.* He berates God, then asks God's forgiveness. Not something we expect from a heretofore normal, troublemaking kid.

- Go to a place in your story where the tension is high. Now increase the heat. Ratchet up the conflict.
- Make a list of possible actions and reactions for your character. Push beyond the familiar. Allow yourself to come up with possibilities you would never have considered. The more surprising, the better (usually these will come when you force yourself to keep listing, so make the list at least ten items long).
- Sit back and choose an action or reaction that seems fresh and alive. Don't fear the unknown. Work the action into your scene. See if you can work others in elsewhere.

Unselfishness

We care about people who care about others. We like characters who don't just think of their own self-interest all the time. A Lead who shows concern for those not as well off as himself creates a strong bond.

Compare two Woody Allen movies. In *Scoop*, Scarlett Johansson plays an American journalism student in London. In her first scene she gets drunk and sleeps with a celebrity to get an interview.

Woody Allen plays a third-tier magician who gets Johansson as a volunteer one night. In the disappearing chamber she is visited by the ghost of a famous journalist who gives her a scoop on a serial killer.

She enlists Allen to help her track the suspect.

But we don't care.

Why? Because all we know about the Lead is that she is a woman of questionable morals and ethics with a nice bod. Her sidekick holds no particular interest for us, either. He isn't doing too badly, apparently, even with his less-than-impressive shtick.

What was missing here?

Now consider one of Allen's more successful films, *Broadway Danny Rose*. Here Allen plays a very similar character to the one he played in *Scoop*, a fast-talking but unimpressive Brooklynite. Yet we care deeply about Danny Rose. Why?

Because Danny is a talent agent to those without a chance, like a blind xylophone player and a one-legged tap dancer. He genuinely cares about his charges, and that's the key: We like characters who care about others.

- Is there a minor character in your story your Lead can care about? If not, create one.
- Your Lead doesn't have to be a saint about this. He can have inner conflict or annoyance about his caring. It's his actions that count.
- A useful technique is the "pet the dog" beat (see chapter seventeen).

The Secret Ingredient: Honor

Honor can be defined as strong moral character shown by adherence to ethical principles. It is an inner quality that motivates right action, even in the face of terrible odds.

In *High Noon*, Will Kane (Gary Cooper in an Oscar-winning role) is the retiring marshal of a small Western town. He's just married a Quaker woman (Grace Kelly), and they're about to ride out to start their quiet lives together.

Then Kane gets the terrible news: The killer he helped put away has been pardoned. And he's announced he's coming to town on the noon train to take care of Will Kane once and for all. And he's bringing three other gunmen to help him in his deadly task.

Maybe he should stay, Kane says. But the townspeople herd him and his wife onto a buckboard and rush him out of town.

A half mile later Kane pulls up the horse. He tells his wife he has to go back. If he doesn't, the killers will hunt them down. The two of them will be on the run for the rest of their lives.

But it goes even deeper than that. The really important theme is that Kane knows he won't be able to live with *himself* if he runs, let alone with his wife. He's a man who cannot live with dishonor, because to do so is worse than death. He has to go back. And for this he risks losing Grace Kelly. Grace Kelly! Talk about a virtue holding sway over a soul!

The key moment in the film occurs just before Act III and the climactic shoot-out. Kane has tried unsuccessfully to gather a posse. The town he had served so well has let him down. He is alone, and four gunmen will soon arrive to kill him. He will almost surely die.

In the livery stable he begins to crack. What has he done? He's given up a wife and a future, for what? For honor? Is that worth anything?

He sees a horse and saddle and wonders if he should just get on and get out.

In walks Harvey (Lloyd Bridges), the young deputy who has bristled under the shadow of the great Will Kane. A coward at heart, Harvey wants nothing more than to have Kane leave town so he can take over his role as the big man. He's even tried to take Kane's former lover for his own, but she now holds him in contempt.

Harvey sees immediately what Kane is thinking and happily starts saddling the horse. "No one'll blame you," he says. "Sure, this is what you've got to do."

And in that moment Will Kane sees what he'll become if he leaves. His dishonor will turn him into Harvey. His life will effectively end, even if he stays physically alive.

Kane refuses to get on the horse. This angers Harvey so much he tries to knock Kane out. They fight, and Harvey is the one who ends up on the ground.

Kane stays to face the killers, and you'll have to watch the movie to see what happens.

But it is that one moment, that interior reflection, where Kane fights the most important battle. As the essayist Michel de Montaigne put it, "It is not for outward show that the soul is to play its part, but for ourselves within, where no eyes can pierce but our own."

Honor is found in another literary classic, Herman Melville's *Moby-Dick*, in a most unlikely place. Ishmael is astonished when Queequeg, the cannibal harpooner, risks his own life to save a young greenhorn from drowning. The astonishment comes from Queequeg's nonchalance about it all. He accepts no congratulations and seeks no reward, just some water to wash off the brine and a place to smoke his pipe. Ishmael seems to peer into the native's mind, catching the thought that we are simply all in this together, and we have to look out for each other. That's just what people do.

The essence of a character comes out in those moments when, under moral stress, one must make a choice. Will it be honorable or dishonorable?

When Rick Blaine (Humphrey Bogart) gives up the love of his life, Ilsa (Ingrid Bergman), in *Casablanca*, it is a transcendent and perfect ending. Blaine has made a sacrifice because to take another man's wife, even though she is willing, is too much dishonor to abide. They may not regret it now, Blaine says to Ilsa, but they will soon, and for the rest of their lives. In this way, the anti-hero Blaine becomes a real hero and shoves off with his new friend, Louis (Claude Rains), to rejoin the war effort.

Contrast that with *An American Tragedy*, the Theodore Dreiser classic that was magnificently made into the film *A Place in the Sun*. Clyde Griffiths starts with one dishonorable act that leads to his inevitable downfall. Early in the novel, goaded by some of his fellow bellboys to visit a brothel, Clyde has a choice to make. He's curious but a little scared, because of his background. His parents were staunch Christians and brought him up that way.

Clyde, Dreiser writes, puts thoughts of his parents "resolutely out of his mind." Thus the choice is made.

After the experience in the brothel, Clyde has thoughts of shame, thinking back on his parents' teachings from the Bible. Yet the experience was "lit with a kind of gross, pagan beauty or vulgar charm for him." Honor is always pitched as a battle of two extremes.

Clyde has made his choice. He seduces the tragic Roberta, consents to marry her (to save his own rep) when she conceives, then lets her drown so he can be free to pursue another woman.

As thoughts of seeing Roberta dead come to Clyde, Dreiser calls it "the devil's whisper."

When our characters show us the full fire of that inner battle, we have the makings of great fiction. For whether the choice is ultimately for honor or dishonor, we will see the consequences, and the reader will be instructed without being taught.

- Define the ethics of your character. This doesn't have to be made explicit in the story, but if you know what they are, your character will act accordingly.
- Construct or rewrite a scene that forces the character to make a moral choice. Make up strong reasons *not* to act honorably. Show us what the character does as a result.

GETTING PHYSICAL

When describing characters, professional writers are of two minds. Some believe in giving a full visual description. They want to control the picture in the mind of the reader. This used to be the popular view. Thus, the beginning of *The Maltese Falcon*, by Dashiell Hammett, goes like this:

> Samuel Spade's jaw was long and bony, his chin a jutting v under the more flexible v of his mouth. His nostrils curved back to make another, smaller v. His yellow-grey eyes were horizontal. The v *motif* was picked up again by thickish brows rising outward from twin creases above a hooked nose, and his pale brown hair grew down—from high flat temples—in a point on his forehead. He looked rather pleasantly like a blond Satan.

The other view, much more popular today, is minimalist. It recognizes that readers are going to form their own picture regardless, and that will be more powerful than what you, the author, can come up with.

Under this view, you select only those details that are essential, that truly characterize. One or two telling details are worth more than a whole page of standard description.

Award-winning novelist Athol Dickson makes an important point about tying the details of description, whatever they might be, to the deeper goals of the story. "In my last two novels and in my work in progress," Dickson says, "all three protagonists have had physical characteristics that play an important role in conveying the story's central conflict. One is an African-

American orphan with blue eyes seeking his roots, one returns to a hostile home disguised by long filthy hair and a bushy beard, and one longs for loving acceptance in spite of being self-described as 'mousy.' These physical characteristics do more than ground the character within the reader's mind; they also serve as frequent reminders of the character's struggle."

Choose description wisely, no matter how much you use, and make it do "double duty." You don't simply describe; you describe in such a way that you add to the mood or tone of the novel. Nothing generic. Descriptions should do more than create a picture—they should support the other things you're doing in the story.

In Donald Westlake's *361*, the Lead loses an eye in chapter one. He gets a glass eye in chapter two. Later, when trying to convince an old man to talk, he pops out the glass eye and uses it for shock value. It works. The old man keels over and dies.

This is getting double duty out of character traits.

- Make a list of all the physical traits of your character.
- Make a list of the moods you want to create, the way you want readers to feel as they progress through the story.
- Now, connect the traits with the mood words, and find ways to tweak them so they're consistent with each other.

THE CHARACTER CHECKLIST

For each of your main characters, consider the following:

- Sex:
- Age:
- Occupation:
- Point of vulnerability:
- Current living conditions:
- Personal habits: dress, manners, etc.:
- Physical appearance and how she feels about it:
- Where she grew up:
- Main attitudes about people and events:
- Main shaping incidents in past influencing present life:
- Dominant attitude:

- What her parents are like:
- Her relationship with other family members:
- Schooling and her performance there:
- Others think of her as:
- What she likes to do in her free time:
- She is passionate about:
- The one thing she wants more than anything else:
- Her major flaw:
- Her major strong point:
- What I love about this character:
- The secret to be revealed:

GETTING INSIDE

Bonding with characters is achieved through intimacy. The more we know and understand characters, especially the Lead, the stronger our desire to follow them through an entire novel.

The greatest intimacy is achieved when we are privy to the thoughts and feelings of the characters. When we get to go inside their heads.

Thoughts

When you render a character's thoughts, you are providing a direct link to what makes him tick. It's secret knowledge. The other characters don't know the thoughts, but the reader does. For this very reason, thoughts are powerful tools in fiction. But because of their power, they must be used judiciously.

You need to pick your spots carefully. Some of those spots would include the following:

- moments of great emotional intensity
- crucial turning-point scenes
- beats where the character must analyze a situation
- challenges that cause the character to reflect on herself
- impressions upon meeting another character or arriving at a location
- scenes where the character is alone and reacting to actions that just happened

Writers show the thought life of characters in two ways: italicized and nonitalicized.

The italicized way looks like this:

> Margie burst into the Red Canary. She paused a moment and cased the joint. *Where is he? Is he hiding? I'll bet he's hiding.*
> She went to the bar and sat.

The reader instantly knows that what is in italics is what Margie thought. Notice two things here. First, the thoughts are written in present tense. And second, there is no attribution, as in: *Where is he?* she thought. The attribution is usually superfluous.

When using italics, the words are always the words the character is thinking in the moment.

Note that italics are harder to read, and for that reason you should keep these relatively short.

The other way to do it is simply to use the attribution without italics:

> Margie burst into the Red Canary. She paused a moment and cased the joint. Where is he? she thought. Is he hiding? I'll bet he's hiding.

A variation on thought rendition is to give us the thoughts in past tense, so it flows along with the narrative:

> Margie burst into the Red Canary. She paused a moment and cased the joint. Where was he? Was he hiding? It was a good bet that he was hiding.

Notice that you don't need an attribution here. Because we see the action first (Margie bursting in), we know that the thoughts are hers.

> Sitting behind his drawing board in the third bedroom of his development house in Pinecrest Manor, he asked himself, What the hell do I want out of life?
> I want to be happy, of course, but that's pure rubbish. Everyone wants to be happy.
> —STRANGERS WHEN WE MEET, BY EVAN HUNTER

The above examples are in third-person point of view. First person, of course, offers endless opportunities for thought life because you're in the head of the character from the start. She is the one who is doing the narrating:

I walked into the Red Canary and looked for him. I kept thinking *He's hiding. I know he's here somewhere, but he's hiding.*

*

I walked into the Red Canary and looked for him. I kept thinking he's hiding. I know he's in here, but he's hiding.

*

I walked into the Red Canary and looked for him. I kept thinking, *You're here, aren't you, Bob? You hiding, Bob? I know you. You're hiding.*

Find a spot in your manuscript where the character is thinking. What style have you chosen? Play with it. If you've used italics, try it the other way, and vice versa.

Can you do away with an attribution by showing the character in action, followed by the thought?

Try compressing the thought as much as possible.

As an exercise, expand the thought beyond all reason. Write quickly and fill a whole page with inner life. Then pick the best lines to keep.

FIRST-PERSON POV WARNING

When writing in first-person point of view, there's a great temptation to let the character go on and on about her thoughts and feelings. This can slow down the story, even one that's "character driven." Compress thoughts and feelings as much as possible.

Feelings

Fiction is an emotional exchange; at least it should be. The reader primarily feels a story, living it vicariously through the character. When the character feels something we can relate to, that creates empathy, a powerful bonding agent.

Jerry Cleaver calls emotion the "active ingredient" of fiction. "Fiction is about people who are desperate, driven, in crisis," he writes. Character emotion establishes empathy, sympathy, and identification.

And, as he was looking, it happened again to him. It was something that had started with the first warm days of spring. All colors seemed suddenly brighter, and with his heightened perception, there came also a deep, almost frightening sadness. It was a sadness that made him conscious of the slow beat of his heart, of the roar of blood in his ears. And it was a

sadness that made him search for identity, made him try to re-establish himself in the frame of reference in time and in space.
—*CANCEL ALL OUR VOWS*, BY JOHN D. MACDONALD

Feelings can be directly described, as in the above example. You can also show feelings through actions. Hemingway was a master at this.

In his short story "Soldier's Home," a young man back from World War I is having trouble getting back in tune with his family and hometown. One morning at breakfast his mother is giving him a talking to. The young man "looked at the bacon fat hardening on his plate."

That's a perfect picture of his inner life at the moment, and a metaphor of his life's prospects.

You don't always have to render the feelings of your characters, but you must know what they are in every scene. That way, the actions and dialogue will have an organic complexity that breathes life into fiction.

Add layers of feeling to your characters by answering questions like the following. These may be expanded or adjusted the more you learn and grow as a writer:

- What does your character yearn for? What does he think about when he's got time to dream?
- What's stopping the character from getting what he yearns for? Come up with a list of several possibilities.
- Choose one of the obstacles to the character's yearning. Now think up a scene where the character is faced with that obstacle. The obstacle is strong. How does the character react?

Here's how that might play out. The character, Frank, is a middle school science teacher. He yearns to do something adventurous, like skydiving.

What stops him? Some possibilities are:

- his own fear of flying
- his domineering father
- lack of money

Let's say it's his domineering father. Write a short scene where the father tells Frank he's stupid to even think about jumping out of a plane.

How will Frank deal with it? One thing for sure, he won't be a wimp. No wimps!

He has to do something.

Suppose you have him scream at the father in defiance. Or storm out without speaking, determined to live his own life. This is how you push past the mundane in your characters and scenes.

Use Inner Life to Show Character Change

The best plots show us not only actions, but the effect of the actions on the characters, especially the Lead. Use inner life to give us a window into how the character is changing.

In Stephen King's *The Girl Who Loved Tom Gordon*, the lost girl, Trisha, knows that her mother will soon be frightened by Trisha not being with her. King writes:

> The thought of her fright made Trisha feel guilty as well as afraid.

That is one line of interior life, and the story goes on. Later, we get a much more detailed look inside Trisha:

> The world had teeth and it could bite you with them anytime it wanted. She knew that now. She was only nine, but she knew it, and she thought she could accept it. She was almost ten, after all, and big for her age.
>
> *I don't know why we have to pay for what you guys did wrong!* That was the last thing she had heard Pete say, and now Trisha thought she knew the answer. It was a tough answer but probably a true one: just because. And if you didn't like it, take a ticket and get in line.
>
> Trisha guessed that in a lot of ways she was older than Pete now.

Showing inner change can be implicit or explicit, but you as the writer should know what your characters are feeling at every stage of the novel.

THE PULL-BACK TECHNIQUE

Often in your first draft your major characters, your Lead in particular, won't "jump off the page," and won't seem all that unique or worth following. You may have created some great plot moments for the Lead to suffer through, but to increase reader interest you need an interesting character.

To deepen the character during revision, try the pull-back technique:

1. Spend some time brainstorming about your Lead. Make a list of main character traits that come across.

2. Now, take each of those traits and ask yourself, what is an action absolutely outrageous and extreme the character might do under the full sway of that trait? Force yourself to come up with a list of at least five actions.

3. If you've let yourself go, you'll have two or three very surprising actions. These actions are likely not worth putting into the manuscript. Why? Because they're so over-the-top they'll probably throw off the balance of the character or plot. But you've tapped into some good stuff here. Can you still use some of it?

4. Yes. Just pull back 25 percent. This is a technique I learned as an actor. It was very easy to overact emotional scenes, to go too far. When I learned the 25 percent pull back, it made a tremendous difference.

Here's how the process might work. Let's say I have a lawyer who is struggling to make it and has a criminal matter he needs to handle. The evidence is not falling his way. He faces recalcitrant witnesses. He's having personal trouble, too. His fiancée has just broken up with him.

One of his traits is speaking his mind when he's angry. Perhaps being a little too honest. Now I ask, what is something the character might do under full sway of this trait? I come up with a list:

- yell at a judge
- scream at TV cameras outside the courtroom
- call a policeman a liar in open court

I need to press these further:

- throw a law book at the judge
- throw a chair through a window
- cut the D.A.'s tie off with scissors during the trial

That last one came out of nowhere but is the most original in my mind.

Now, I have to assess this. I decide that if my lawyer literally performs this action, it would impact the plot too much. It would make the character a little too over the top. So I pull back 25 percent. How?

Maybe he bumps into the D.A. outside the courtroom and, after an exchange, grabs his tie and throws it in his face. That's pulling back, and it works here.

MINOR CHARACTERS

Your hero walks into a bar (this is not a joke!). He needs some information from the bartender. A beefy man, the bartender, is cleaning a glass with a cloth. Hero shows a picture to the bartender, asks him if he knows who the guy is.

"Yes," the bartender says, then blows into the glass. He gives your hero a name and your hero walks out.

And your reader yawns and puts down the book.

What's happened here is something we've seen innumerable times. A clichéd minor character—doing clichéd things—who adds nothing to the tension of the story. He's used to convey information only, to give your protagonist a link so he can move on to another scene.

It's an opportunity wasted. Because minor characters can add spice to your novel, that extra spark that distinguishes the best fiction. So put a little effort on your minor characters. Here's how.

Allies and Irritants

Supporting players should serve one of two purposes in a story. They either help or hinder the main character. They are *allies* or *irritants*. If they aren't one or the other, what are they doing in the story except taking up space?

Consider Peggotty in Charles Dickens's *David Copperfield*. She's David's beloved nanny who reappears at various times to offer him much-needed support. She is an ally.

By way of contrast there is Miss Murdstone, the cruel sister of David's stepfather. She is, of course, an irritant, someone standing in the way of David's happiness.

Neither character is wasted. Each functions to illuminate a different side of David's character.

When you conceive a minor character this way, you open up wonderful plot opportunities. In *Carrie*, Stephen King uses an irritant early in the book:

> Tommy Erbter, age five, was biking up the other side of the street. He was a small, intense-looking boy on a twenty-inch Schwinn with bright red training wheels. He was humming "Scooby Doo, where are you?" under his breath. He saw Carrie, brightened, and stuck out his tongue.
>
> "Hey, ol' fart-face! Ol' prayin' Carrie!"

Carrie glares at Tommy and makes the bike fall over, hurting Tommy.

He has clearly irritated her, but he also serves another purpose—as a premonition of Carrie's later, telekinetic revenge. This character is put to the best possible use.

Make sure this is true even for the "cogs," those characters who are necessary to move the story along—doormen, cabdrivers, bartenders, receptionists—the people we meet every day and who your protagonist will have to deal with from time to time.

What if the cabdriver is the type who won't stop talking? Your hero is desperately trying to get to the other side of town to stop a nuclear device from going off, and the cabdriver wants to drive and chat leisurely about the Jamaican bobsled team. This irritation adds to the suspense.

A little thought will unveil innumerable plot possibilities.

Sound and Sight

Individualize each of your minor characters by giving them distinct audio-visual markers.

Audio is how characters sound, and each character should speak a little differently from the others.

In *David Copperfield*, Barkis comes to life through a single phrase that is now part of the lexicon. He asks David to deliver a marriage proposal to Peggotty. "Barkis is willin'," he says. Endearingly unique.

Distinctive audio markers come from really hearing the characters in your head. Give them voices and syntax. We know all we need to about Tommy Erbter from his language (*Scooby Doo, where are you? Hey, ol' fart-face!*).

The *visuals*—physical appearance, dress, mannerisms, tics, eccentricities, and so forth—also set a character apart. And because there is an infinite variety of visuals, you can give each minor character his due. In *Tripwire*, Lee Child describes a private investigator who has come to Key West to find Child's hero, Jack Reacher.

> He was old. Maybe sixty, medium height, bulky. A doctor would have called him overweight, but Reacher just saw a fit man some way down the wrong side of the hill. A man yielding gracefully to the passage of time without getting all stirred up about it. He was dressed like a northern city guy on a short-notice trip to somewhere hot. Light gray pants, wide at the top, narrow at the bottom, a thin crumpled beige jacket, a white shirt with the collar spread wide open, blue-white skin showing at his throat, dark socks, city shoes.

This character talks to Reacher for a couple of pages, then disappears. Later, he turns up dead. That's it for him.

So why give him a whole paragraph of specific description? First, it adds to the reality of the scene. But second, it gives us some spice—primarily, a sympathy factor. Here's a private investigator about to retire. When he's murdered, Reacher feels somewhat responsible. And that helps explain why Reacher tries to find out what's going on.

Audio-visual markers help you avoid the biggest mistake writers make with minor characters—the dreaded cliché, like our bartender, or the macho truck driver, the tough-talking waitress, the mousy accountant. So each time you have to come up with a minor character, ask:

- What is his purpose in the story?
- What audio-visual markers can I attach to him?
- How can I make each marker more unique or memorable?
- How am I avoiding cliché?
- What plot possibilities—a twist, a revelation of my protagonist, a setup, a premonition, a mood—does the character offer?
- How can the character irritate my protagonist? Or help him in a unique fashion?

Let's go back to our bartender, the big guy who polishes a glass. Instead of that, why not a petite woman? Rather than cleaning a glass, maybe she's juggling limes, or playing with a knife.

And she is in no mood to give anyone any information.

Suddenly, our story seems fresher. Delicious plot possibilities arise. This is what the spice of fiction can do for your novel.

Apply liberally.

OPPOSITION CHARACTERS

Fiction readers thrive on danger. They want to see your protagonist challenged, threatened, uneasy. Sure, there's pleasure in vivid prose. But sooner or later (preferably sooner) your protagonist must be opposed or the story starts to drag.

Without a strong opponent, most novels lack that crucial emotional experience for the reader: worry. If it seems the hero can take care of his problems easily, why bother to read on?

Not every story needs a *bad guy* opponent, of course. An opposition character can be someone who merely holds a position contrary to the protagonist's. In the film *The Fugitive*, Harrison Ford's wrongly convicted doctor is chased by the dedicated lawman, played by Tommy Lee Jones. Both are on the side of "right," but the letter of the law makes them opponents.

Most times, though, your opponent is going to be one who operates from a negative set of values. If so, make sure he's a fully realized, well-rounded character.

What Makes Bad Guys Run

The great temptation in creating bad guys is to make them evil through and through. You might think that will make the audience root harder for your hero. More likely, you're just going to give your book a melodramatic feel. To avoid this, get to know all sides of your bad guy, including the positives.

Ruthless Hollywood player Sammy Glick is described by the narrator of Budd Schulberg's *What Makes Sammy Run?* like this:

> Nine times out of ten I wouldn't have even looked up, but there was something about the kid's voice that got me. It must have been charged with a couple of thousand volts.

The raw energy of this kid, all of sixteen years old, attracts awe, if not affection:

> I never saw a guy work so hard for twelve bucks a week in my life. You had to hand it to him. He might not have been the most lovable little child in the world, but you knew he must have something. I used to stop right in the middle of a sentence and watch him go.

When the narrator, newspaper veteran Al Manheim, offers to guide Sammy into a cub reporter's job, we're struck by Sammy's direct response:

> "Thanks, Mr. Manheim," he said, "but don't do me any favors. I know this newspaper racket. Couple of years at cub reporter? Twenty bucks. Then another stretch as a district man. Thirty-five. And finally you're a great big reporter and get forty-five for the rest of your life. No thanks."

Sammy is a kid on the way up, ambitious and, we sense, able to get what he wants. We usually like, or at least admire, such traits.

A bad guy ought to be competent. He gets results. If he doesn't, he's not threatening. Sammy Glick rises to the top through his ability to use people and situations. He's a shark in the Hollywood pool and eats those in his way.

A dose of charm makes the opponent even more dangerous. This can be the hyper, turned-on allure of a Sammy Glick, or the deadly, spider-to-the-fly magnetism of Dr. Hannibal Lecter in *The Silence of the Lambs*. In both cases, another level of dread is added to the plot.

The Sympathy Factor

Dean Koontz, who's given us many a chilling villain, once said, "The best villains are those that evoke pity and sometimes even genuine sympathy as well as terror. Think of the pathetic aspect of the Frankenstein monster. Think of the poor werewolf, hating what he becomes in the light of the full moon, but incapable of resisting the lycanthropic tides in his own cells."

Koontz proves his own point in rendering one of his creepiest creations, Thomas Shadduck in *Midnight*. Shadduck is the evil genius behind horrible biological experiments performed on the people of a small town.

When we first meet Shadduck, he's floating in a sensory deprivation chamber in the grip of a weird vision: his desire to meld man and machine into cybernetic organisms. It's literally an erotic experience for him.

So Koontz doesn't give us a mustache-twirling villain of pure evil. Shadduck's motivation is visionary—perverse though it may be.

Well into the book, Koontz gives us an extensive flashback that explains how Shadduck came to be the twisted villain he is. As a young boy he fell under the spell of Don Runningdeer, an employee of his father's. The mental manipulation Shadduck suffered creates sympathy, even though his acts in the book remain evil. A truly remarkable villain is the result.

You can provide the same for your novel if you'll spend some time doing the following. First, catch a glimpse of your bad guy in visual form. Let your imagination create the physical impression for you. Chances are you'll come up with a rather standard image, but that's okay. This is just the raw clay.

Now, start molding. Ask what her objective is. Just as a good lead character must want something in order to drive him through the story, the opposition character must want an objective that is opposed. The old rule about a good plot is "two dogs and one bone."

But don't stop there. Dig into her motivation. Why does she want, to the point of obsession, her objective? Why must she have it?

Next, create a background for your villain that generates some sympathy. I like to create a major turning point from childhood for my opposition, often a powerful secret that can emerge later in the book. Even if it doesn't, I get to know my villains a lot better because of it.

Digging Deeper

Here are deepening questions you can ask about your opposition character.

- What is he good at? How does this help him get what he wants?
- What admirable qualities does he possess?
- What do other characters think of him?
- Why might people be drawn to him, or at least be fascinated by him?

Your hard work will be rewarded when your readers keep turning pages to find out just how your hero will overcome this complex, memorable villain.

KEY POINTS

- Lead characters must be active, not passive. No wimps!
- Grit, wit, and it make dynamic Leads.
- Strong Leads have a distinct *attitude* about what's going on, and they always surprise us.
- Unselfishness and honor are two very sympathetic traits.
- Remember to show us the inner life of the Lead.
- Minor characters must serve a purpose. Are they allies or irritants?
- Give as much attention to your opposition as you do your Lead.
- Sympathy for a villain deepens a story.

Exercise 1

Write an obituary for your Lead, as if the character has died in the middle of your story. No more than 300 words or so, just as you might find it in a newspaper.

Exercise 2

We know people best by watching what they do. It follows that the sooner I see my story people doing things, the sooner I get to know them. That's why I let my imagination create a movie for me to catch the characters in action. Follow these steps:

- Close your eyes and "watch" your character. See the character in rich detail and describe what you see. Be a journalist—record this information as if for a distant reading audience.
- Place your character in a scene, any scene, and once again watch. Let the action happen. Watch other characters and events pop up on your inner movie screen. Let all manner of tough conflict take place and see what your character does.
- Create another character to describe the first character. One of the ways we get to know people is to listen to what others say about them. Get to know each of your own characters this way. You'll "hear" some surprising things.
- Conceive your characters as extremes first, and only later "pull back" to the point where they fit their roles. This will keep your characters from being drab. Let them have their passions and obsessions. What do they reveal to you?

Note that none of this has to have ANYTHING to do with the story you want to write. In fact, it's better if it doesn't. The only point of the exercises is to get to know your character so when you place her in your story you'll know who you're writing about.

Another key to these exercises is this: Let as much of this happen without judgment or criticism. Only later, with lots of rich material, will you make editorial decisions.

Exercise 3

Figure out the year your character was born. Write down that year and place *Born* next to it.

List key years for the character: i.e., Elementary school, high school, college, first job, military service.

Research those years. What was happening? The main stories, the hit TV shows, songs, and movies. Whatever it is from popular culture that the character would have been aware of. These incidents can often come into play, as memories or influences, in the story.

CHAPTER 3

Plot and Structure

Plot is simply the stuff that happens to your characters. It is the record of the incidents that challenge the well-being of your Lead.

Structure is where you place those incidents along the novel's narrative timeline.

You imagine a plot and build a structure.

Structure makes your plot accessible to the reader. While you are free to play with structure, understand that the more you experiment, the harder the reader has to work.

I wrote an entire book called *Write Great Fiction: Plot & Structure*. While a full detailing of all the elements I cover there is beyond the scope of this tome, I do want to summarize the two non-negotiables of plot and structure: The LOCK system and the three acts.

THE LOCK SYSTEM

I came up with the acronym LOCK to help fiction writers grasp the essentials of a strong narrative. If the LOCK elements are in place, the story will be solid, guaranteed. Your job after that is to make the story soar, using your imagination and the techniques you learn to give your novel fresh wings.

Briefly, here are the four essentials:

L Is for Lead

Readers want to bond with a Lead character. That is their access into the story world. There are four main things you can give a Lead to create this bond:

- identification
- sympathy
- likeability
- inner conflict

Identification

This means the Lead is like us. Someone we can relate to on a human level. Not perfect, just as we are not perfect. Someone with flaws and quirks in addition to strengths. Another word for *identification* that is sometimes used is *empathy*.

Sympathy

This aspect goes further than identification/empathy. It creates an emotional "rooting interest" in the Lead character. It makes the reader care deeply about the Lead and her challenges.

Four ways to establish sympathy are:

1. **JEOPARDY.** You do this by putting the Lead in a situation where there is imminent trouble, either physical or psychological. Let's say your Lead is a ten-year-old boy. He's new at school. Physical jeopardy could be the bully who targets him that first day. Psychological jeopardy could be that the boy's father, his only living parent, is dying of cancer. Either of those situations creates sympathy right off the bat but can also happen at points well into the story.

2. **HARDSHIP.** If the Lead has to face some misfortune in life not of her own making, sympathy abounds. Think of Forrest Gump, who has both mental and physical challenges as a boy.

3. **THE UNDERDOG.** People love rooting for the determined Lead with the odds stacked against him. Like Rocky Balboa. Like several John Grisham protagonists.

4. **VULNERABILITY.** Readers worry about a Lead who might be crushed at any time. Stephen King's Lead in *Rose Madder* is a perfect example. Lacking real-world experience or skills because her psycho husband has kept her a virtual prisoner for years, Rose must figure out how to survive on her own, get a job, and most of all keep from being found by her policeman husband, who knows how to track.

Likeability

A likeable Lead is, very simply, someone who does likeable things. A person who cares about others, who isn't selfish, who is witty, and who doesn't take himself too seriously. All likable characteristics.

Not all Leads are likeable, of course. When rendering a negative Lead (someone who does things we *don't* like), substitute *power*. Characters who have power over their world and other characters—because of charm, intelligence, or competence in their field—fascinate.

Inner Conflict

A character with an interior, emotional struggle engages our attention. Inner conflict is a fight between two opposing emotions. Many times it is fear on one side, telling the Lead not to act; on the other side is moral or professional duty, or perhaps self-image.

We don't identify with people or characters who are perfectly balanced under moments of great stress. Inner conflict is a strong bonding agent between reader and character.

O Is for Objective

The objective is crucial because it gives the story forward motion. It spurs your Lead into action. It means something is at stake for him. Otherwise, why should a reader bother with reading the book? We don't want a three-hundred-page character sketch.

An objective is a *want*. A strong want. A want that is so crucial to the character that he must have it or suffer deep loss.

Objectives can come in two forms: to *get* something or to *get away* from something.

Most stories involve the *get something* type of objective.

A cop story is about the cop trying to get the bad guy.

A legal thriller is usually about the lawyer trying to get the truth, or get an acquittal for his client.

A romance is about the characters trying to get love.

A character-driven novel may be about the Lead trying to get equilibrium in his soul, as in *The Catcher in the Rye*.

The other type of objective, to *get away* from something, is a staple of action stories—like the fugitive Dr. Richard Kimble trying to get away from

Sam Gerard, the U.S. Marshal (combined with a *get-something* objective, i.e., to get the real killer).

Prison escape stories, and many caper novels, are obviously getaways.

A character may also be trying to get away from her past, or her parents, or anything else holding her back in life.

In light fare, the objective may seem trivial to us, but it must be crucial to the characters. The reason *The Odd Couple* works is that being a happy slob is almost a life-and-death matter for Oscar. He wants to *get away* from Felix but can't because Felix is suicidal and needs care. Of course, the comedy comes when, in Act III, Oscar is ready to kill Felix himself.

C Is for Confrontation

To get the most out of your story engine, you need opposition to the Lead's objective.

Novels are about confrontation. That's how you obey Hitchcock's axiom and keep the dull parts out.

With confrontation in place, you can construct scenes that have organic unity. They relate to this struggle between the Lead and the opposition.

If your story begins to veer off course or drag, look back at these two elements: objective and confrontation. Make sure they are solidly in place. Write scenes that move the Lead forward into the brick wall of the opposition.

There is an old saying about writing conflict: "Get your protagonist up a tree. Throw rocks at him. Then get him down."

Now, there are different kinds of opposition, but in a novel you almost always want it to be personal. Another character with a strong reason to stop the Lead.

Yes, stories have been written about characters against nature, society, or themselves. All of these are valid but most often serve better as subplot material.

When learning to write, make your opposition personal.

Adhesive

Something needs to hold the opposing parties together. This is *adhesive*, which prevents the Lead or opposition from walking away from the fight.

Think about it.

Let's say you have an abused wife. She decides to leave her husband and take an apartment in town, divorce him, and start life over again.

If the husband, the opposition in this case, lets her go, thinking maybe he's better off without her, end of story. She has no reason to leave town. He has no reason to bother her. Nothing is forcing these two into mortal combat.

So you add adhesive.

In the case of Stephen King's *Rose Madder*, the adhesive is psychopathology. The husband is psycho. He is an insane control freak and, it so happens, a cop who knows how to track.

The wife not only has to leave town, she has to get as far away as she can. And the husband can't rest his troubled mind until he finds and kills her.

Here are some other ways to establish adhesive:

- **DUTY.** If a character is bound by a moral or professional duty, that will be an automatic adhesive. A mother seeking a kidnapped child has a natural moral duty not to give up. A cop on a case, or a lawyer with a client, has professional duties.
- **PLACE.** If the opponents can't physically get away from each other, that's adhesive. Casablanca is a place people can't easily get out of. So is the Overlook Hotel in *The Shining*.
- **SELF.** In a literary novel, where the character might have mainly an interior struggle, the adhesive is self. We can't escape ourselves. The issue must be resolved or the character will die inside.

• •

Here's what I want from a book, what I demand, what I pray for when I take up a novel and begin to read the first sentence: I want everything and nothing less, the full measure of a writer's heart. I want a novel so poetic that I do not have to turn to the standby anthologies of poetry to satisfy that itch for music, for perfection and economy of phrasing, for exactness of tone. Then, too, I want a book so filled with story and character that I read page after page without thinking of food or drink because a writer has possessed me, crazed me with an unappeasable thirst to know what happens next.

—PAT CONROY

K Is for Knockout

Readers of fiction want to be knocked out at the end. Endings are critical. A great ending might save an otherwise flat book. If you read a great story only to be disappointed at the end, the whole experience feels wasted.

Knockout is also a metaphor for the final battle, or final choice, your character faces.

All the forces of the story are against her. How will she get through to victory?

That's what readers want to know.

The ending doesn't have to be upbeat to be powerful, of course. Sometimes it can even be ambiguous or bittersweet.

The key is leaving the readers satisfied in an unpredictable way. (See chapter seven on Beginnings, Middles and Ends.)

THREE-ACT STRUCTURE

For purposes of self-editing, you need to understand at least the following fundamentals of each act.

ACT I

- Introduce the Lead in a compelling way.
- Present the story world—tell us something about the setting, the time, and the immediate context.
- Establish the tone the reader will rely on. (Is this to be a sweeping epic or a zany farce? Action packed or dwelling more on character change? Fast moving or leisurely paced?)
- Compel the reader to move on to the middle. (Just why should the reader care to continue?)
- Introduce the opposition. (Who or what wants to stop the Lead?)

ACT II

- Deepen character relationships.

- Keep us caring about what happens.
- Set up the final battle that will wrap things up at the end.

ACT III

- Present the final battle.
- Tie up loose ends.
- Leave readers with a feeling of "resonance" (satisfied in a unique way).

How you achieve forward motion and readability in each act is covered in chapter seven.

You "stitch" the three acts together via what I call "a disturbance and two doorways."

The disturbance is anything that happens in the very beginning of your book that represents a change or challenge to the lead's normal pattern of living. It can be something small, like a late-night phone call, or something large, like an auto accident.

Because dullness is life going on as usual, the opening disturbance hooks the reader.

The first doorway, the one that gets us from Act I to Act II, should occur no later than one-fifth of the way into the novel. It is the incident that forces or thrusts the Lead into the major trouble of the middle.

Act II is where most of the novel will take place, the battle of the opposing forces.

About three-quarters of the way into the book, or even later if you wish, you pass through the second doorway to get to Act III. This is usually a major setback, crisis, clue, or discovery, something that forces or enables the final battle.

The three-act structure looks like this:

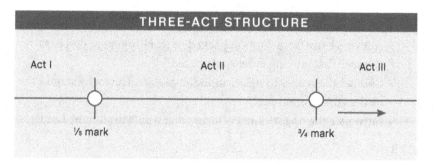

THREE-ACT STRUCTURE

Act I Act II Act III

⅕ mark ¾ mark

MYTHIC STRUCTURE

Ever since George Lucas acknowledged that his classic film *Star Wars* was partly inspired by the works of Joseph Campbell, interest in the mythic structure has taken off. Several good books have been written on this subject. Two I would recommend are *The Writer's Journey* by Christopher Vogler and *The Key* by James N. Frey.

The classic myth structure is actually fairly easy to understand. There are some minor variations, but here is one suggested template:

Hero in His Ordinary World

The story begins with the Lead character in his ordinary world. In classic myths, there is something "about" this Lead, a prophecy or circumstance of birth that presages great things.

In the novel, your Lead might be an ordinary person. But you can give her an extraordinary past and a yearning about the future. Then place her in an everyday setting to begin the story. The ordinary world is disturbed almost immediately by the call.

The Call

The hero is called to an adventure or quest, but it is really about his destiny. When King Arthur pulls the sword from the stone, he is called to be the rightful King of England.

Any incident in your novel that offers the Lead a chance to move out from her ordinary world would fulfill this function.

In many myths, the call is at first resisted. Something has to motivate the hero to answer.

Answering the Call

There is a dilemma within the hero whether to answer the call or not. He resists. But then something happens that compels or forces the decision to move from the ordinary world.

In *Star Wars*, Luke would like to leave the planet where he lives with his aunt and uncle, and look for the Princess. Maybe become a Jedi. A strange hologram in a droid showing Princess Leia asking for help is the call to adventure. But Luke's loyalty is to his family, so he resists the call.

Then the Imperial Forces kill his aunt and uncle and scorch the farm. There is no longer anything holding Luke back. He is compelled to answer the call.

Tasks and Challenges

Now out of the ordinary world, the hero is faced with various tests, tasks, challenges, and battles.

Jason is asked to sail to Colchis and find the Golden Fleece. But he must first build a ship and gather a brave crew. Then, under sail, he has to survive the test of the clashing rocks. He must meet the challenge of King Aeëtes to yoke fire-breathing bulls. And so on.

In your novel, your Lead must spend most of the book fighting battles on her way toward a worthy objective.

A Tutor

King Arthur had Merlin. Luke Skywalker had Obi-Wan Kenobi, then Yoda. All heroes can use a little help out there in the dark world.

The tutor can't solve the hero's problems for him. The whole point of the mythic journey is that the hero learns and then applies the lessons that help him make it through the dark world on his own.

Allies and Opponents

Along the way, the hero will befriend or coerce allies, those who can aid him in his tasks. Sometimes he will think someone is an ally who is really a traitor (a character sometimes referred to as the "shapeshifter"). There are many variations among these kinds of characters.

Talisman

Many of the great myths and legends involve a talisman that gives the hero the power or protection he needs to prevail in the ultimate test. Perseus had the shield of Athena. Arthur had Excalibur. In the *Star Wars* movies, Luke Skywalker had "The Force." Whatever it is, this element provides both strength and motivation for action.

In the novel, this will often simply be the acquired knowledge and skill to ultimately overcome the final test. It may also be an "icon" that provides an emotional lift.

Jefferson Smith looks upon the Lincoln Memorial before jumping into the final battle with the political machine in *Mr. Smith Goes to Washington*. The view inspires him (something that has been set up in an earlier scene).

Final Test

At last there is an epic battle, where the hero is tested once and for all.

Luke going into battle with the Death Star.

King Arthur in the great battle with Sir Mordred.

A legal thriller might pit the hero against the greatest trial lawyer in the country in one final courtroom showdown.

A crime novel has the detective facing a most clever killer on the killer's own turf.

The Return

Many times the hero returns to his ordinary world, carrying with him a message and becoming an inspirational example for the community.

MYTHIC STRUCTURE APPLIED

Consider *The Wizard of Oz*. We meet Dorothy in her ordinary world, a Kansas farm. Yet she yearns for something else, something "over the rainbow." She is given the chance to run off with Professor Marvel but refuses the call out of loyalty to her aunt with whom she lives.

But a twister makes the decision for her.

Landing in Oz, she is faced with the task of getting back home. She is given help by a tutor, Glinda, the Good Witch of the North, who gives her a start, to "follow the yellow brick road." Glinda gives Dorothy a talisman, the ruby slippers, as a going-away present.

Out in the dark world, Dorothy picks up three allies—the Scarecrow, the Tin Woodman, and the Cowardly Lion. She is opposed by grumpy trees and the wizard's guard. Not to mention the flying monkeys.

In the final test with the Wicked Witch of the West, Dorothy prevails by way of a bucket of water.

Finally, she returns, with the wisdom that "there's no place like home."

This little overview of the mythic structure is actually quite powerful. Myths tap into our hard wiring. By recognizing these elements in the context of your novel, you'll be creating potent points of connection with your readers.

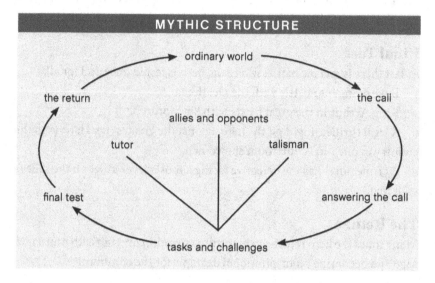

PATTERNS OF PLOT

It will also help your plot sense to understand familiar patterns. As you do further research in each pattern, you may find that one of these works best for your story. They can also be jumping-off points for a plot you'll create.

Don't hesitate to borrow plot patterns. All plots have been done. What makes them fresh are your characters, voice, style, and themes.

For deeper study, you may see my own *Plot & Structure*, or two other Writer's Digest Books titles: *Story Structure Architect* by Victoria Lynn Schmidt and *20 Master Plots* by Ronald B. Tobias.

Here are some patterns that have stood the test of time:

The Quest

The Lead is on a quest for something vital, crucial to his happiness in this world, or crucial to someone with whom he has allegiance.

Like Sir Galahad searching for the Holy Grail.

On this quest, the Lead will encounter various opponents and enemies. Perhaps there is one enemy overall who is leading the opposition.

A quest story is a microcosm of everyone's journey through life. We all face challenges in this "dark world." We will identify with someone on a quest, so long as it is made of crucial importance to that character.

Revenge

This is an old pattern, one we all relate to on a visceral level. It has been the pattern of a number of memorable novels and films, such as Alexandre Dumas's *The Count of Monte Cristo*.

It's also the pattern found in the 1953 Fritz Lang film *The Big Heat*, where Glenn Ford plays a cop whose wife is murdered by thugs working for a crime boss. We can well understand his drive to get the bad guys for this.

Love

Another oldie—two people in love. But something keeps them apart. It may be family, as in *Romeo and Juliet*. Or social class, as in the film *It Happened One Night*.

The lovers struggle throughout the story to get together.

Sometimes they start off not liking each other (this is the pattern of the Doris Day/Rock Hudson movies *Pillow Talk* and *Lover Come Back*).

The lovers end up together—happy.

Or not—sad.

Change

Here the story is about how a character must change in order to live a more fulfilling life. If he doesn't change, his prospects will be dire.

A Christmas Carol is a change story. Scrooge must change or he'll die unloving and unloved.

The film *On the Waterfront* is about change. Will the waterfront thug Terry Malloy change from living like an animal to caring about other people?

The change pattern makes a great subplot. In *The Fugitive*, the lawman, Sam Gerard, tells Richard Kimball he "doesn't care" whether he truly killed his wife. His job is just to bring the fugitive in.

By the end of the film, though, we see that Gerard really does care. He says to Kimball, "But don't tell anybody."

Adventure

Simple structure here. The character longs for adventure, goes out and tries to find it.

And runs into trouble as a result.

The aftermath of adventure is somewhat like the change story, because the character will gain some insight into himself as a result of his adventure.

Maybe that insight is that it's best not to seek adventure. As Dorothy says at the end of *The Wizard of Oz*, "There's no place like home."

The Chase

Somebody is on the run. Maybe that somebody is the Lead, as Richard Kimball is in *The Fugitive*. Somebody is chasing the person on the run, like Sam Gerard in *The Fugitive*.

Either of these characters could be the Lead. All you need is a reason for the chase.

That can be professional duty, as it is with a U.S. Marshal.

Or it can be a duty to a loved one. The reason Kimball keeps running is not just to stay alive; it's to find out who killed his wife.

Or the one doing the chasing is a psycho, as in *Rose Madder*. Rose has to stay on the run or she'll be murdered by her husband.

One Against

The idea of one person standing up against a huge opponent is a popular plot pattern.

Ken Kesey's *One Flew Over the Cuckoo's Nest* is a perfect example of this. Randall McMurphy is institutionalized and becomes the one patient willing to stand against Nurse Ratched.

Spencer Tracy, in the film *Bad Day at Black Rock*, must stand against an entire town that will kill to keep a shameful secret.

Almost always, the one against is standing up for the community, for some great moral principle. We relate to the Lead because we want that principle vindicated.

One Apart

The one apart Lead is the classic anti-hero, who wants to be left alone. He has his own code to live by. But then things happen that force him to come out of his self-imposed exile for a time.

At the end of the story, he may decide to rejoin the community, as Rick does in *Casablanca*. Or he may go back to being alone, as Ethan does in the John Ford film *The Searchers*.

Power

The quest for and exercise of power is a fascinating plot pattern. We all have an attraction to power, which is not always a good thing (that, indeed, is the whole theme of The Lord of the Rings trilogy).

The powerful getting their just desserts is satisfying, as is the relinquishment of power for a greater good.

In *The Godfather*, Michael Corleone gains ultimate power, but at the cost of his soul.

In my novel *Deadlock*, a Supreme Court judge who is the key swing vote steps down for the greater good of the country.

Death Overhanging

A gripping plot of any kind involves the overhanging possibility of death, and three kinds of death are possible.

First, of course, is physical death. If you're writing action or suspense, we need to feel that the Lead may suffer actual demise at various places in the book. The stakes are highest here, of course.

But there is also psychological/spiritual death. The character who will die inside if the objective is not met. This is what drives *The Catcher in the Rye*. Holden needs to find out if life is worth living. If he doesn't, he not only will die inside, he might just die physically by killing himself.

Finally, there is professional death, which occurs when what the character does for a living is in jeopardy. This is what you find in the film *The Verdict*. Paul Newman plays an alcoholic lawyer who gets one last case, one he really cares about. If he loses this one, it's over for him as a professional.

All three aspects of death are seen in the movie *High Noon*, which is why it has endured. Will Kane, the marshal, may lose his life, of course, because he has to face four gunmen alone. If he runs away, which everyone is urging him to do, he will certainly die inside (cowardice) and as a lawman (duty).

Your plots will strengthen exponentially when you raise the stakes to involve some sort of death overhanging.

KEY POINTS

- The essential elements of plot are Lead, Objective, Confrontation, and Knockout.
- Your Lead is the access point for your readers.

- The objective—to get or to get away from something—must be essential to the Lead's well-being.
- Confrontation comes from an opposition character who is stronger than the Lead.
- A knockout ending satisfies and creates resonance.
- Mythic structure is solid and has stood the test of time.
- The essential elements of structure are the beginning, middle, and end. They are stitched together by the disturbance and two doorways.
- A gripping plot has death overhanging (physical, psychological/ spiritual, or professional).

Exercise 1

Reread a favorite novel with the LOCK System in mind. Analyze:

- how the author establishes a bond between you and the Lead
- how the author establishes the objective and makes it super important to the Lead
- how the author creates confrontation and opposition that is stronger than the Lead, thus creating tension
- the elements that go into making the ending a satisfying one

Perhaps in the book some of the above points will be weak. Can you identify them? How would you do things differently and better? Don't be intimidated by the last question. Just by exercising your brain on this you'll be working those craft muscles.

Exercise 2

Watch one or more of the following movies and analyze the structure:

- *Star Wars*
- *High Noon*
- *Sunset Boulevard*
- *It Happened One Night*
- *Wall Street*
- *Willow*
- *True Grit*
- *The Wizard of Oz*
- Spider-Man trilogy
- The Lord of the Rings trilogy

Note in each where the disturbance occurs in the first act, and where the two doorways come into play. What moves us between acts? If a film or book seems to drag, it's usually because it is off structurally.

CHAPTER 4

Point of View

Among novelists there seems to be a continual confusion over point of view. Even veteran writers sometimes get in a fog about it. Writing teachers constantly catch their students in the dreaded "point of view violation"—or "head hopping" as it is sometimes known.

Readers, however, don't seem to mind. There aren't a flood of e-mails streaming into publishing houses or author websites asking for money back because of a POV lapse.

Still, it's readers we must care about. Because when POV isn't handled correctly, the impact of the story is diluted in a subtle and almost subconscious way. At the end of the book a reader might say, "Hey, that was a pretty good yarn." But he may not experience that "Wow" factor we're going for. Why not? The reason comes from the central concern of any POV, and that is bonding with the characters through *intimacy*.

There is a range of intimacy in POV. The most intimate is first person, where the narration is coming from the head of the character. We get the closest possible connection to the thoughts and feelings of the Lead.

By way of contrast, the omniscient POV is usually the least intimate. While the omniscient narrator can roam freely and go into any character's head, that very freedom prevents the close focus on one character.

Between first person and omniscient is third-person POV, which comes in two forms—limited and unlimited. Limited means you stick with one POV throughout the book. You don't stray into the perceptions of other characters. Unlimited means you can switch POV to another character in another scene.

Finally, a variation on the omniscient POV is cinematic, rarely used except in some genre fiction. Dashiell Hammett's *The Maltese Falcon* is the prime example of this style.

(By the way, I'm not even going to mention second-person POV, which is as rare as the blue-footed booby. My advice is not to try it at home, or anywhere else for that matter.)

Most literary novels choose first person these days, for good reason. Since character internality is the motor of literary plots, using first person is a natural choice.

Third person is most popular for commercial and action-driven books.

But this doesn't mean there is any one right answer. The answer for you is what best fits your book.

Let's have a look at your choices.

OMNISCIENT

The omniscient POV is the least intimate because you, the author, take up the burden of telling the story.

Being omniscient, you are free to float over your story, describing things, telling us what's going on in any character's head or heart at any time. Note the word *telling*. When the omniscient voice tells us what a character is feeling, the intimacy is diminished because we don't feel along with the character. That's a danger with the omniscient voice—it tempts you to take shortcuts.

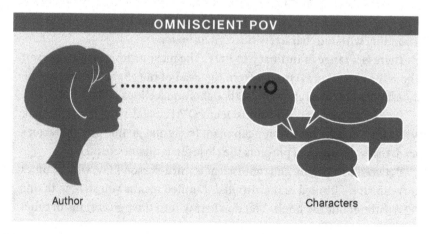

OMNISCIENT POV

Author

Characters

This is not to say you should never use the omniscient POV. For historical novels and sweeping epics, it can be a very good choice. It was good enough for Charles Dickens. In chapter one of *Bleak House*, after describing the foggy and muddy streets of London, Dickens continues:

> With the images of mud and fog in place, we move into the slow, ponderous motions of the Chancery court. The scene itself, even the way the characters speak, feels like slogging through mud. And the depiction of the law as an enterprise of obfuscation rather than clarity is itself a fog.

A little later, the action of Chancery court is detailed:

> "Several members of the bar are still to be heard, I believe?" says the Chancellor with a slight smile.
>
> Eighteen of Mr. Tangle's learned friends, each armed with a little summary of eighteen hundred sheets, bob up like eighteen hammers in a piano-forte, make eighteen bows, and drop into their eighteen places of obscurity.
>
> "We will proceed with the hearing on Wednesday fortnight," says the Chancellor. For the question at issue is only a question of costs, a mere bud on the forest tree of the parent suit, and really will come to a settlement one of these days.

Only an omniscient narrator can tell us what eighteen lawyers have in their possession, and what all eighteen look like as they "bob up."

A little later in the scene:

> Suddenly a very little counsel with a terrific bass voice arises, fully inflated, in the back settlements of the fog, and says, "Will your lordship allow me? I appear for him. He is a cousin, several times removed. I am not at the moment prepared to inform the court in what exact remove he is a cousin, but he *is* a cousin."
>
> Leaving this address (delivered like a sepulchral message) ringing in the rafters of the roof, the very little counsel drops, and the fog knows him no more. Everybody looks for him. Nobody can see him.

In chapter two, Dickens introduces us to two characters, Lady Dedlock and her husband, Sir Leicester Dedlock:

> Sir Leicester Dedlock is with my Lady, and is happy to see Mr. Tulkinghorn.
>
> "It would be useless to ask," says my Lady, with the dreariness of the place in Lincolnshire still upon her, "whether anything has been done."

Within the scene, Dickens drops into both "heads" and tells us what's going on there. Dickens, of course, used all the tools of his craft to compel interest in his tale. And he was writing to an entirely different audience. Today, omniscient POV is not as frequently employed.

In their book *Self-Editing for Fiction Writers*, Renni Browne and Dave King suggest the omniscient choice was a weakness in Larry McMurtry's *Lonesome Dove*. An otherwise successful novel, the book shows that a great plot can overcome some minor deficiencies.

But why make anything deficient?

These days, the safest bets are first person and third person.

FIRST PERSON

First person is the character telling us what happened.

> I went to the store. I saw Frank. "What are you doing here?" I said.

Obviously, this POV requires everything to be seen through the eyes of one character. The Lead can only report what she saw, not what Frank saw or felt (unless Frank sees fit to report these items to the Lead). No scene can be described that the narrator has not witnessed—although you can have another character tell the narrator what happened in an "off-screen scene."

You can use past or present tense with first-person POV. The traditional is past tense, where the narrator looks back and tells his story.

But the narrator can also do it this way: *I am going to the store. I see Frank. "What are you doing here?" I say.*

There is an immediacy of tone here that, when handled well (as Steve Martini does in his Paul Madriani legal thrillers), is quite compelling.

One can also choose to write first-person POV for various characters in different chapters. Some authors put the name of the POV character at the start of the chapter, then proceed to write in that narrator's voice.

This requires great skill, of course, because each voice must be different, each perspective unique.

The most important aspect of first person is *attitude*. There must be something about the voice of the narrator that makes her worth listening to—a worldview, a slant, something more than just a plain vanilla rendition of the facts.

Here are two examples of attitude from Lisa Samson. In her novel *Quaker Summer*, Heather Curridge is living in the lap of luxury, wondering what life is really all about and what she has to do with any of it.

> Six-thirty a.m., and the forty-five minutes before I must awaken my son stretches in front of me like a sun-warmed path to beach. I'm never alone it seems, even with just one living child (and I wanted ten, but those thoughts are definitely for another day, or maybe next year). I feel so confined, as if my skin has thickened, hardened like the dried-up skin of a past-due tangerine and inside this shell I'm fighting to be free, to be young and full of hope that I'm made for something more.
>
> More than motherhood?
>
> Justifiably so, the women at my old church would never understand these thoughts. Any woman who wanted more than motherhood wanted too much. But something inside me claws with puckered lips and shiny-bright eyes, believing it will drag not just me, but all those I love right along with it onto a new roller coaster with longer drops to go speeding down, but greater vistas from which to view the world.

In Samson's *Straight Up*, Fairly Godfrey is a New York design consultant, a widow at an early age, assuaging her grief over her deceased husband by a life of many dates:

> My contact lens ripped! Right in half like a slightly dried-out Jell-O saucer. And I'm out of replacements. So I rolled it around on my fingers, figuring I might as well have a little of that curious fun I used to have when I was a child and the thermometer broke.
>
> Lucky me, I may land myself in a cancer ward someday due to the effects of the mercury I allowed to skate and pill across my palm.
>
> So there I sat at the Tavern with Braden, who said we needed to celebrate the finishing of his M.B.A. He's a Mr. Smarty Pants. Did I tell you Braden's only twenty-three? A whiz kid. My boy toy.
>
> Man, he looked cute, that brown, curly JFK Jr. hair sweeping his brow.

Two completely different voices. The author's voice is submerged in character. That's how it's done.

Technical Note

A first-person narrator is usually telling the story in *past tense*, so she knows everything that has happened. Presumably, then, she could report on things that she couldn't have perceived at the time.

Let's say there's a scene with the narrator facing a bar. The door to the bar is behind her. She could say *Just then Billy walked in* even though she hasn't turned around yet. Why? Because she's telling the story in past tense and knows it was Billy.

But it is still preferable to write the narration as if it were in real time. This places the reader within the scene in the most organic and gripping way.

So the line would be rewritten something like this: *I heard the door open and turned. It was Billy.*

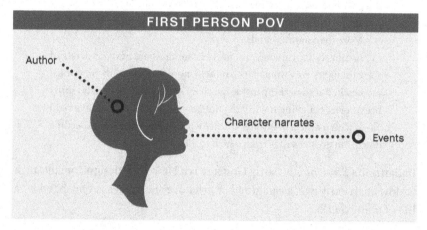

FIRST PERSON POV

Author

Character narrates

Events

THIRD PERSON

Third-person POV is a good choice for most current fiction. The biggest problem writers seem to face with third person is keeping that POV consistent throughout a scene. It's easy to lapse and suddenly have the POV switch to a different character or to a perspective the character can't see.

In the *limited* variety of third person, you stay with one character throughout. You never take on another character's POV. Done well, this can be nearly as intimate as first person. James N. Frey, in *How to Write a Damn Good Novel II*, has an opinion on this. "Don't believe the pseudo-rules about what you can do in first vs. third person," Frey writes. "Virtually *anything* you can do in first person you can do in third and vice versa."

If you allow other characters to have a third-person POV (unlimited) you obviously spend less time in the head of a single character. You spread the intimacy around.

I recommend the discipline of "one scene, one point of view." If you need to change POV, you should start a new chapter or leave white space to signal the switch.

Here's an example of third person from David Morrell's *Creepers*:

> Balenger's muscles relaxed. Knowing there'd be other tests, he watched the creepers fill their knapsacks. "What time are you going in?"
> "Shortly after ten." Conklin hooked a walkie-talkie to his belt.

The POV character is Balenger, so we can know that his muscles relax. Another character wouldn't be able to know that about Balenger. We are also informed what Balenger knows is coming.

Conklin is not a POV character, but we can see what Balenger sees, which is Conklin hooking the walkie-talkie to his belt.

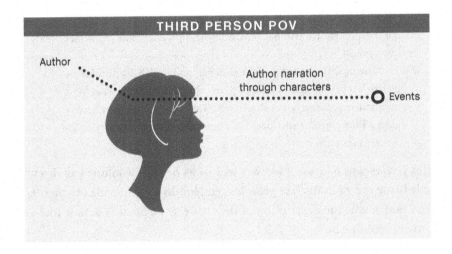

CINEMATIC

Cinematic POV is a description from the outside, as if a movie camera were set up to film the proceedings. You don't deliver the thoughts of the characters. It differs from the other points of view in that we never "drop into the head" of the character to reveal thoughts and emotions. It's all done as if looking at the physical details through an open window or on a movie screen.

```
┌─────────────────────────────────────────────────────────────┐
│                   CINEMATIC PERSON POV                        │
│                                                               │
│                                              ┌─────────────┐  │
│                                              │             │  │
│                                              │  Events on  │  │
│   Author  ●●●●●●●●●●●●●●●●●●●●●●●●●●●●●●●○     │ "The Screen"│  │
│                                              │             │  │
│                                              └─────────────┘  │
│                                                               │
└─────────────────────────────────────────────────────────────┘
```

Almost always the cinematic POV focuses on one main character.

Here's an excerpt from Dashiell Hammett's *The Maltese Falcon*, a novel in the cinematic style:

> Spade sank into his swivel-chair, made a quarter turn to face her, smiled politely. He smiled without separating his lips. All the v's in his face grew longer.
>
> The tappity-tap-tap and the thin bell and muffled whir of Effie Perine's typewriting came through the closed door. Somewhere in a neighboring office a power-driven machine vibrated dully. On Spade's desk a limp cigarette smoldered in a brass tray filled with the remains of limp cigarettes.

This is cinematic because if we were in Spade's head he wouldn't have been able to see the v's in his face grow longer. Nor do we get Spade's thoughts. And notice how the description of the cigarette on Spade's desk is like a camera zooming in.

BENDING POV RULES

Writers have great discussions among themselves about various writing "rules," especially on the knotty question of POV. Well, it's good to know what's what, and who's who, and keep that POV straight. But the occasional break in a POV rule, when done for a purpose, can help you. For example, a little omniscience at the beginning of a chapter, which then drops into third person, is fine. In *Small Town*, one of the masters of the craft, Lawrence Block, does this in chapter four:

> L'aiglon D'or was on Fifty-fifth between Park and Madison, and had
> been there for decades. A classic French restaurant, it had long since
> ceased to be trendy, and the right side of the menu guaranteed that it
> would never be a bargain. The great majority of its patrons had been
> coming for years, cherishing the superb cuisine, the restrained yet el-
> egant décor, and the unobtrusively impeccable service. The tables, set
> luxuriously far apart, were hardly ever all taken, nor were there often
> more than two or three of them vacant. This, in fact, was very much as
> the proprietor preferred it. …
>
> Francis Buckram saw he was a few minutes early and had the cab
> drop him at the corner.

Block begins with an omniscient view of the setting, which is interesting
and helps set the mood. Then he gets us to the POV of Francis Buckram.

But what about dropping in a little omniscience in the *middle* of a scene?
Block does that as well in *Small Town*. In the midst of a scene where third-
person POV has been established, Block gives us a description of the POV
character from the omniscient perspective.

> He stood six-two, a bear of a man, big in the chest and shoulders, with a
> mane of brown hair and a full beard that he trimmed himself. His waist
> was a little thicker than he'd have liked, but not too bad.

And then he goes on with the scene. Now, a POV police alarm might go off
somewhere. "Bear of a man" is the author's voice and evaluation, and the
character is not reflecting on his grooming habits or weight; that's Block
again. But this is hardly a moving violation. It enables Block to get the description in and move on. And it is brief.

Lesson one: Rules exist for a purpose. They work. When you know them
well you can also pick spots where a slight modification might help.

Lesson two: If you do break a rule, keep it brief.

Lesson three: It's not a bad thing to strictly follow POV rules the rest of
your career.

Becoming proficient at POV takes time. Relax, do the exercises at the end
of the chapter, continue to get feedback, and enjoy the process.

When you do nail POV, and you will, you'll feel a command over your
fiction that has heretofore eluded you. It's a nice feeling.

KEY POINTS

- Point of view refers to whose head you are "in."
- The most intimate POV is first person. Least intimate is omniscient.
- A good bet for beginners is third person.
- Don't play with POV until you have plenty of experience!

*Exercise 1**

Read the following section and try to identify all the places where POV shifts or is improperly used. (Check the appendix for the answers.)

Frank ran into the room, hoping Sarah was still there.

She was, waiting impatiently. "Quick," he said, "we've got to get out of here!"

Sarah sighed. "What is it this time?"

"The cops. They're coming." Why couldn't she just do what he said? He went to the window and looked down at the street, watching for cop cars.

Sarah got up from the easy chair and said, "You're paranoid, you fool. It's your meds." It was always the meds with him, every time.

Frank spun around as the first black-and-white pulled up to the curb.

"It's not paranoia if everyone is after you!" he screamed. "Look at me when I talk to you."

I'll look at you when I'm good and ready, Sarah thought. She walked into the kitchen. She was a lovely woman of thirty, popular among her friends. Just not with her husband at the moment.

Another black-and-white pulled up in front of the apartment building.

Frank and Sarah heard the bullhorn. "We know you're in there! Come out with your hands up."

They freaked.

Sarah knew this meant prison.

Frank knew what Sarah knew, because he was omniscient.

*Exercise 2**

Here's a clip of first-person POV. Underline the places where the POV is violated.

---

*Indicates that answers and/or possible revisions to the exercises are included in the appendix

I walked into the deli, looking for her. The place was packed, the people busy with their own food and own problems.

Then I saw her. She had her back to me, sitting in a booth by the wall.

With a determined look I went to the booth and sat across from her.

She was not pleased.

"How you doing, Sarah?" I said.

"How do you think I'm doing?" She shook her head disgustedly.

A waiter with a plate of scrambled eggs came up behind me, said, "I see you've got a friend," and put the plate in front of Sarah.

"I'll have coffee," I said.

Coffee is one of those products with a fascinating history. It was primarily known in the Muslim world, but gradually made its way to Europe by way of the Dutch. It was in the Dutch East Indies that European coffee was largely grown. Its health benefits have been debated, but current scholarship indicates that moderate use is beneficial.

Sarah didn't like having company. "What are you doing here?"

"I came to find out what you know," I said, my blue eyes flashing.

Sarah reached in her purse and fumbled for a key. She tossed it on the glass table, where it clanked in front of me.

"That's all you need to know," she said.

CHAPTER 5

Scenes

In the English countryside they have stone walls to keep in the sheep. Some of these walls have been around for centuries and are amazing architectural achievements. The flat stones are not uniform. They differ in color and shape, yet they fit together to form the whole.

Your scenes are like the stones in an English wall. I prefer that image to bricks, because bricks all look the same. You want your scenes to vary in shape and feel, but when you step back they should all fit together.

You don't want any stones sticking out at odd angles or cracked through the center. If you make each scene stand on its own and contribute to the story in an essential way, your novel will be structurally solid.

But if you have weak scenes your story may crumble.

In this chapter we'll look at approaches to self-editing scenes so your edifice will stand the test of time.

WHAT DOES A SCENE DO?

Your scenes must do one or more of the following:

- move the story through action
- characterize through reaction
- set up essential scenes to come
- sprinkle in some spice

In addition to these purposes, each scene must have a degree of *intensity*. This doesn't mean equal intensity throughout. You don't want the cartoon feel of a coyote chasing a roadrunner in every scene.

But something does have to be at stake in the scene; something has to matter. Even when the characters are taking time to breathe or reflect or re-group, the underlying story question needs to roil, like the bad goo under the streets of New York in *Ghostbusters II*.

It is best to approach scenes as primarily involving action and reaction, setup, and spice, which are examined below.

ACTION SCENES

An action scene is any scene where a character is trying to get somewhere, solve a problem, move forward in the story. Action doesn't always mean a car chase or shoot-out, though those certainly qualify. An action scene takes place when you have an objective, obstacles, and an outcome.

Objective

Each action scene must have a *scene objective*. That is, from whatever point of view you're in, there must be a moving force in the scene trying to make something happen.

- A cop is questioning a witness, trying to get information.
- A mother who has lost a child is trying to forget her pain.
- A Navy SEAL is trying to kill five assassins at once.
- A man is drinking to keep from confronting the fact that he has cheated on his wife.

And so on. In addition to that, you need some sort of ...

Obstacle

What person, place, thing, or circumstance is keeping the POV character from gaining the objective?

- The witness is lying to the cop, and even has a gun.
- The mother keeps seeing her missing child in every object in the house.
- Assassins are good at what they do. That's why they're assassins.
- Alcohol dulls, but doesn't destroy, the conscience.

As you can see, the opposition element can be outer (as in another character) or inner (as in the character's psychology and thought patterns).

Further, you can have social opposition. Any group of people who have an interest in the status quo can provide this. For instance, Rick Dadier in

Evan Hunter's *The Blackboard Jungle* is a teacher who thinks he can make a difference in a tough school. Most of the other teachers, and the administration, don't think so. This makes for several tense scenes in the book and movie.

Finally, nature itself can provide opposition in a scene. It can provide the basic opposition for an entire novel or script, as in Stephen King's *Storm of the Century*. Don't ever get stuck on an island off the coast of Maine in winter if King is writing the story. He's liable to drop a pathological killer in there.

Nature or circumstance can be a great obstacle when time is of the essence. The character needs to get to town, but the bridge is out. Or a storm puts a tree across the road. Or the car itself breaks down.

The nice thing about being an author is you get to choose.

Outcome

Each scene has to end at some point. In general a scene can end:
1. well
2. not so well
3. terribly

In the realm of fiction, the worse the scene ends, either overtly or implicitly, the better.

Because people read to worry. They want to watch a Lead they've bonded with go through the trials and tribulations of the story. The more success, the less worry.

Design your scenes, for the most part, so the Lead is in a worse position after the scene is over.

She doesn't get the information she wants.

Worse, she gets some information that hurts her.

Worse still, she is knocked out by a hammer.

There is an infinite variety of bad outcomes to choose from.

This doesn't mean that the occasional scene can't end well. For breathing space, have something good happen from time to time.

But get her back into trouble as soon as possible.

REACTION SCENES

Where action is mainly about forward progress, reaction is mainly about emotion. It's a window into how the character is dealing with the story issues around her. Reaction scenes can be complete unto themselves. Or you can put a reaction *beat* into an action scene. When you break it down, the reaction unit goes like this:

Emotion

When something happens to us, our first reaction is often an emotional one. This is part of what makes us human. Our emotions are there to protect us and give us instant direction. Sometimes it's a wrong direction, but there you are.

Your Lead finally gets into the hotel room and finds her husband dead. Emotion is first. The greater the stimulus, the more explicit you make the emotional reaction.

Analysis

When the emotions cool, the character must decide what to do. In the case of the woman and her husband's body, she has some options:

- hide the body
- call the police
- tell the mother-in-law
- sit and do nothing

Decision

Finally, a decision must be made or the story stalls. This decision leads to the next objective, or action scene. The following diagram shows the perpetual plot motion that action and reaction provide.

Dwight Swain, in *Techniques of the Selling Writer*, and Jack Bickham in *Writing and Selling Your Novel*, cover action/reaction in depth (they call it scene and sequel). For further study, I recommend these books.

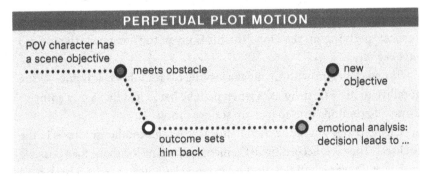

PERPETUAL PLOT MOTION

POV character has a scene objective •••••••••••••• meets obstacle

outcome sets him back

emotional analysis: decision leads to ...

new objective

SETUP

A scene that's primarily used for setting up other aspects of the story should itself contain all the elements of an action or reaction scene. Such scenes should be relatively short and come early in the story.

For example, a writer may need to set up the family life and a particular trait of one of the characters so when a kidnapping takes place, the trait may come into play later. Let's say the victim is a five-year-old boy with a fear of the dark.

Select a POV character and create a scene that utilizes or mentions this trait. Say it's the mother, the Lead in your story. You might create a scene where she is arguing with her husband, and they're startled by the boy screaming in his room. She goes to comfort him, thinks about his fear, then comes back to the husband.

Like spice, below, setup information should be "marbled" into a scene, carefully spread throughout the whole.

SPICE

Spice is an ingredient best used sparingly. You can sprinkle it in just about any scene, and sometimes (rarely) make it the basis of an entire scene. Stephen King did this in his novella *The Body* when he had one of the characters make up a pie-eating story.

The plot stops, but the added spice draws us in further.

Used within a scene, spice can often be the difference between an average scene and a truly memorable one.

An example is a scene from Francis Ford Coppola's *The Godfather*, which was adapted from Mario Puzo's novel. In the film, after Don Corleone has been shot, Sonny orders a hit on Paulie, a low-level soldier they suspect of giving up the Don. The hit is given to Clemenza, the rotund *capo regime*.

The spice begins with Clemenza leaving his middle-class home, saying goodbye to his wife, who asks when he'll be back. Just like a guy going to work. She reminds him to pick up some cannoli.

Clemenza gets in the car that Paulie is driving. Another soldier is in the backseat. They are, according to Clemenza, scouting locations for a possible mob war. There's small talk in the car, some laughter, then on a back road

Clemenza tells Paulie to pull over. "I have to take a leak," Clemenza says, and walks over to the weeds.

We now get a long shot of the car from the side. We see Paulie at the wheel, and only the weeds and, in the distance, the Statue of Liberty.

A hand comes up from the back of the car, holding a gun. Two shots to the head.

Clemenza zips up and goes back to the car and says to the hit man, "Leave the gun. Take the cannoli."

The hit man hands the little box of cannoli to Clemenza, and they go their merry way.

What makes this scene so strong and memorable is the spice of opposites. The normal family man routine mixed with a mob hit. That's what spice can do.

SCENE TENSION

Every scene in your novel should have tension, whether that comes from outright conflict or the inner turmoil of character emotions.

You create outer tension by remembering scene structure and giving the POV character a scene objective. What does he want, and why? It has to matter to him or it won't matter to us.

Next, what keeps him from the goal? It may be the opposing action of another character or a circumstance in which he finds himself.

Finally, make most scenes come out with the character suffering a setback. This ratchets up the tension for the scenes to follow.

Even in scenes that are relatively quiet, characters can feel inner tension—worry, concern, irritability, anxiety.

In Evan Hunter's *The Moment She Was Gone*, Andrew Gulliver's twin sister, a schizophrenic, is missing. Andrew and his mother, brother, and sister-in-law take stock.

The sister-in-law tries to lighten things:

> "Then maybe she's hiding out in St. Patrick's Cathedral," Augusta says.
> "Or the Museum of Modern Art."
>> I hate it when my sister-in-law tries to be funny about Annie. I think she does this only to gain further favor with Aaron, who by the way has never thought any of our sister's little escapades were in the slightest bit

comical, even when they really were. As for example, the time she peed on a cop's shoes in Georgia.

"Or maybe we ought to go look for her guru," Augusta adds, compounding the felony.

"Augusta, you're not being funny," I say.

By throwing Andrew's irritability against Augusta's "humor," Hunter increases the overall tension in the story.

Every scene should have one or more of the following elements:

CONFLICT
- **INNER:** The character's emotional argument with himself.
- **OUTER:** Obstacles to the objective:
  a. Character: Another character or group of characters with a different agenda.
  b. Social: Rules or circumstances of the community.
  c. Natural: Anything about the physical setting.

TENSION
- **UNCERTAINTY:** The character doesn't have enough information.
- **WORRY:** The character has more than enough (bad) information.
- **DOUBT:** The character doesn't have confidence in her abilities, other characters, or the circumstances.

SCENE PATTERNS

Consider your scene openings. Once the novel is rolling along, you want to jump into scenes fairly quickly.

A logical pattern of a scene goes like this:

> A = the opening description, to set the scene
> B = the characters coming on stage
> C = the actual meat of the scene, the conflict or central point

Many times you can get right to the characters and drop in description as needed. A scene pattern might look like this: B, A, C, or C, B, A.

Here's an example of a traditional scene:

A

The bar was dimly lit and smelled of stale beer. Country music was blaring, some song about lost trucks. Two or three people looked his way.

B

Steve decided the best thing to do was order a beer and look like he belonged. Then he'd approach Manfred and suggest they talk. That way, there was less of a chance it would look like he was trying to start something.

He got the beer at the bar, taking note of the gilded wall mirror with various liquor bottles lined up in front of it. He thought of the old Westerns, the way a six-gun would wipe out the glass and send people diving. He wished he had one right now, just in case. Manfred was not going to be happy to see him.

Steve took one more sip, wiped his mouth with the back of his hand, and walked over to Manfred's table.

Manfred's red hair was hidden under a black cowboy hat. His pale blue eyes were trained at a big-screen TV showing the Bears game.

C

"Manfred?" Steve said.

Two eyes shot bullets. "What?"

"Can we talk?"

"I'm watching the game."

Steve pulled out a chair. "Won't take a second."

"Don't even think about sitting down."

And we're into the conflict of the scene. This pattern is fine and always usable, but it's a little clunky, like Grandma's shoes. You can vary the pattern and achieve a better effect, even cut what isn't necessary. Here's an example of a different pattern:

"Manfred?" Steve said.

Two eyes shot bullets. "What?"

"Can we talk?"

"I'm watching the game."

Manfred glowered under his black cowboy hat. Only a bit of his red hair was visible. The big-screen TV showing the Bears game competed with the country music coming from behind the bar.

Steve pulled out a chair. "Won't take a second."

"Don't even think about sitting down."

We're at a point in the book where we know who Steve is, know where he's going. We started the scene with the conflict. Now we can drop in details of the setting as we see fit.

• •

The most debilitating thing about writing is that the voice inside us, the voice we trust more than others, says, "You're not good enough, you're not smart enough, what you wrote yesterday really stinks." What aspiring writers should keep in mind is that we all hear that voice, and sometimes that voice lies to us. In fact, when it comes to writing, that voice almost always lies to us. Midway through a book you are going to read back and think, "This is awful." Now it may be awful, but it also may be wonderful and you've simply read it so many times your ear has gone deaf. Don't listen to that voice.

—RANDY WAYNE WHITE

GETTING HIP

In *Plot & Structure* I have a section on getting HIP to your scenes. HIP stands for *hook, intensity,* and *prompt.* Let me briefly reiterate.

Hook

Where you begin a scene is just as important as where you begin the novel. You don't want to give a reader any reason to put your book down. You may think you have some time to take a break once you're rolling along. No breaks.

Create something at the beginning of a scene/chapter that pulls the reader in. You can introduce a new character. This is what Steve Martini did in three consecutive chapters in *The Jury*:

CHAPTER SIX
Jimmy de Angelo is forty-seven, a former street cop turned detective.

CHAPTER SEVEN
William Epperson is the mystery man in our case.

CHAPTER EIGHT

Dr. Gabriel Warnake is a private consultant under contract to the county crime lab.

Dialogue is another good hook technique, as it means something is happening now.

> "Don't turn on the light," she said.
>
> I didn't dare. Didn't want to be seen from the street. The apartment smelled of last night's pizza.

You can use setting to begin a scene if you make it interesting enough, and then you get right to the action. Here's how Max Phillips does it in *Fade to Blonde*:

> Halliday's office was in one of those modernistic buildings that look old six months after they're built. It had a two-story lobby with a streaked glass wall in front and steel and terrazzo staircase in back. Everything was covered in dusty green bathroom tile. It was trying hard not to seem cheap. It looked like Rebecca's boarding house in a ten-dollar suit. As I climbed the stairs …

How you open a scene is a matter of *strategy*. What is the feel you want your book to have? Is it fast moving or does it take its time? Is it more about the interior character life or outward threats? Is your intended readership those who like commercial fare or literary fiction?

You will choose scene openings accordingly.

Do you want a leisurely opening for your scene? One that sets the mood and then eases into the action?

> The next morning was fiercely windy and as he crossed into Texas passing some purple beehives and a sign that read SEE THE WORLD'S LARGEST PRAIRIE DOG, 3 MI WEST, the wind increased, banged at the car with irregular bursts and slams. Tumbleweeds, worn small by a winter's thrashing, rolled across the road in the hundreds. Sheets of plastic, food wrappers, sacks, papers, boxes, rags flew, catching on barbwire fences where they flapped until a fresh gust tore them loose. The landscape churned with detritus.
>
> —*That Old Ace in the Hole*, by Annie Proulx

Proulx gives us another page or so of description like this, before the scene action begins, all in keeping with the tone of the story.

Notice the details, building one upon the other, all adding to the mood. This is double duty at work. Not just descriptions, but ones that are relevant to the strategy.

Another good use of the leisurely opening is to show the passage of time.

> It was the rainiest May ever. A sense of ordinary life had established itself by late winter, had risen from the chaos and comfort of schedules and lazy weekends, school vacations, colds and flus and dentist appointments, long sleepy Saturday mornings of drawing together in Mattie's bed. In early spring, they threw off their jackets and tore outside. The garden was in full crazy bloom and the children were growing like Topsy, too, as Isa always said. They now spend three weekends a month with Nicky and Lee …
> —*BLUE SHOE*, BY ANNE LAMOTT

In Medias Res

A good default setting, even in literary fiction, is to start a scene as close to the central action as possible. By central action I mean the heart of the scene, the reason you're writing it. What Raymond Obstfeld calls the "hot spot."

In medias res means "in the middle of things," and that's what you should go for. Often you can cut some flab off the opening of a scene and make it move a little faster. For example, a chapter might begin like this:

> It was warm on Tuesday. The sun beat down on the pavement like Lucifer's hammer. The whole city seemed drenched in a torpor unrelenting in its somnolence. Don fought the traffic all the way into the heart of the city but happily found a lot that didn't cost a second mortgage to park.
> He walked up Main Street, starting to sweat in his white cotton shirt. The Massingale Building was right there where it always was. Funny, he thought. Did I expect it to move? Expect it to hide from what I'm about to do?
> He took the elevator to the fourth floor and walked to Suite 415.
> Clearing his throat, Don drew his gun and charged in.
> "Nobody move!" he shouted.

Now, there's nothing necessarily wrong with this opening. It all depends on your strategy. But if this is supposed to be a fast-moving action type of novel, you have other ways to do it.

> Don drew his gun and charged into Suite 415.
> "Nobody move!" he shouted.

You can then marble in the description you want to use throughout the scene.

Don can notice the stifling heat, for example, because the building's air-conditioning system is down.

Another way to start is like this:

> "Nobody move!" Don shouted. He pointed his gun at the startled receptionist in Suite 415.

Vary your openings. Don't always lead off with the same rhythms. Use dialogue, thoughts, and description, but always put them close to the hot spot.

Establish Viewpoint

Your scene openings must quickly establish the viewpoint character. Whose scene is this? Readers need to know.

Next, tell us what is important to that viewpoint character. What is her agenda? What is her objective? The whole reason she's "onstage" in the first place?

You can do this explicitly or implicitly.

EXPLICIT
Margie walked into the Red Canary looking for Bob. She was going to lay him out once and for all. Let him know exactly what she thought of him. Take her for granted, would he?

IMPLICIT
Margie walked into the Red Canary. She looked around. Where was Bob? She noticed her hands clenching and unclenching. She paused, trying to slow her breathing.

You use the implicit opening when, from the scenes preceding, it's obvious what the character is feeling and thinking.

The exception to this is when the action in the scene is meant to be a surprise. Perhaps we don't know how Margie feels about Bob but will find out when she hits him over the head with a pitcher of beer.

But most of the time you want readers clued in on who wants what in the scene, so they can enjoy the tension of wondering how things will turn out.

Intensity

Remember Hitchcock's axiom: You don't want dull parts in your fiction, and dull parts are those without trouble.

The greater the trouble, the greater the intensity.

You want to have some sort of tension in every scene, though it doesn't have to be of the highest sort. That would wear out the reader. Modulating tension is one of the keys to writing fiction. You give your readers some breathing room, too.

But when they breathe, let it be with a tight chest.

Always look at your scenes to see if there are ways you can ratchet up the tension a few degrees. Can you:

- Make the stakes more important?
- Make the odds greater?
- Make the characters care more?
- Make the incidents more challenging?
- Bring in a surprise character?
- Have the setting or weather provide an obstacle?

Prompt

The last paragraph or line of your scene has one purpose: to get the reader to read on. It prompts him forward in some fashion.

While there are going to be innumerable possibilities for you at the end of each scene, here's a list of some:

- a mysterious line of dialogue
- an image that's foreboding (like the fog rolling in)
- a secret suddenly revealed
- a major decision or vow
- announcement of a shattering event
- reversal or surprise—new information that suddenly turns the story around
- a question left hanging in the air

Greg Iles uses foreboding—literally!—for this scene ending from *Sleep No More*. This scene is early in the suspense novel. John Waters is a young husband and father, with what seems to be the perfect life. But then he happens to encounter a stunningly beautiful mystery woman at his daughter's soccer game, one who reminds him of a lover he had before he was married.

> Waters turned back to the dark river, his gut hollow with foreboding, his
> mind roiling with images of two women, neither of whom was his wife.

Iles capitalizes on this to create a scene ending that hints of dark tones to come (the use of the word *dark* in relation to the river is the right choice of word). And the images of two women roiling in his mind, with the reminder that he has a wife he's not thinking of, is a recipe for disaster to come.

A sense of foreboding—or discomfort, anger, frustration, confusion—is inner trouble for the character, and trouble is always enticing for the reader.

Here are some chapter-ending lines from an early Stephen King novel, *Christine*:

> It was bad from the start. And it got worse in a hurry.
>
> *
>
> That's what I thought. But that time I was wrong.
>
> *
>
> "Dennis," he said, "I'll do what I can."
>
> *
>
> That night I didn't get back to sleep too quickly.
>
> *
>
> But I'm a little older now.
>
> *
>
> We went up, and tired as I was, I lay awake a long time. It had been an eventful day. Outside, a night wind tapped a branch softly against the side of the house, and far away, downtown, I heard some kid's rod peeling rubber—it made a sound in the night like a hysterical woman's desperate laughter.
>
> *
>
> It was a question he shrank from. He was afraid of the answer.

Work on your HIPs. It will pay off in greater readability. It will give your book an irresistible forward motion, and that's what you want. Challenge your readers. Make them miss appointments because they can't put your book down.

THE PRESSURE COOKER

Legendary screenwriter Paddy Chayefsky was, in the 1950s, called "the bard of the commonplace." He wrote about ordinary characters (as in the film *Marty*) who become sympathetic through their everyday struggles.

He did this by placing them in a pressure cooker.

An example is his film *Middle of the Night* with Fredric March and Kim Novak. It's about a middle-aged widower, successful but lonely, and a twenty-four-year-old girl, beautiful but nervous. Ordinary people surround them—his sister and daughter and son-in-law (Martin Balsam), and her mother and sister. Also a fifty-nine-year-old salesman at March's work (who attempts suicide).

All of them seem ordinary yet interesting in their ordinariness because their anxieties are understandable to us (we know we have, or would have, the same) and pressed to the *limit* in the story. March is desperately lonely and tries to hide it (the tension shows in a wonderful phone call scene early on). Finally he breaks and practically begs the girl to love him.

She is anxious, almost to a neurotic degree. She has been used by men physically (including her ex-husband) and she *does* have passions. She wants to be truly loved but is afraid if she does love March he will eventually abandon her. He, on the other hand, is constantly worried about her being attracted to another man.

Balsam has a great scene as a henpecked husband with a controlling wife who finally bursts and makes a plea that his wife cares more for her father than she does for him.

Novak's mother is tightly wound and tries to convince Novak to dump March and go back to her ex-husband.

Each scene has some sort of this tension built in. It's like the characters are pressure cookers. The anxieties cause them to tremble inside a little, and these anxieties gradually build until the characters explode to relieve the pressure.

So, in every scene, ask about the characters' inner anxieties:

- Are they understandable, human?
- Are they on the way to being pressed to the limit?
- How can you show, subtly or overtly, the pressure?
- What will be the consequences of the explosion?

MOVE AROUND

Avoid "talking heads." That is, two characters talking where nothing else is taking place. Give a scene some sort of motion, either with the characters themselves or something around them.

I was writing a scene once where my Lead, a lawyer, visits a client who runs a lumberyard. They meet in the yard, then the client invites the Lead into his office to talk. That seemed natural, as the reason for the scene is mainly for the lawyer to tell the client he has to pull out of the case.

A couple of things hit me. First, one reason we create static scenes is because the main purpose is to exchange story information verbally. So we get the characters into a place where they can talk. Logical, but static.

Then I remembered one of the things I like most about my favorite TV show, *Law & Order* (the Moriarty/Noth/Orbach years). When the detectives interview witnesses, they usually go to their place of business and interview them as the witness is walking around working. It's a great way to avoid talking heads and also provides some opportunities for conflict, as in "I have to get back to work now" (at which point Orbach says something like, "Maybe we'll talk at the precinct next time.").

So I rewrote the scene as a "walk and talk." Here's part of it:

> Pete was holding a clipboard and talking on a cell phone out in the yard. Stacks of lumber in various cuts and sizes created a bunker feel, as if this might be ground zero against a military attack. Sam felt besieged, and a bit like a traitor.
>
> It hurt even more when Pete smiled at him and checked out of his call. "Sam, nice surprise."
>
> Pete's grip was strong this time, invested with optimism. Sweat glistened on his arms.
>
> "Moving a lot of wood?" Sam said in a feeble attempt at small talk.
>
> "If that Valley Circle development goes through—you know the one out at the end of Roscoe—we'll move a whole bunch."
>
> "That'd be nice."
>
> "We could use it. Walk and talk?"
>
> "Sure."
>
> Pete clipped his cell phone on his belt and started walking toward the north end of the yard. "You have some news," Pete said.
>
> "Yes."
>
> "Good?"
>
> "In the long run, I think it will …"
>
> A forklift loaded with 2 × 10s rumbled past them, drowning Sam's words. He didn't want to shout.
>
> Pete's face clouded. "You think we'll lose."
>
> "No."
>
> "What then?"

"Pete, I have to pull out."

"I thought we—"

"Something's happened to my family, Pete."

Pete nodded. "The legal thing with that guy? Listen, I don't care—"

"Thing is, I can't give my best to you because of it. I've tried, but you need somebody who can give a hundred percent."

A man in a blue work shirt and baseball hat shouted to Pete from the loading bay. "Hey Mr. Harper, you want us to house that load of air-dried?"

"Do it," Pete answered.

"Which space?"

"Just pick one!"

Now Sam felt a double dose of guilt. He'd become a workplace irritant. "I'm sorry, Pete. I shouldn't have bothered you here."

UNDERSTANDING SUMMARY

Our discussion of scenes would not be complete without an explanation of *summary*. Whereas *scene* gives the feeling of happening in real time, in front of you—think of watching a scene on a movie screen, for example—*summary* is the author or narrator merely relating what happened, telling us about it rather than showing us beat by beat.

Summaries are essential for fiction because not everything needs to be shown. For example, Mary and her husband, Frank, have an argument. Frank storms out and slams the door. Mary decides to go to the store to buy some groceries. At the store, she'll run across an old boyfriend, who will make new moves on her.

The obvious scenes are the argument and the scene in the store. Those are scenes we'll want to see beat by beat. But getting Mary to the store doesn't need to be shown, because it would only slow things down.

Summary is the way to get Mary from the first scene to the next in short order. Such summaries are also called *transitions*.

Here's how it works, picking up at the end of the argument scene:

"You can just stick it where the sun don't shine!" Frank grabbed his coat.

"You can't talk to me that way!" Mary said, "Where do you think you're going?"

"I'm going to my mother's, if it's any of your business."

> "You will not leave this house."
>
> Frank opened the door. "I guess it's true what they say. A boy's best friend is his mother." He slammed the door behind him.
>
> Mary stood there for a moment, feeling like a prize fool. She saw the flowers he'd brought home the night before. She picked up the vase and slammed it to the floor.
>
> *I'd better calm down.*
>
> She grabbed her car keys.
>
> Ten minutes later she was walking down the cracker aisle at Ralph's.

That last line is *summary*. It spares us from seeing Mary walking out the door, getting in her car, backing out, taking a right on Olive Street, and so on. We don't need that. We just need to get her to the store.

Summary does that for us. It can also be used to set up a scene.

If the story is really about Mary meeting her former boyfriend, Lance, and you don't want to dwell on the argument with Frank, use summary:

> Mary wondered if she should really go through with this. Meeting Lance at Starbucks was a risk. But she and Frank had gone through another of their frequent arguments, the kind that ended with her breaking a vase. It was getting expensive living with Frank. She hoped Lance would buy the coffee.
>
> She pulled into a parking spot in front of Starbucks and her heart spiked. Lance was sitting at a table, looking right at her.

Finally, you can use summary if you need to cover a lot of ground quickly, as Stuart Woods does in *Short Straw*:

> "Amigo," Vittorio replied, "what are the three best hotels in Puerto Vallarta?"
>
> "Well, Señor, there are many fine hotels, but if I must, I will name three." He did so.
>
> "Okay, let's start with those." Vittorio broke the seal on the box containing his guns, which he had checked through, and returned them and the magazines to his holsters. The first two desk clerks took his money and denied all knowledge of Barbara Eagle, under any name. At the third hotel, the clerk came up with a guest named Barbara Kennerly.

How can you tell if you're using summary? Always ask, does what I'm writing have the possibility of present-moment dialogue? If it does, you're writing a scene. If not, you're in summary. For example:

> John and Stephanie arrived at the little town of Dos Zapatos on July 14. This was where they were going to spend their vacation. It had been decided. By John, of course. He had read that the town was named back in 1912. Pancho Villa shot a shoemaker because he had only one of Villa's shoes ready.

That's summary. The information about the town doesn't give us the possibility of present-moment dialogue. This does:

> Stephanie stared out the window at the dirty little town called Dos Zapatos. "This is where you wanted to spend our vacation?" she said.
> "What's wrong with it?" John said.
> "Oh, nothing that a little civilization won't cure. You and your Pancho Villa fixation."
> "Aren't you intrigued by that? He shot a shoemaker here just because one of his shoes wasn't ready."
> "That's so exciting."

FLASHBACKS

A lot of writing teachers warn about flashbacks. Some simply echo Sinclair Lewis who, when asked how best to handle flashbacks, said, "Don't."

That's a bit extreme. Many novelists successfully utilize flashbacks. You can, too, if you approach them with great care.

The first question to ask about a flashback scene is, *Is it absolutely necessary?* Be firm about this. Does the story information have to come to us in this fashion?

Be wary of starting your novel in the present and going too soon to flashback. If the flashback is important, consider starting with that scene as a prologue or first chapter.

These are guidelines. In the hands of a good writer, a gripping first chapter, followed by a compelling flashback, can work—see the first two chapters of Lee Child's *Persuader* for an example.

If you've decided a flashback scene is necessary, make sure it works *as a scene*; that is, it must be immediate, confrontational. Write it as a unit of dramatic action, not as an information dump. Not:

> Jack remembered when he was a child, and he spilled the gasoline on the ground. His father got so angry at him it scared Jack. His father hit

him, and yelled at him. It was something Jack would never forget … [and more of the same]

Instead:

Jack couldn't help remembering the gas can. He was eight, and all he wanted to do was play with it.

The garage was his theater. No one was home. He held the can aloft, like the hammer of Thor. "I am the king of gas!" he said. "I will set you all on fire!"

Jack stared down at the imaginary humans below his feet.

The gas can slipped from his hand.

Unable to catch it, Jack could only watch as the can made a horrible *thunking* sound. Its contents poured out on the new cement.

Jack righted the can, but it was too late. A big, smelly puddle was right in the middle of the garage.

Dad is going to kill me!

Desperate, Jack looked around for a rag, anything to clean up the mess.

He heard the garage door open.

Dad was home.

You get the idea. A well-written flashback scene will not detract from your story. Readers are used to novels cutting away from one scene to another. They will accept a cut to a flashback if it's written with dramatic flair.

Getting In and Out

How do you get in and out of a flashback so it flows naturally? Here's one way that works every time.

In the scene you're writing, when you're about to go to flashback, put in a sensory detail that triggers the memory in the point-of-view character:

Wendy looked at the wall and saw an ugly, black spider making its way up toward a web where a fly was caught. Legs creeping, moving slowly toward its prey. The way Lester had moved on Wendy all those years ago.

She was sixteen and Lester was the big man on campus. "Hey," he called to her one day by the lockers. "You want to go see a movie?"

We are in the flashback. Write it out as a dramatic scene.

How do we get out of it? By returning to the sensory detail (sight, in this case). The reader will remember the strong detail and know he's out of flashback.

> Lester made his move in the back of the car. Wendy was helpless. It was all over in five minutes.
>
> The spider was at the web now. Wendy felt waves of nausea as she watched it. But she could not look away.

Watch Out for "Had"

Watch out for the word *had* in your flashback scenes. Use one or two to get in, but once in, avoid them. Instead of:

> Marvin had been good at basketball. He had tried out for the team, and the coach had said how good he was.
>
> "I think I'll make you my starting point guard," Coach had told him right after tryouts.
>
> Marvin had been thrilled by that.

Do this:

> Marvin had been good at basketball. He tried out for the team, and the coach said how good he was.
>
> "I think I'll make you my starting point guard," Coach told him right after tryouts.
>
> Marvin was thrilled.

Flashback Scene Alternative

An alternative to the flashback scene is the back flash. These are short bursts in which you drop information about the past within a present moment scene. The two primary methods are dialogue and thoughts.

First, dialogue:

> "Hey, don't I know you?"
>
> "No."
>
> "Yeah, yeah. You were in the newspapers, what, ten years ago? The kid who killed his parents in that cabin."
>
> "You're wrong."
>
> "Chester A. Arthur! You were named after the president. I remember that in the story."

Chester's troubled background has come out in a flash of dialogue. This is also a good way for shocking information from the past, or a dark secret, to be revealed at a tense moment in the story.

Now, thoughts:

"Hey, don't I know you?"

"No." Did he? Did the guy recognize him? Would everybody in town find out he was Chet Arthur, killer of parents?

"Yeah, yeah. You were in the newspapers, what, ten years ago?"

It was twelve years ago, and this guy had him pegged. Lousy press, saying he killed his parents because he was high on drugs. They didn't care about the abuse, did they? And this guy wouldn't, either.

We are in Chester's head for this one, as he reflects on his past. If you want to do a full flashback scene, thoughts can also operate as a transition point.

The skillful handling of flashback material is one mark of a good writer. Using back flashes as an alternative is usually the mark of a wise writer.

KEY POINTS

- Scenes are the building blocks of fiction. Make each one count.
- An action scene needs a viewpoint character with an objective and obstacles.
- A reaction scene (or beat) needs a viewpoint character reacting emotionally, analyzing the situation, and making a decision on what to do next to gain his objective.
- Setup and spice should be used sparingly and placed within real scenes.
- Open your scenes *in medias res*. Use a variety of styles.
- End most of your scenes with things getting tougher for the Lead.
- Use summary for transitions and setup.
- Flashbacks should be as compelling as any scene.

*Exercise 1**

In the following scene, underline: (1) the POV character, (2) his objective, (3) the opposition, and (4) the outcome.

When the sun came up, Sam thought about driving over to Roz's and getting Heather himself. His wife talked him out of it, and he knew she was right. This thing needed some natural flow.

Besides, with no sleep, he couldn't be sure he'd be rational or understanding. He might end up chasing a dog down the street, or biting a mailman.

So he went into the office. But working was like slogging up a muddy hill in ankle weights. Sam tried to clear out the brain cobwebs with a triple latte, but after the early morning run-in with Heather, anything he tried to concentrate on was a boulder he could barely move. *Call me Sisyphus.*

There was one thing he decided, though, and there was no going back in his mind. He finished his coffee and went to Lew's office.

"Hey, what's up, pard?" Lew was twiddling a pencil in his right hand as he tapped at his keyboard with the other.

"I can't do it, Lew."

"Do what?"

"Give up on Harper. I'm taking it all the way."

Lew threw the pencil on the desk. "That's disappointing."

"I'm sorry. That's just the way it's going to be."

"Just like that?"

"I've been thinking about this a long time."

"So we don't make decisions together anymore?"

"You wanted to take the decision away from me, Lew. You made the pronouncement that it was up to me, but you didn't really want me to stay on this case. But I took it on, and it's my obligation as a lawyer—"

"Will you stop with the law school ethics? You're not a One-L."

"I happen to believe in what I'm doing."

Lew shook his head. "I'm not pleased. But I think you already knew I wouldn't be." He was silent for a moment. "Alright. Do what you have to do. But we are not waiving our fee. Now get out of here and go do some work, will you?"

Work. Yes. Sam would do what he always had in the past—work his tail off. He was never the smartest one in his class at law school, he knew that. But he made sure nobody would outwork him, and nobody did.

He was going to work at getting his daughter back, getting justice for Sarah Harper, and making life come out even again. Raw effort, that would do it.

*Exercise 2**

See what you can do to add a hook to the following scene opening:

It was cold that Monday. The weatherman had reported it. He said it was going to be cold, very cold. John had watched the report in the morning, sipping his coffee. He knew it was going to be one of the coldest Mondays on record.

He took care to get dressed warmly. He put silks on under his clothes. He made sure there was an extra layer over them, too. He didn't want to be cold.

It was cold in the garage. When he opened the door to the garage he was hit with it. He knew this was going to be one cold day, all right.

He got in the car, started it, used the garage door opener to open the garage door. He waited until it was all the way open, then he started to back out.

John reached down to turn on the heater but kept going. Then he felt the bump. And heard the scream. He stopped the car and jumped out.

The old man lay motionless on the driveway.

"No," John said. "Don't be dead. Please don't be dead."

CHAPTER 6

Dialogue

Here's a little secret: Dialogue is the fastest way to improve your fiction.

That's right.

Because sodden, overwritten dialogue sticks out of a manuscript like a garrulous uncle at Thanksgiving.

But if you put crisp dialogue in your characters' mouths it will make your manuscript look more professional. Immediately.

In most of the manuscripts I read from new writers, the dialogue is clunky. It doesn't sound realistic. When it does sound realistic, it is often because the dialogue is an attempt to be real-life speech without fictional purpose, and that doesn't work either.

Sometimes there are too many attributions or adverbs. Sometimes there is too much "happy talk," dialogue without tension or conflict.

The dialogue itself may be too "puffy." There are words in the dialogue that could be cut, contributing to dynamism and readability.

The solutions to these various problems are not difficult to understand or apply. And if you practice them, you will easily make your manuscript sharper. This will be noticed.

It will help you enormously to understand that dialogue in fiction is just another form of *character action.*

Speech is physical. Characters speak. When they speak, it should be because they are trying to further their agendas in a given scene.

Dialogue in fiction is not space filler, as it often is in life. It is not a way to kill time. If you think of dialogue as action, you'll avoid elementary mistakes.

THE 8 ESSENTIALS OF GREAT DIALOGUE

Every dialogue exchange in your novel must be intentional. You need to know why you're writing it. The following essentials will enable you to assess any line of dialogue you write from now on.

1. It Is Essential to the Story

If dialogue isn't essential to your story, why is it in there?

Dialogue must do one or more of the following three things: Advance plot, reveal character, and reflect theme.

To advance the plot, dialogue needs to give us essential story information. It needs to give us exposition, or background, or help us understand what's going on in a scene:

> "Bill," Shelia said. "What are you doing here? I thought you were in Baltimore."
>
> "We have some unfinished business, sweetheart."

We know from the above that Bill was supposed to be in Baltimore, at least as far as Shelia is concerned. Also, that he has something on his mind that doesn't sound particularly nice.

Dialogue also fills its essential role when it helps reveal character and character relationships. In *The Maltese Falcon*, Sam Spade, private detective, talks in a clipped manner. The dandy, Joel Cairo, has a more refined way of speaking:

> Spade said: "Let's go some place where we can talk."
>
> Cairo raised his chin. "Please excuse me," he said. "Our conversations in private have not been such that I am anxious to continue them."

We can tell a lot just by listening to how people speak.

Dialogue can also illuminate theme, so long as you're not heavy-handed about it. What is the theme of *The Maltese Falcon*? Greed and lies and the power of money. Yes, all these, but for Sam Spade, what is it? It is that he will not be played for a sap. To do that would be losing all self-respect and the ability to go on as a man and detective. The theme is that only a personal code, clung to, can save a man from self-destruction.

> She put a hand on his hand on her shoulder. "Don't help me then," she whispered, "but don't hurt me. Let me go away now."

"No," he said. "I'm sunk if I haven't got you to hand over to the police when they come. That's the only thing that can keep me from going down with the others."

"You won't do that for me?"

"I won't play the sap for you."

Not even for love:

"... Now on the other side we've got what? All we've got is the fact that maybe you love me and maybe I love you."

"You know," she whispered, "whether you do or not."

"I don't. It's easy enough to be nuts about you." He looked hungrily from her hair to her feet and up to her eyes again. "But I don't know what that amounts to. Does anybody ever? But suppose I do? What of it? Maybe next month I won't. I've been through it before—when it lasted that long. Then what? Then I'll think I played the sap. ..."

In Lawrence Block's short story "A Candle for the Bag Lady," Matt Scudder interviews the manager of the low-rent tenement where the victim, Mary Alice Redfield, lived. The manager, an old woman named Mrs. Larkin, reflects,

"I got used to having her about. I might say Hello and Good morning and Isn't it a nice day and not get a look in reply, but even on those days she was someone familiar to say something to. And she's gone now and we're all of us older, aren't we?"

"We are."

"The poor old thing. How could anyone do it, will you tell me that? How could anyone murder her?"

I don't think she expected an answer. Just as well. I didn't have one.

2. It Comes From One Character to Another Character

Imagine the following scene: A woman, Mary, has come home from visiting her husband in the hospital. She plans to go back in an hour. As she sits down with a cup of coffee, trying to control her emotions, there is a knock at the door. She answers.

Ted stood there.

"Oh hello, Ted, our family doctor from Baltimore," Mary said. "Please come in."

Ted walked through the door.

"Mary," Ted said, "I'm so glad you were at home here on Mocking-bird Lane."

"I am too, Ted. I am comforted that you're here. Having a doctor who is six feet, four inches and in good shape, but even better knows what he's talking about, is a wonderful thing for a forty-year-old woman in crisis to have visit her."

Here's the good news: I am certain none of you will ever write dialogue that bad. But you must be aware of writing this way more subtly.

What's happening here is the author is slipping information to the reader (actually knocking the reader over the head!). Dialogue can be an excellent way to impart information, but it must be done in a way that doesn't violate this rule: Fictional dialogue must truly be from one character to another and not be seen as a blatant attempt to give information.

See Essential of Great Dialogue #7, later in this chapter.

3. It Has Conflict or Tension

All dialogue should contain tension or conflict.

Let me repeat: All dialogue should contain tension or conflict.

Now wait, you may be thinking. What about dialogue between a husband and wife who have a happy marriage? Or two friends sitting down over lunch to discuss the day? Or simply two people who are on the same side in the story? Are you telling me such dialogue should have tension or conflict?

Yes.

Let's use Hitchcock's axiom here: Great dialogue has the dull parts taken out. No tension or conflict = dull.

Your Lead should be dealing with change, threat, or challenge from the get-go. At the very least, then, whenever she is in dialogue with another character, that inner tension is present.

Tension and conflict can be modulated for any effect.

Imagine Mary in our previous scene. This time she's having coffee with her neighbor, Babs, at the kitchen table. Mary's husband, Frank, is still in the hospital. Here is one way the scene might go:

"How is that new toaster working for you?" Babs asked.

"Oh, it's marvelous," Mary said. "I'm really glad I got this one. It's at Target, on sale."

"Really? I may just have to get one for myself."

"Do. You'll love it. You'll absolutely love it."

Babs took a sip of her coffee. "Mm, this is good. What blend?"

"French Roast."

"I adore French Roast."

"Me, too."

Blah, blah, blah. The dialogue may also go something like this:

"How is that new toaster working for you?" Babs asked.

"Hm?"

"The toaster. How's it working?"

"It toasts."

"Yes?"

"Yes. It toasts."

"I didn't mean to—"

"What do you think it does?"

Babs took a sip of her coffee. They sat in silence for a long moment.

4. It Sounds Just Right for the Piece

Sometimes I encounter a writer who wants to show off in dialogue by putting in some character talk that jumps off the page and says *Listen to me! I'm brilliant dialogue!*

That means the dialogue doesn't go with the overall tone of the narrative. It pulls us out of the story rather than keeps us in it.

Make it your goal not to show off, but simply to show. Period.

This doesn't mean your dialogue can't, at times, be memorable. (See Tool for Great Dialogue #9, later in this chapter.)

In Robert B. Parker's *Double Play*, ex-Marine and World War II vet Joseph Burke meets another Marine named Anthony in a bar:

"You're a strong guy," Anthony said. "How 'bout you be a fighter. My brother Angelo could fix you up with some easy fights."

"How easy?"

"Easy enough to win," Anthony said.

"These guys going in the tank?"

"Sure."

"And?"

"And we build you a rep," Anthony said.

"And?"

"And we get you couple big money fights, and maybe me and Angelo bet some side money and ..."

The terse dialogue fits the mood of two tough ex-Marines talking about fighting. The single-word sentences are like jabs, and the last line is a small flurry.

Compare that to Robin Lee Hatcher's *The Victory Club*, a story that takes place on the home front during World War II. Grocer Howard Baxter befriends Lucy Anderson, whose husband is fighting overseas.

> "A penny for your thoughts, Mrs. Anderson."
>
> A flush of embarrassment warmed her cheeks. "I was just feeling envious. Of Mrs. Wright and her car. It's been so long since I've gone anywhere except on foot or by bus. I'd love to just get into a car and take a drive."
>
> "That's understandable." He raised an eyebrow. "I don't suppose you'd care to drive to McCall with me next Saturday. There's plenty of snow in the mountains and the lake may still be frozen over, but the roads should be in good shape. We could go up, have lunch at the lodge, then drive back before dark."
>
> "You own a car?"

The tone here is lush, filled with emotions and details, just right for two people making contact during trying times.

Of course, the mood in any scene can change, and your dialogue can signal that. The key is to vary the cadences in keeping with the tone.

5. It Sounds Just Right for Each Character

Once you establish a character, the dialogue must sound right for him. There are four primary aspects to consider here.

- **VOCABULARY.** The sort of words a character uses tells us a lot about his background. A character who knows such words as *expatriate* and *deleterious* has a good education. Someone who has dropped out of school early probably won't know as many five-dollar words.
- **FAVORITE WORDS AND EXPRESSIONS.** Peer and professional groups have pet expressions or lingo they like to use. These undergo change, of course, so keep that in mind

   Cops no longer talk about "gats."

   Surfers no longer "hang ten."

   You need to keep up on the latest expressions via Internet slang sites and by talking to people who represent the group.
- **REGIONALISMS.** Such as the "Ayuh," that pops up in Stephen King characters from Maine. In Texas, you don't just talk to someone, you "visit."

"Supper" sometimes means "dinner." And so on.

- **DIALECT AND SYNTAX.** Writing out dialect phonetically is frowned upon these days. Don't try to re-create the sound of a thick accent. Instead, a word or two for suggestive purposes will help the reader catch the sound. Don't have a character say, "Wah ah jus' luhv't when a yung'n lak y'sef sets'n dan bah the far."

Preferred would be: "Why, I just love it when a young'n like you sets on down by the fire."

The one phonetic word, *young'n*, gives the major clue.

You can set up a thick accent simply by saying so in the narrative—*He spoke with a thick southern accent*—and then writing dialogue like the above.

On occasion you can point out how a specific word sounds:

> "Why, I just love it when a young'n like you sets on down by the fire."
> The last word sounded like *far*.

Syntax is about the order of the words, which is a good way to indicate that someone's native language is not English.

How might someone from Japan, learning English, say the following?

> Can you tell me where the bathroom is, please?

Might be:

> Please, where is bathroom?

In his novel *End of Story*, Peter Abrahams has a dishwasher in a New York restaurant who is recently from Eastern Europe. He says to a character who is a writer, "How is going the writing?"

Later he says, "I myself have idea for novel."

The writer answers, "You never mentioned that."

"You are never asking," he says.

6. It Isn't Real-Life Speech

One mistake many beginning writers make is to try to re-create real-life speech on the page.

Fictional dialogue must give the *suggestion* of real speech, but every word must be purposeful. Real-life speech is filled with hesitators (um, uh, y'know) and tangents. And small talk, to fill space.

While there are times you may choose to render dialogue with hesitators, do so only when it's integral to the character or scene. A character may say *y'know* when nervous or trying to hide something.

7. It Is Compressed

In the past, bloated dialogue was tolerated in fiction. Here, for example, is an exchange from Theodore Dreiser's *An American Tragedy* (the narrative portions have been omitted). In this exchange, Clyde, a young man of about twenty, is trying to get Roberta to give herself to him sexually. She is from a conservative Christian background.

> [Clyde]: "It's getting cold, isn't it?"
>
> [Roberta]: "Yes, I should say it is. I'll soon have to get a heavier coat."
>
> "I don't see how we are to do from now on, do you? There's no place to go any more much, and it won't be very pleasant walking the streets this way every night. You don't suppose we could fix it so I could call on you at the Gilpins' once in a while, do you? It isn't the same there now as it was at the Newtons'."
>
> "Oh, I know, but then they use their sitting room every night nearly until ten-thirty or eleven. And besides their two girls are in and out all hours up to twelve, anyhow, and they're in there often. I don't see how I can. Besides, I thought you said you didn't want to have anyone see you with me that way, and if you came there I couldn't help introducing you."
>
> "Oh, but I don't mean just that way. Why wouldn't it be all right for me to stop in for a little while? They wouldn't need to know, would they? There wouldn't be anybody there now, would there?"
>
> "No, no, I can't let you do that. It wouldn't be right. I don't want to. Someone might see us. Somebody might know you."
>
> "Oh, who would be likely to see us anyhow, at this time of night? There isn't any one around. Why shouldn't we go there for a few moments if we want to? No one would be likely to hear us. We needn't talk so loud. There isn't anyone on the street, even. Let's walk by the house and see if anybody is up."

Compare that to this exchange from Robert Crais's *Hostage*:

> The Watchman held the phone to Talley's ear again.
>
> "Jane?"
>
> "What's going on, Jeff? Who are these people?"

"I don't know. Are you all right? Is Mandy?"

"Jeff, I'm scared."

The Watchman took back the phone.

"That's enough."

"Who the hell are you?"

"Can we let you go? You past your shock and all that, we can turn you loose and you won't do something stupid?"

"You can let go."

These days, the more compressed the dialogue, the better. Unless a character has a strong reason to give a speech or run off at the mouth, strive for crispness in word choice.

On those occasions where you do have a speech or extended monologue, find ways to break it up for the reader. You can do this by cutting to thoughts, action beats, and interruptions.

"Four score and seven years ago," the president said, "our fathers brought forth on this continent a new nation, conceived in liberty and ..."

Oh no, thought Jasper. He's going to make a speech.

"... the proposition that all men are created equal."

Jasper kicked a dirt clod. *Equal my foot.*

"Now we are engaged in a great civil war, testing whether that nation, or any nation so conceived and so dedicated, can long endure."

"Excuse me," Jasper shouted. "But what does this have to do with the price of tea in China?"

The president paused, glared at Jasper, then gave a quick nod. Two blue uniformed soldiers grabbed Jasper's arms and wrestled him to the ground.

"We are met on a great battlefield of that war," the president said.

"I got your battlefield," Jasper shouted. "Right here!"

8. It Is Rich With Subtext

In great dialogue, what is unsaid is as important as what is spoken out loud. In *Reading Like a Writer*, Francine Prose writes:

When we humans speak, we are not merely communicating information but attempting to make an impression and achieve a goal. And sometimes we are hoping to prevent the listener from noticing what we are not saying, which is often not merely distracting but, we fear, as audible as what we are saying. As a result, dialogue usually contains as much or even more subtext than it does text. More is going on under the surface than on it. One mark of bad written dialogue is that it is only doing one thing, at most, at once.

In any given exchange there is the tip of the iceberg (what is being said "onscreen") and the part underneath the surface.

The underneath, while it can't be seen, manifests itself above the surface, subtly, adding layers that the reader absorbs subliminally.

The layers below the surface consist of *story, character,* and *theme.*

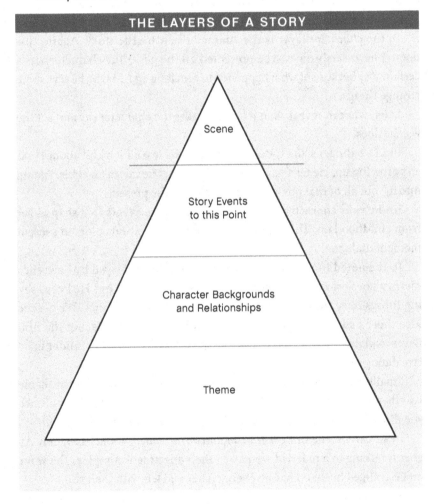

THE LAYERS OF A STORY

Scene

Story Events to this Point

Character Backgrounds and Relationships

Theme

What has happened in the story so far will affect the present. This can be what has been presented or part of the backstory (whether presented or not).

For example, in the early scenes in *Casablanca*, we don't know why Rick is so mysterious about why he's running a saloon in this part of the world. When Renault, the French captain, asks him the question, Rick says it's for his health. He came to Casablanca for the waters.

"Casablanca is in the middle of the desert," Renault says.

Rick replies, "I was misinformed."

Only later do we learn about that part of the iceberg, that he was dumped by the love of his life.

In the *character* layer is the character's entire life story. Again, this doesn't necessarily have to be presented on the page. The character acts a certain way because of what happened to him long ago. Maybe he says some strange things.

Later, you can reveal what it is that makes the character say and act the way he does.

In J.D. Salinger's *The Catcher in the Rye*, we learn bit by bit about Holden's growing up. He tells us at the very start that he doesn't feel like "going into it," but all of that obviously affects him in the present.

Know your character's deep background—the events that shaped her from childhood on. This will result in subtle shades and colors in present moment dialogue.

In the noted film noir *Born to Kill*, the character played by Lawrence Tierney goes crazy with anger sometimes, and kills. Why? He keeps saying things like, "Nobody's gonna make a monkey out of me." We get the idea there's something in his background that caused this, but the film never explains what it is. It doesn't have to, however, for it to render effective dialogue.

Finally, there's *theme*. Many writers say they don't know what their theme is as they write that first draft. It only emerges later. If that's true for you, once you discover a theme, you can go back and work that into the dialogue.

In an early scene in Ross Macdonald's *The Underground Man*, Lew Archer is talking to a married woman in their apartment complex. The woman's estranged husband has just berated her and left with their son.

Archer, who hasn't been hired by anyone, asks the woman questions like he would with a client. He keeps going. But she's not a client. At least not yet, anyway.

Later we discover how lonely he is. That explains the scene and why he kept her talking, and it gives it poignancy in retrospect.

That is what subtext does. It deepens and enlarges the canvas, but in soft tones, supporting the surface music.

12 TOOLS FOR GREAT DIALOGUE

Now you know the essentials of great dialogue. Here are twelve nuts-and-bolts techniques that will help you write it.

1. Orchestrate Exchanges

Good dialogue begins before a single line is written. It begins when you first start to develop your cast of characters.

Orchestration means you create characters who are sufficiently different from each other to allow for conflict and tension. Since dialogue is best when it is an extension of action, you give your characters different agendas in a scene, and the dialogue almost takes care of itself.

The movie *City Slickers* is a good example of orchestration. Billy Crystal, Bruno Kirby, and Daniel Stern play three friends who leave New York because of various crises in their lives and go on a cattle drive in the West. Much of the comedy comes from the interplay between the three friends. They are very different.

Crystal is the wisecracking ad man who tries to get out of things with charm and wit. Kirby is the macho guy who wants to fight and prove he's a man all the time. Stern is just a loser who can't make anything go right in his life.

There's a scene early on where Crystal is trying to learn how to throw a lasso. He can't get it right. Kirby chides him. Crystal says it's not a competition. Kirby disagrees, saying *life* is a competition, that everything is a competition. Then Stern wanders over and the two friends ask him what he's been doing. "Just watching them castrate a horse," he says.

The lines fit and become funny because the characters are different. The dialogue helps in the characterization.

2. Assign Roles: Parent, Adult, Child

In his book *Writing Novels That Sell*, Jack Bickham included a helpful tool adapted from the school of psychology known as transactional analysis.

Now, I know nothing about this school, except that it was founded by Dr. Eric Berne and popularized in a book called *Games People Play*. So this tool is perhaps best described as being "loosely suggested" by transactional analysis.

The idea is this: In any interaction between people, each person tends to inhabit a role, and speak and act consistently with that role.

The three roles are parent, adult, and child:

- The parent (P) is the seat of authority, the one with the power. He lays down the law. What he says goes. End of issue.
- The adult (A) is the most "objective" role. It is a rational and even-tempered one who can see things as they are. "Let's be adults about this," she's likely to say.
- The child (C) is not rational but emotive. He's selfish and "wants what he wants when he wants it."

What I find helpful about this model is that in any given scene you can put the characters into one of these roles—or give them shades of any role—and create tension between them.

I create, either on paper or in my head, a little grid:

CHARACTER 1	CHARACTER 2
P	P
A	A
C	C

I decide which role Character 1 will be (primarily) and which role Character 2 will be (primarily). Obviously, the transaction with the least amount of conflict is this one:

Why? Because adults are the most even minded and able to "get along."

But what if we have:

Now we have potential for conflict. P wants to teach, direct, and guide A. A will resist, for good and rational reasons.

P may then take things a step further, getting frustrated with A for not bowing to authority. The dialogue or action heats up.

Now these roles aren't static. A character, for reasons associated with his goal in the scene, may try to assume a different role while the conflict is going on.

A, for example, may be drawn into a conflict by assuming more of a P role. Then it's like two rams butting heads. Or, A may try to gain sympathy by pouting like a C. Or throwing a tantrum.

There's an infinite variety of permutations, based on the intensity with which the characters feel their roles and the changes that can happen within a scene.

For example, in Neil Simon's *The Odd Couple*, Felix Unger (the neat freak) and Oscar Madison (the slob) have just seen the weekly poker game break up. It happened because of Felix and his fussiness, though he is oblivious.

Now Oscar is ready for the fight that's been building.

When this part of the scene opens, Felix is the A. He's analyzing the situation and discussing it rationally.

Oscar is in no mood to be an A. He's a C. The scene continues:

> FELIX: That's funny, isn't it Oscar? They think we're happy ... [he starts cleaning up]
> OSCAR: I'd be immensely grateful to you, Felix, if you didn't clean up just now.
> FELIX: It's only a few things.

In the movie, Oscar then says, "I'm not through dirtying up for the night," and throws some cigarettes on the floor—a very childish thing to do.

Oscar then points out the irony that, "Unless we come to some other arrangement, I'm gonna kill you. That's the irony."

Felix asks what's wrong, and Oscar begins a rant. He lets it all out. In the middle of it Felix straightens a picture on the wall. Oscar says he *wants* it crooked, it's his picture! So he makes it crooked again.

At this point, Felix changes tactics. He becomes childlike and moans, "I was wondering how long it would take."

He begins to pout. Oscar now assumes the role of A, trying to get him to stop pouting.

On it goes, back and forth. It's worth watching that scene in the movie to catch the dynamics of P, A, and C on dialogue.

Try doing it yourself a few times, and you'll see great possibilities that you otherwise might have missed.

3. Drop Words

Leaving off words is a favorite technique of dialogue master Elmore Leonard. By simply excising a single word here and there, he creates a feeling of verisimilitude in his dialogue. It sounds like real speech, though it is really nothing of the sort. All of Leonard's dialogue contributes, laser-like, to characterization and story.

Here's a standard exchange:

> "Your dog was killed?"
>> "Yes, run over by a car."
>> "What did you call it?"
>> "It was a she. I called her Tuffy."

This is the way Elmore Leonard did it in *Out of Sight*:

> "Your dog was killed?"
>> "Got run over by a car."
>> "What did you call it?"
>> "Was a she, name Tuffy."

It sounds natural, yet is lean and meaningful. Notice it's all a matter of a few words dropped, leaving the feeling of real speech.

As with any technique, you can overdo it. Pick your spots and your characters. Your dialogue will thank you for it.

4. Cast the Character

Dialogue for me never really comes alive until I can see and hear the character.

If I don't have a visual and a voice, my dialogue comes out generic. It sounds a lot like me as if I were playing that character.

So a quick way to get that sight and sound is to cast the character in your mind. Here you have a great advantage. You may use any actor in history, or anybody you know personally, and the reader will never know that's who you had in mind.

And yet the dialogue will come out fresh on the page.

Another twist to this exercise: Just to see what happens, try casting your character with an actor of the opposite sex. What would your male truck driver sound like if played by Grace Kelly?

You might be pleasantly surprised.

If not, don't use it. That's the fun of being a writer.

5. Act It Out

Before going into writing, I spent some time pounding the boards as an actor. I took an acting class in New York, which included improvisation. Another member of the class was a Pulitzer Prize-winning playwright. When I asked him what he was doing there, he said improvisational work was a tremendous exercise for learning to write dialogue.

I found this to be true. But you don't have to wait to join a class. You can improvise by doing a Woody Allen.

Remember the courtroom scene in Allen's movie *Bananas*? Allen is representing himself at the trial. He takes the witness stand and begins to cross-examine, asking a question, running into the witness box for the answer, then jumping out again to ask another question.

I suggest you do the same thing (in the privacy of your own home, of course). Make up a scene between two characters in conflict. Then start an argument. Go back and forth, changing actual physical location. Allow a slight pause as you switch, giving yourself time to come up with a response in each character's voice.

Another twist on this technique: Do a scene between two well-known actors. Use the entire history of movies and TV. Pit Lucille Ball against Bela Lugosi, or have Oprah Winfrey argue with Bette Davis. Only you play all the parts. Let yourself go. And if your local community college offers an improvisation course, give it a try. You might just meet a Pulitzer Prize winner.

6. Curve the Language

I learned this technique from Danny Simon, Neil's older brother, who taught a comedy writing class for many years in L.A. Both Neil and Woody Allen credit Danny Simon with teaching them how to write narrative comedy.

Simon didn't like "joke jokes" in comedy, funny lines inserted just to be funny. They had to be organic, tied to the story. So to get a funny line, you work with what the character would naturally say, then just "curve" it a little.

Here's an example of the process. You're writing *The Godfather,* and Michael Corleone has come to Las Vegas to tell the older, more established Moe Greene that the Corleone family is buying out his interest in the casinos. Moe Greene is outraged. What does he say in response? At first, you might write out the line in plain vanilla, as it occurs to you:

> "I'm Moe Greene! I was running this place when you were in high school!"

Not good enough. So you tweak it:

> "I'm Moe Greene! I made my bones when you were in high school!"

A little better. But we can do more with it. In the movie the line is:

> "I'm Moe Greene! I made my bones when you were going out with cheer-leaders!"

That's curving the language. In an old *Seinfeld* episode, Elaine is suddenly being hit on by Jewish guys. She's told this is "shiksa appeal." So she goes to a rabbi to ask about it. The rabbi tells her it's a myth.

Her reply might be something like this:

> "Something's going on here, because every Jewish guy I see is making a play for me."

Blah. Curve it. What would be a substitute for "Jewish guy"?

> "Something's going on here, because every able-bodied Israelite I see is making a play for me."

Curve it some more:

> "Something's going on here, because every able-bodied Israelite in the county is making a play for me."

The line in the show:

> "Something's going on here, because every able-bodied Israelite in the county is goin' pretty strong to the hoop."

7. Place Exposition Within Confrontation

Many writers struggle with exposition in their novels. Often they heap it on in large chunks of straight narrative. Backstory, what happens before the novel opens, is especially troublesome. How can we give the essentials and avoid a mere information drop?

Use dialogue. First, create a tension-filled scene, usually between two characters. Get them arguing, confronting each other. Then you can have the information appear in the natural course of things. Here's the clunky way to do it:

> "I am in love with Jeffrey," Sondra said.
>
> "Why are you attracted to him?" asked Mabel.
>
> "Why? Oh, so many reasons. The way his teeth sparkle and his eyes glisten. The lilt of his voice on a summer's day. His strong arms enfolding me."
>
> "You're such a romantic!"
>
> "Yes, but then Jeffrey is, too. He writes me love poems, you know."

And so on. We get the information that Sondra is in love with Jeffrey. We get an idea that she has her head in the clouds. But there's too much fat here. One way to convert this into confrontation might go like this:

> "Why do you keep staring off like that?" Mabel said.
>
> "Sorry," Sondra said, "I was just thinking ..."
>
> "Yeah?"
>
> "Of Jeffrey."
>
> "Oh, please! Is that why you're so out of it?"
>
> "What do you have against Jeffrey?"
>
> "What do I have against slime, you might ask."
>
> "Mabel!"
>
> "You really like this guy?"
>
> "I'm in love with him."
>
> "Here, here's the number of my shrink ..."

This may not be your way to approach it. That's okay. There are countless ways to do it, all more interesting than the original exchange. Just keep in mind that if your dialogue characters are "on the same page" mentally and emotionally, your dialogue won't be compelling.

Often, this is a good way to convey something positive and sympathetic about a character to the reader.

8. Employ the Sidestep

One of the most common mistakes new writers make with dialogue is creating a simple, back-and-forth exchange. Each line responds directly to the previous line, often repeating a word or phrase (an "echo"). It looks something like this:

"Hello, Mary."

"Hi, Sylvia."

"My that's a wonderful outfit you're wearing."

"Outfit? You mean this old thing?"

"Old thing! It looks practically new."

"It's not new, but thank you for saying so."

This sort of dialogue is called *on the nose.* There are no surprises, and the reader drifts along with little interest. While some direct response is fine, too much of it renders your dialogue bland.

Thus, the *sidestep*, where you avoid the obvious or direct:

"Hello, Mary."

"Sylvia. I didn't see you."

"My that's a wonderful outfit you're wearing."

"I need a drink."

I don't know what is going on in this scene since I've only written four lines of dialogue. But this exchange is immediately more interesting and suggestive of currents beneath the surface. I might even find the seeds of an entire story here.

You can also sidestep with a *question:*

"Hello, Mary."

"Sylvia. I didn't see you."

"My that's a wonderful outfit you're wearing."

"Where is he, Sylvia?"

Hmm. Who is "he"? And why should Sylvia know? (Go ahead and find out for yourself if you want to.) The point is there are innumerable directions the sidestep can go. Experiment. Look at a section of your dialogue and change some direct responses into off-center ripostes. Like the old magic trick ads used to say, you'll be pleased and amazed.

Here's a simple on-the-nose exchange:

"Are you ready to go, dear?"

"Yes, darling, just a moment."

Possible responses:

A. THE NON-RESPONSE
"Are you ready to go, dear?"
"I was so humiliated."

B. ANSWER WITH A QUESTION
"Are you ready to go, dear?"
"Why must you always do that?"

C. THE UNEXPECTED
"Are you ready to go, dear?"
"I saw you downtown today."

D. INTERRUPTIONS
"Are you ready to—"
"Please, Arthur, just stop it."

Note: You show interruptions with the *em dash*. An ellipsis (…) is for a voice trailing off on its own.

E. SUDDEN PUNCH
"Are you ready to go, dear?"
"I want a divorce."

9. Use One Gem Per Act

We've all had those moments when we wake up and have the perfect response in a conversation that took place the night before. Wouldn't we all like to have those *bons mots* at a moment's notice?

Your characters can. That's part of the fun of being a fiction writer. I have a somewhat arbitrary rule—one gem per quarter. Divide your novel into fourths. When you polish your dialogue, find those opportunities in each quarter to polish a gem.

Lawrence Block once gave the following line to a cop describing a suspect. The suspect is reportedly ugly. *How ugly?* someone asks.

"God made him as ugly as he could then hit him in the mouth with a shovel."

10. Say It With Silence

A powerful dialogue device is silence. It's often the best choice, no matter what words you might come up with. Hemingway was a master at this. Consider this excerpt from his short story "Hills Like White Elephants." A man and a woman are having a drink at a train station in Spain. The man speaks:

> "Should we have another drink?"
>
> "All right."
>
> The warm wind blew the bead curtain against the table.
>
> "The beer's nice and cool," the man said.
>
> "It's lovely," the girl said.
>
> "It's really an awfully simple operation, Jig," the man said. "It's not really an operation at all."
>
> The girl looked at the ground the table legs rested on.
>
> "I know you wouldn't mind it, Jig. It's really not anything. It's just to let the air in."
>
> The girl did not say anything.

In this story, the man is trying to convince the girl to have an abortion (a word that doesn't appear anywhere in the text). Her silence is reaction enough.

By using sidestep, silence, and action, Hemingway gets the point across. He uses the same technique in the famous exchange between mother and son in the story "Soldier's Home":

> "God has some work for everyone to do," his mother said. "There can be no idle hands in His Kingdom."
>
> "I'm not in His Kingdom," Krebs said.
>
> "We are all of us in His Kingdom."
>
> Krebs felt embarrassed and resentful as always.
>
> "I've worried about you so much, Harold," his mother went on. "I know the temptations you must have been exposed to. I know how weak men are. I know what your own dear grandfather, my own father, told us about the Civil War and I have prayed for you. I pray for you all day long, Harold."
>
> Krebs looked at the bacon fat hardening on the plate.

Silence and bacon fat hardening. We don't need anything else to catch the mood of the scene. What are your characters feeling while exchanging dialogue? Try expressing it with the sound of silence.

11. Let It Flow

When you write the first draft of a scene, let the dialogue flow. Pour it out like cheap champagne. You'll make it sparkle later, but first you must get it down on paper. This technique will allow you to come up with lines you never would have thought of if you tried to get it right the first time.

In fact, you can often come up with a dynamic scene by writing the dialogue first. Record what your characters are arguing about, stewing over, revealing. Write it all as fast as you can. As you do, pay no attention to attributions (who said what). Just write the lines.

Once you get these on the page, you'll have a good idea what the scene is all about. And it may be something different than you anticipated. Good! You're cooking. Now you can go back and write the narrative that goes with the scene, and the normal speaker attributions and tags.

I've found this technique to be a wonderful cure for writer's fatigue. I do my best writing in the morning, but if I haven't done my quota by the evening (when I'm usually tired), I'll just write some dialogue, fast and furious. It flows and gets me into a scene.

With the juices pumping, I find I'll often write more than my quota. And even if I don't use all the dialogue, it's a good exercise. The more dialogue you write, the better you'll get at it.

12. Minimize

This is the opposite of the let-it-flow exercise. Here, you make a copy of your scene and go through it, cutting as much as you possibly can. Cut words, cut lines, replace words with silences and action beats. See how close to a silent movie you can make the scene.

Doing this will almost always make your dialogue better, sharper. You can now add back what you wish.

DIALOGUE AS A WEAPON

It's often helpful to think of dialogue as a type of weapon, especially when the conflict is running high.

Verbal weapons are employed by characters who are trying to outmaneuver each other. There's a whole range of weaponry to choose from—threats, epithets, pouting, name calling, dodging—virtually anything from the arsenal of human interaction.

John D. MacDonald's classic *The Executioners* (basis for the two *Cape Fear* movies) is about a lawyer, Sam Bowden, whose family is stalked by the sadistic rapist Max Cady. Cady's first act is poisoning the family dog, Marilyn. Sam hasn't been totally upfront with his wife, Carol. She challenges him:

> "I'm not a child and I'm not a fool and I resent being ... overprotected."

Her volley is direct, telling him she *resents* the coddling. Sam responds:

> "I should have told you. I'm sorry."

Sam's apology is meant to diminish his wife's anger. But his words ring hollow to her, and she continues to advance:

> "So now this Cady can roam around at will and poison our dog and work his way up to the children. Which do you think he'll start on first? The oldest or the youngest?"
>
> "Carol, honey. Please."
>
> "I'm a hysterical woman? You are so damn right. I am a hysterical woman."

Carol uses sarcasm, Sam tries again to soften her up, and she responds with a bitter observation and a curse word. Sam the lawyer tries another tack:

> "We haven't any proof it was Cady."
>
> She threw a towel into the sink. "Listen to me. *I* have proof it was Cady. I've got that proof. It's not the kind of proof you would like. No evidence. No testimony. Nothing legalistic. I just *know*."

Seeing that this has no effect on her husband, Carol quickly shifts and brings out her heavy artillery:

> "What kind of a man are you? This is your *family*. Marilyn was part of your *family*. Are you going to look up all the precedents and prepare a brief?"

She has attacked both his manhood and his profession. Sam attempts an answer but Carol cuts him off (interruptions are good weapons, too):

> "You don't know how—"
>
> "I don't know anything. This is happening because of something you did a long time ago."
>
> "Something I had to do."
>
> "I'm not saying you shouldn't have. You tell me the man hates you. You don't think he's sane. So *do* something about him!"

Carol wants instant action and Sam knows he can't provide it. The stress of the situation brings out weapon-like dialogue.

Don't forget that silence can be a weapon as well. In William E. Barrett's *The Lilies of the Field*, a German nun wants wandering handyman Homer Smith to stay and build a chapel for her small order. He just wants to get paid for a small job and move on. He confronts Mother Maria Marthe:

> "I want to talk to you," he said. "I've been doing work for you. Good work. I want pay for what I do."
>
> She sat silent, with her hands clasped in front of her. Her small eyes looked at him out of the wrinkled mask of her face but there was no light in them. He did not know whether she understood him or not.

If one character knows what holds great importance for another character, he can often turn that into his strongest weapon. After the silent treatment, Homer decides to play hardball. He directs the nun to a Bible verse, *The laborer is worthy of his hire*, and explains, "I'm a poor man. I work for wages."

Not to be outdone, and using the same weapon, Mother Maria Marthe shows Homer another passage: *And why take ye thought for raiment? Consider the lilies of the field, how they grow; they toil not, neither do they spin. And yet I say unto you that even Solomon in all his glory was not arrayed like one of these.*

Homer realizes he is dealing with one crafty nun who has won the initial tussle.

Not every scene, of course, is going to involve stark conflict. Some scenes are preludes to conflict. But even then characters can use dialogue to position themselves for the battles yet to come, when their more potent weapons will be employed.

Consider the dialogue in Edward Albee's play *Who's Afraid of Virginia Woolf?* It is almost entirely about language as a weapon, as when George plays his sadistic game, "Get the Guests." He throws fact after embarrassing fact in the faces of the young couple visiting his home, reducing them to emotional rubble.

Of course George and his wife Martha save the most lethal weapons for each other. The drama never flags because the dialogue escalates in its violent intent.

Indeed, when it's really clicking, dialogue can be described in combat terms. There are thrusts and parries, roundhouse punches and uppercuts, retreats and advances.

In this brief exchange from the classic *Casablanca* (script by Julius J. and Philip G. Epstein, and Howard Koch) Major Strasser, the Nazi official (played by Conrad Veidt in the movie), is questioning Rick, the saloon owner (Humphrey Bogart).

Strasser obviously has the more powerful position and uses oily charm to communicate. Rick, on the other hand, couldn't care less about the show of authority.

> STRASSER: Do you mind if I ask you a few questions? Unofficially, of course.
> RICK: Make it official if you like.
> STRASSER: What is your nationality?
> RICK: I'm a drunkard.

We can sense here not simply gamesmanship but the contempt Rick holds for this entire process. His last answer, a mere three words, perfectly conveys his attitude. It's a little firecracker he tosses into the Nazi's mailbox.

A few lines later, Strasser lobs a grenade:

> STRASSER: We have a complete dossier on you. "Richard Blaine, American. Age thirty-seven. Cannot return to his country." The reason is a little vague. We also know what you did in Paris. Also, Herr Blaine, we know why you left Paris.

At this point Rick takes the dossier from Strasser's hand.

> STRASSER: Don't worry. We are not going to broadcast it.
> RICK: Are my eyes really brown?

Again, Rick shows his contempt with an acerbic remark. The cat-and-mouse game begun here elevates to become the main plot of the story.

Not every scene, of course, is going to involve such stark conflict. Some scenes are preludes to conflict. But even then characters can use dialogue to position themselves for the battles yet to come, when their more potent weapons will be employed.

Finding the Right Words

How do you know what verbal weapons a character is likely to use? And when? How can you anticipate the various moves opposing characters are likely to make?

It's easy if, before writing a scene, you have a few things in mind.

First, what are the characters like? If a character is the *charge-ahead* type, he'll speak that way. His words will be forceful, direct. Sam Spade in Dashiell Hammett's *The Maltese Falcon* is like that. Here he confronts the odd little intruder, Joel Cairo:

> "I've got you by the neck, Cairo. You've walked in and tied yourself up, plenty strong enough to suit the police, with last night's killing. Well, now you'll have to play with me or else."

But the dandy Cairo, smelling faintly of gardenia, uses fancier verbiage:

> "I made somewhat extensive inquiries about you before taking any action, and was assured that you were far too reasonable to allow other considerations to interfere with profitable business relations."

We know, simply from the words used here, that these are two very different characters.

Next, be sure to assign your characters objectives in every scene. Without conflicting objectives—be they overt or subtle—your scene is in danger of falling flat. Knowing what each character wants, however, allows you to choreograph the dance—the ups and downs, the feints and jabs.

The chapter in *The Maltese Falcon* from which the above dialogue was lifted begins with Cairo pointing a pistol at Spade. The dynamic changes radically when Spade elbows Cairo in the face and takes the gun.

Cairo must now convince Spade to take the case of the missing black bird. The bulk of the chapter is about his verbal attempts to do it. Spade finally accepts and returns Cairo's gun—which Cairo promptly points at him again. Another shift.

Finally, you'll find a list of synonyms helpful, for words like *punch*, *dodge*, *thrust*, or any other fighting verbs you like. Go wild. You can later refer to this list when writing a scene. One of those words may suggest the perfect verbal weapon for one of your characters to use.

ATTRIBUTIONS

An attribution tells the reader who is speaking. Almost always, the simple *said* should be your default setting. Some writers, under the erroneous impression that *said* isn't creative enough, will strain to find ways not to use it. This is a mistake.

Said is almost invisible to the reader but for its primary use as a tag to tell us who is speaking. It does its work and stays out of the way. It lets the dialogue do the heavy lifting.

So the reader barely notices it. Any substitute causes the reader to do a little more work.

In the past, adverbs were often used liberally in dialogue. For example, a random page in Thorne Smith's 1929 novel, *The Stray Lamb*, reveals the following:

> "Off again, major," Sandra said resignedly ...
>
> "Not a scrap of evidence left behind," Mr. Long optimistically informed the party ...
>
> "It's a shame we haven't a camera," she observed ...
>
> "That depends," answered Thomas consideringly ...

Needless to say (I write disapprovingly), such effulgent grammar is frowned upon today.

Don't be hesitant about using *said*. In a two-person dialogue scene, you can skip attributions, and should, when it's clear who is speaking. Don't do this:

> "Let's drive right up and say hello," he said.
>
> "Oh, that sounds just super to me," she said.
>
> "You don't have to use that tone of voice," he said.
>
> "I shall, whenever the notion strikes me," she said.
>
> He said, "I might strike you myself."
>
> She said, "Don't threaten me, or I shall call Papa."
>
> "Go ahead and call him," he said.
>
> "Don't think I won't," she said.

Depending on where you are in the scene, you might be able to get away with just one attribution. For example, if you've established this couple is in the car and driving, the dialogue may proceed like this:

"Let's drive right up and say hello," he said.

"Oh, that sounds just super to me."

"You don't have to use that tone of voice."

"I shall, whenever the notion strikes me."

"I might strike you myself."

"Don't threaten me, or I shall call Papa."

"Go ahead and call him."

"Don't think I won't."

The first *he said* establishes who is speaking. In the rest of the dialogue, therefore, the reader knows who says what. Don't go on too long in this fashion. Put in an occasional attribution or action tag as a reminder.

Action Tags

Because dialogue is a form of action, we can utilize the physical to assist the verbal. This is called the *action tag*.

The action tag offers a character's physical movements instead of *said*, such as in Lisa Samson's *Women's Intuition*:

Marsha shoved her music into a satchel. "She's on a no-sugar kick now anyway, Father."

He turned to me with surprise. "You don't say? How come?"

Marsha jumped right in, thank you very much. "She saw a special on one of those health news spots on WJZ that sugar is actually a poison."

I shook my head. "Marsha, come on."

The action tag can follow the line as well:

"Come along, dear." Harriet spun toward the door.

This is not to be done every time, of course. Too many action tags will wear the reader out. Variety is called for, and often the best choice is no tag at all. If the reader knows who is speaking—because of alternating lines or a distinct manner of speech—that's often enough.

But in keeping with the idea of dialogue as action, look for ways to let your tag add to the dynamics of a scene. You'll be giving the reader more bang for the written buck.

So instead of this:

"What shall we do for the next two hours?" Smith said nervously.

Do something like this:

> Smith pulled at his eyebrow. "What shall we do for the next two hours?"

In life, talk may be cheap. Not so in fiction. Make every word count by viewing a character's speech as an expansion of his actions.

QUESTIONS AND EXCLAMATIONS

When a character asks a question, should the attribution be *he asked* or *he said*? Some feel the question mark makes *asked* redundant.

Still, *asked* is almost as invisible as *said*, so if you want to use it for variety on occasion, go ahead. But I advise against synonyms like *queried* or *inquired*.

Exclamation points in fiction, in my view, should be used rarely, and only when conveying an inner thought or a line of dialogue. (Or if you're writing a Hardy Boys book! Where chapters end with an exclamation point to get young readers to read on!)

An inner thought would be something like this:

> She peeked out the window.
> *It was Tony!*

In dialogue, while it is sometimes acceptable to use *said* after an exclamation point, beware of contexts where *said* is too sedate:

> "You monster!" she said.

The *said* here works against the exclamation point. If it's clear who is speaking, you can dispense with the attribution:

> "You monster!"

Or you can use an action tag:

> She raised the ax. "You monster!"

KEY POINTS

- Think of dialogue as an *action*. It is something the character does to further her agenda.

- Dialogue isn't "real-life speech." It's intentional but with the sound of realism.
- All dialogue should have conflict or tension, even if it's only within one of the characters.
- Subtext—story, background, character, theme—deepens dialogue.
- Orchestrate your characters so they don't sound alike.
- Hide exposition inside confrontational dialogue.
- Use *said* as your default attribution. Only rarely should you use other attributions and adverbs.
- Use action tags for variety.

*Exercise 1**

Here's an exchange between two characters. I've put one of the speakers in bold:

"Good evening."

"Good evening."

"I didn't know you were coming."

"I hadn't made any plans, but I got an invitation."

"Wonderful. Nice night, isn't it?"

"Lovely."

"Don't you just love it when the breeze holds the scent of honeysuckle?"

"Oh yes."

Using the sidestep tools from this chapter, see what tension you can add just by changing the boldface dialogue.

Exercise 2

Choose two characters who are violently opposed to one another. What sex are they? What ages? Why are they enemies? Now, set them at a dinner party where one walks in. Keep the first line, but play with the others by doing the sidestep. Build on what you've done. Write more of the dialogue. Let it flow.

Drop some words in the exchanges. Does it sound better?

Find a place for a silent reaction. Is the subtext clear? What is the character doing in the silence that's a clue to what she is thinking?

Finally, choose one line of dialogue for a gem. Make up several variations, then choose the best one. Does it sparkle? Sure it does. You're on your way to becoming a dialogue whiz.

*Exercise 3**

Take the following speech and turn it into part of a scene. Make up what you need:

> I am certain that my fellow Americans expect that on my induction into the Presidency I will address them with a candor and a decision which the present situation of our people impel. This is preeminently the time to speak the truth, the whole truth, frankly and boldly. Nor need we shrink from honestly facing conditions in our country today. This great Nation will endure as it has endured, will revive and will prosper. So, first of all, let me assert my firm belief that the only thing we have to fear is fear itself—nameless, unreasoning, unjustified terror that paralyzes needed efforts to convert retreat into advance. In every dark hour of our national life a leadership of frankness and vigor has met with that understanding and support of the people themselves, which is essential to victory. I am convinced that you will again give that support to leadership in these critical days.

Extra Credit

Try writing a scene just in dialogue. No action beats or descriptions at all. Let the dialogue itself paint the mood.

Now, write a scene while listening to a "mood tune." This can be any type of music you want. Movie soundtracks are a rich source of various mood tunes. The tune should color the way your dialogue turns out.

Take the scene you just wrote and rewrite it, only with a piece of music that is as opposite from the original piece as you can find. What does this do to your scene?

CHAPTER 7

Beginnings, Middles, and Ends

There is a complex academic phrase for the unfolding of a complete novel. It is: beginning, middle, and end.

Try to remember that.

I like the way one wag modified this: beginning, *muddle*, and end.

There's trouble in the middle.

This is why the three-act structure works. Stories have to begin, they have to play out, and they have to end.

Even if you want to play around with structure in your novel, understanding why the three acts work will help you make informed decisions.

Each portion of your book presents special challenges.

Your beginnings must grab.

Your middles must hold.

Your ends must satisfy.

Not easy tasks! But that's what editors and readers want, so that's what you're going to give them. Here's how.

BEGINNINGS

The opening pages of your book, starting with line one, are absolutely key. They are usually the first things an editor or agent reads (because if the writing isn't strong, they don't have to read the rest of your proposal). And readers browsing in a bookstore usually give attention to the first page or two to see if they want to buy.

They are, in other words, giving you a chance to grab them.

Do it.

Don't waste a single paragraph getting warmed up. A weak opening plants the idea of thinking "No." A strong opening will establish momentum. True, you have to keep writing strong, but those opening lines buy you time.

Before we get into fixes, let's consider what makes a good opening.

In a word, it's *disturbance.*

Because that's what fiction is really about. A Lead character's life gets a thrashing, and we read to see how he deals with it.

Consider this opening line:

> Tuesday was a fine California day, full of sunshine and promise.

What is the reader feeling at this point? While it's not going to turn her off necessarily, it certainly isn't going to turn her on.

And to think that line was written by Dean Koontz!

Yes, Koontz, the master of the grabber opening, wrote those words. Only I added a period and cut the line in half. Here's the full opening line from Koontz's *Dragon Tears*:

> Tuesday was a fine California day, full of sunshine and promise, until Harry Lyon had to shoot someone at lunch.

And the hook is in.

What causes a disturbance is anything that is *change or threat of change to a character's equilibrium.* That's why opening lines that carry the potential for disturbance also work.

> On the morning that he received the letter, Matthew Cowart awakened alone to a false winter.
>
> —JUST CAUSE, BY JOHN KATZENBACH

What's in the letter? There's always potential disturbance in that. And why is Matthew Cowart alone? *False winter* is a mood detail that adds to the portent.

Literary fiction, of course, doesn't need to leave all the fun to the genres. Anna Quindlen, for example, knows how to capture readers right from the get-go:

The first time my husband hit me I was nineteen years old.
> —*BLACK AND BLUE*

Jail is not as bad as you might imagine.
> —*ONE TRUE THING*

These lines relate to something in the narrators' past, both disturbing to the equilibrium.

She heard a knocking, and then a dog barking.
> —*THE PILOT'S WIFE*, BY ANITA SHREVE

A knocking would have been a mild disturbance. The barking dog adds urgency.

Lines of dialogue can be an effective way to open a novel or story. They generate immediate tension (or they should), and that creates instant reader interest. Sometimes just thinking up dialogue to start a story (as Koontz did in the earlier example) will get the imagination flowing.

The only warning here is not to let the dialogue go on too long without identifying the speakers and the situation. Readers will give you a few lines, but after that they want to know who is saying what and why. But artfully done, opening dialogue can do "double duty" and give us information without sounding dull.

Here, for example, is the opening of *The Transposed Man*, a pulp novel by the famed writing teacher Dwight V. Swain:

> "Name?"
> "Robert Travers."
> "Occupation?"
> "Mining engineer."
> "Place of residence?"
> "Seven Base, Jovian Development Unit, Ganymede."
> "Reason for visiting Luna?"
> "I'm checking on performance of the new Dahlmeyer units in the Mare Nubium fields. We're thinking of adapting them for use in our Trendart field on Ganymede."
> "I see ..." The port inspector fumbled through my papers. "Where's your celemental analysis sheet?"

We know several things even before we get the identity of the second speaker. We know this is some sort of official questioning. We know the name of the guy being questioned (Robert Travers). We know also, from some of the words used, that this is a science-fiction story (so the opening also gives us the "story world"). And there is conflict developing, especially with the last line.

In the opening to my novel *Final Witness* I wanted to suggest the middle of a courtroom cross-examination, but then turn the tables:

"How old are you?"

"Twenty-four."

"Going into your third year?"

"Yes."

"Second in your class?"

"Temporarily."

"Isn't it true you have a motive to lie?"

"Excuse me?" Rachel Ybarra felt her face start to burn. That question had come from nowhere, like a slap. She sat up a little straighter in the chair.

The tall lawyer took a step toward her. "Motive to lie, Ms. Ybarra."

"No, sir. I don't lie."

"Never?"

"No."

"Come now, Ms. Ybarra, everybody lies, especially when they want a good job."

Feeling like a cornered animal Rachel suppressed the urge to snap. Calm yourself, she thought. Don't lose your cool. "Not everybody," she replied. "Not all the time."

"Can you prove it?" the tall lawyer demanded. "Can you prove you never lie?"

"Why are you asking me all this?"

Alan Lakewood took another step toward her, stopped suddenly, sat casually on the corner of his desk. "It's just a little exercise I go through. I call it my trial by ambush. You want to know what it's like to grill some witness in court, you have to walk in their shoes once. And you have to be ready to take the gloves off, like I just did."

It turns out the tall lawyer was playing a slightly harsh interview game with a young law student applying for a job at the U.S. Attorney's office. Immediate conflict, then a twist.

Here's the opening of Gregory McDonald's *Fletch*:

"What's your name?"

"Fletch."

"What's your full name?"

"Fletcher."

"What's your first name?"

"Irwin."

"What?"

"Irwin. Irwin Fletcher. People call me Fletch."

"Irwin Fletcher, I have a proposition to make to you. I will give you a thousand dollars for just listening to it. If you decide to reject the proposition, you take the thousand dollars, go away, and never tell anyone we talked. Fair enough?"

"Is it criminal? I mean, what you want me to do?"

"Of course."

"Fair enough. For a thousand bucks I can listen. What do you want me to do?"

"I want you to murder me."

Now that makes me want to read on. The dialogue is immediate, interesting, and ends with a zinger.

The First Three Pages

Okay, you've got that killer first line or paragraph.

Now all you have to do is attach a killer book to it.

Which means your next task is to carry on the interest past the three-page mark. You've got the reader on your side.

What do you do to keep him there?

Change or challenge is what we need to begin a story. Something out of the ordinary routine.

Many beginning manuscripts I read start with setting up a nice family day. Mom comes down from the bedroom and starts the coffee brewing, gets the kids off to school (without argument). Maybe a neighbor stops by to chat.

Then, finally, in chapter two perhaps, we get a whiff of trouble.

We need trouble, or at least something showing a change (or disturbance to the routine) from the start.

Cornell Woolrich was a master at first pages. Here are excerpts from two of his stories:

The woman wondered who they were and what they wanted out there at this time of the day. She knew they couldn't be salesmen, because salesmen don't travel around in threes. She put down her mop, wiped her hands nervously on her apron, started for the door.

What could be wrong? Nothing had happened to Stephen, had it? She was trembling with agitation and her face was pale under its light golden tan by the time she had opened the door and stood confronting them. They all had white cards stuck in their hat bands, she noticed.

They crowded eagerly forward, each one trying to edge the others aside. "Mrs. Mead?" the foremost one said.

"Wha-what is it?" she quavered.

—"Post-Mortem"

She had signed her own death warrant. He kept telling himself over and over that he was not to blame, she had brought it on herself. He had never seen the man. He knew there was one. He had known for six weeks now. Little things had told him. One day he came home and there was a cigar-butt in an ashtray, still moist at one end, still warm at the other. There were gasoline-drippings on the asphalt in front of their house, and they didn't own a car. And it wouldn't be a delivery-vehicle, because the drippings showed it had stood there a long time, an hour or more.

—"Three O'Clock"

To vary the pace, you can cross up the reader by starting pleasant, then hitting with a surprise. Woolrich's novel *I Married a Dead Man* opens like this:

The summer nights are so pleasant in Caulfield. They smell of heliotrope and jasmine, honeysuckle and clover. The stars are warm and friendly here, not cold and distant, as where I came from; they seem to hang lower over us, be closer to us. The breeze that stirs the curtains at the open windows is soft and gentle as a baby's kiss. And on it, if you listen, you can hear the rustling sound of the leafy trees turning over and going back to sleep again. The lamplight form within the houses falls upon the lawns outside and copperplates them in long swaths. There's the hush, the stillness of perfect peace and security. Oh, yes, the summer nights are pleasant in Caulfield.

But not for us.

The opening disturbance is anything that puts ripples in the surface of the character's life. It doesn't have to be a major threat. But following Hitchcock's axiom, something needs to happen that takes us out of the placidity of everyday life.

Mythic structure begins with the hero's *ordinary world*. The disturbance is often the *call to adventure*.

In *Star Wars*, Luke is living an ordinary life with his aunt and uncle. But then his uncle buys some secondhand droids. While tinkering with one of them, Luke sets off the hologram of Princess Leia calling for help. This is something different, something strange. It piques interest.

In *The Wizard of Oz*, the opening disturbance comes in the very first shot. Dorothy is running home to the farm with Toto close behind. She is frightened. We learn immediately that it's because Miss Gulch just threatened to have Toto taken away.

A few minutes later, the disturbance intensifies as Miss Gulch rides to the farm and gets custody of the dog.

Very early in your novel you need to have this challenge to the status quo. Some examples I listed in *Plot & Structure*:

- The Lead gets a phone call in the middle of the night.
- The Lead gets a letter with some intriguing news.
- The boss calls the Lead into his office.
- A child is taken to the hospital.
- A car breaks down in a desert town.
- The Lead wins the lottery.
- The Lead witnesses an accident. Or a murder.
- The Lead's wife (or husband) has left, leaving a note.

The Use and Abuse of Prologues

One of the most popular TV shows of the late 1950s to early 1960s was *Peter Gunn*. The series, starring Craig Stevens as a cool, jazz-loving private eye, didn't start with credits. It jumped right in with a shocking incident, usually somebody getting murdered. It lasted about two minutes.

Then the famous Henry Mancini opening theme burst on, with the credits. The rest of the show was about Gunn's getting to the bottom of what happened. This was the proper use of a grabber prologue, because (1) it was short and dramatic in and of itself, and (2) it had something to do with the main plot.

Dean Koontz's *Midnight* begins with a prologue (even though he calls it chapter one). It works for the following reasons.

The opening line:

> Janice Capshaw liked to run at night.

Koontz begins many of his books this way, with a named character in motion and an intriguing detail. Running at night presages mystery.

As Janice runs, Koontz also gives us some details about Janice and the setting. Using mood details like light and fog, an ominous scene unfolds.

> As she ran down the sloping main street, through pools of amber light, through layered night shadows caused by wind-sculpted cypresses and pines, she saw no movement other than her own—and the sluggish, serpentine advance of the thin fog through the windless air.

Koontz also drops in backstory elements: a short paragraph about Janice's childhood, how darkness soothed her, and another about her late husband and how much she misses him.

With these small bits of backstory in place, the reader's sympathy is with Janice as she jogs in the dark. Koontz spends the remainder of the chapter building the suspense of a horrific chase and, eventually, the stunning death of Janice Capshaw. The death has more impact because the background details bonded us, even briefly, to the character.

A prologue can be used to set up the story to come by giving us some essential history mixed with a tone of anticipation. The rather long prologue to Pat Conroy's *The Prince of Tides* is like that. It gives the family background of the narrator, Tom Wingo, and his twin sister, Savannah, who has twice attempted suicide. The prologue wraps up thus:

> The truth is this: Things happened to my family, extraordinary things. I know families who live out their entire destinies without a single thing of interest happening to them. I have always envied those families. The Wingos were a family that fate tested a thousand times and left defenseless, humiliated, and dishonored. But my family also carried some strengths into the fray, and these strengths let almost all of us survive the descent of the Furies. Unless you believe Savannah; it is her claim that no Wingo survived.
>
> I will tell you my story.
> Nothing is missing.
> I promise you.

To write a prologue like that, style is important. The sound of the words and the mood created is what gives this prologue its power.

Backstory

Backstory is any account of events that takes place before the main narrative. This element of fiction must be handled with great care. Use too much of it in the beginning, and the story may bog down. But use none of it and essential character bonding won't take place.

Try for a good balance by starting with action. My rule is: *Act first, explain later.* In fact, it's best to withhold as much information as possible in your opening chapter. Later, you drop in only what is essential.

Quite often I'll read the opening chapter of a young writer's manuscript and it will go something like this:

> Victoria stepped off the stagecoach onto the dusty street of Tumbleweed, New Mexico. The smell of dust assaulted her nostrils. She heard the tinkling of a piano coming from somewhere, then saw the huge sign *Saloon* hovering over her.

All right, we've got a character in action, arriving in town. Good. But shortly after this, maybe halfway down page one, comes the following:

> She thought wistfully of her home in Boston. She missed it already. She had been happy there.
>
> Her father had warned her not to go West. When she was sixteen ...

And then comes page after page of backstory. The true opening has stopped and we are given what I call *backdumping.* Many times the young writer will spend most of that first chapter on backdumps, returning to the present only near chapter's end.

It's an understandable fault. The writer thinks readers must know all about who the Lead character is and how she got here before the story can take off. It's an attempt to bond readers to the character, get them to care, then start up the action.

Understandable, but doomed to failure. The problem is it puts on the brakes. The actual story stalls while we get all the background information.

Readers will wait a long time for full explanations if you give them interesting or troubling circumstances up front. In the meantime, you can drop in some backstory elements to increase the reader's interest in the characters.

Backdrops can be done with skillful dialogue, as Colleen Coble demonstrates in chapter one of *Alaska Twilight*:

Augusta cupped Haley's face in her hands and looked deep into her eyes. "I'm so proud of you. You're brave enough to face it now."

She was in her Doris Day encouragement mode. Haley was in no mood for it. "I'm not being brave," she said. "I want my movies, my friends, the malls, and especially my powdered donuts. This is not my idea of a good time. I'm only here because my shrink said this would help bring closure, so I'm going to see it through. If I reconnect with Chloe, maybe the nightmares will stop."

If the writing is good enough it can make backstory a pleasure to read. In Phil Callaway's wistful novel *The Edge of the World*, the narrator begins chapter two with: *On August 4, 1976, the Rapture of the Church took place. I was sleeping at the time. But before I tell you about it, allow me a little more background.*

Having captured our attention with the first lines, Callaway gives us some family information, but not in plain vanilla language.

I am the youngest. The caboose, my brothers call me. A mistake, my third-grade teacher once said. I sometimes wonder if they'd miss me at all if I packed my bags and hopped a boat bound for my grandparents' homeland of Scotland. But I'm quite sure they would. I may be the caboose, but they seem to like knowing I'm back here.

Both Koontz and Stephen King have used more extensive backstory in the early pages of some of their most successful books.

In *The Dead Zone*, one of King's best, he introduces three characters— Johnny, Greg, and Sarah. Each character starts off in action. Then each is given extensive backstory. On page 9, for example, there's a section on Greg, referring back to his father's rages. This deepens our interest in and sympathy for Greg.

Pages 17 through 21 are dedicated to Sarah's backstory.

The reason these sections work is twofold. First, King starts off with action, then drops back. That's the way it should always be.

Second, the backstory is *essential* detail, contributing to the reader's sense of why the character is involved in the action.

Dean Koontz's first bestseller was *Whispers*, and he actually attributes this success to his conscious decision to deepen his characters. Up to that time, he'd done a lot of action, good action, but felt it was surface level. With *Whispers*, he created deep backgrounds.

Whispers has one of the most famous, chilling action scenes in suspense fiction—the attempted rape of Hilary Thomas by Bruno Frye. He attacks and chases her in her own house, from pages 24 to 41!

But what precedes it? The backstory of Hilary Thomas from pages 7 through 11. Why is this so important? Because it sets us up to care intensely for her in the attempted rape scene. Without it, we'd be watching the action but not be as engaged.

We learn in those pages of her bad upbringing, resulting in an inferiority complex, which she now fights against (a rooting interest is thus established). Koontz takes us back to her dingy Chicago upbringing and how she used her imagination to escape (explaining why she's a writer now).

The backstory ends with a scene where she has reached her dream, a big movie contract. But she can't entirely enjoy it, fearing it won't last, just like everything else in her life to this point. Now we really understand her.

By the time she gets home, on page 24, we are in love with this character. So when she finds Bruno Frye waiting for her, we can't stop reading.

The longer backstory works because the writing of Koontz and King is focused and sharp. So until your own skills are finely honed, err toward shorter backstory.

The Chapter Two Switcheroo

One great technique is the *chapter two switcheroo*. You try out chapter two as your new chapter one and see how much faster things move.

Here's the opening of a manuscript from a writing student:

> "Come on, honey. We're going to be late."
>
> Kathleen Jones stood at the backdoor watching her husband as he jogged up to the patio. William Carter Jones was the love of her life. They had met in junior high school, gone to separate high schools, and met up again in college. Kathleen would have done anything to win the heart of Will. He took her breath away the first day she saw him in their biology lab. Dissecting frogs wasn't the most romantic thing in the world, but they enjoyed being lab partners. Over time, romance bloomed and they promised to live until death parted them. That was twenty-two years ago. Now they had the house of their dreams, a daughter in college, and a revolving back door. Only the wall by the patio showed evidence of all the teenagers that had come in and out of the Jones's home over the years. Many still stayed in touch, but some were lost in the world somewhere. Kathleen prayed to herself every time she passed the pictures.

While dialogue is a great way to open, everything else is backstory and exposition. I suggested the student make chapter two her new opening chapter. If she had *essential* information from chapter one, she could sprinkle it in throughout the novel.

I advised her to be ruthless about leaving out any information that didn't absolutely have to be there.

In the student manuscript, chapter two (which became chapter one) opened like this:

> As the credits rolled and Tammy slept, Fancy wished life was really like the chick flick they had just watched. *But happy endings only happen in the movies.*
>
> Fancy sighed as she shook Tammy.
>
> "Tammy. Time to go get in bed. Come on, it's late."
>
> "I hear you. I'm awake. What time is it?"
>
> "It's after eleven o'clock." Fancy started turning off lights and reached across Tammy to pick up the popcorn bowl.

This is so much better. Something is happening.

MIDDLES

Most of your novel is going to be the middle portion, or Act II. It is the record of the confrontation between the Lead and various forces against her. Middles, of course, are open to infinite possibilities. So just how do you choose what to write?

It depends.

NOP vs. OP

In *Plot & Structure* I discuss the strengths and weaknesses of two approaches. NOP stands for "No Outline People." OP stands for "Outline People."

Some writers like to move along daily, without knowing what's going to happen a few scenes ahead. They reason that if the writer doesn't know what's going to happen, surely the reader won't.

This is a tad misleading, as decisions have to be made *sometime*, and if they're deferred until the actual writing of the scene, that doesn't mean it still won't be predictable.

And the danger is that it will be so off the track that it leads to "rabbit trails," and there will be a whole lot of rewriting to do.

However, if you are of the NOP persuasion, if you can't stand the idea of mapping out a story, don't despair. I would advise you to try to do at least a little mapping, as it will help your structure skills.

But at the very least know your LOCK elements! (See chapter three.)

If you do, then when you dream up scenes on the run, they'll have some relationship to the story engine—the conflict between a crucial objective and a stronger opposition.

Robin Lee Hatcher, who is a prolific NOP, says:

> For me, writing a novel is all about the joy of discovery. If I know too much about how the story will play out or how it will end, then I lose my passion for telling it. So I go to my computer every day, wondering what will happen next. I'm not sure how it happens, but it all falls together in the end.

Sometimes this gets a little scary, Hatcher admits, especially when a deadline is approaching.

> But I have learned, through trial and error, that this is the way I create, the way that works best for me.

If, however, you like the security of an outline, do as much as you can. There are various methods (scene cards, spreadsheets, extended synopses, etc.).

One of the more prolific writers ever, Richard S. Prather (author of the Shell Scott mystery series) said he would try to get "a fresh idea and just keep working with it. I'd fill up about a hundred or two hundred pages, single-spaced, with just plotting stuff. You know, ideas, characters, and bits of dialogue, actions and reactions."

From here, he'd create chapter notes on pages, one or two pages for each chapter. He'd put these in a notebook and write the novel from there.

My advice to OP is to allow your story to "breathe" a little, and if you come to a point where you feel the story needs to veer off a bit, be ready to revise your outline.

Some writers are in the middle (NOOP?) and outline the opening act strongly, then use "signpost scenes" for the rest of the outline (I fall into this camp).

A signpost scene is a scene you know has to be in the book: a major confrontation or complication. It can even be a little vague in your imagination. You might just have a feeling about it. Jot that down on a card or in your outline somewhere. As the story progresses, you'll fine-tune what lies ahead.

Your approach to writing should evolve. As you write that long middle, be aware of the feel of the story, of various techniques, and experiment with different approaches. Keep some notes on what's working for you.

Refer to those notes when you start your next project. Just keep writing.

ENDS

Novels have to end, and they have to end in a way that isn't predictable and is satisfying to the reader.

Endings tie up loose threads, unless you're writing literary fiction, which allows for more ambiguity.

Rules for writing endings can barely exist, because endings are tied to the unique story elements of each novel. Your imaginative powers will be tested most when it comes to creating a satisfying conclusion.

Beginnings are easy. Endings are hard.

It's relatively simple to hook readers from the start. It's a bear to leave them happy that they've read your book after the last page.

"Your first chapter sells your book," Mickey Spillane famously said. "Your last chapter sells your next book."

But it will help if you know the five types of endings:

1. The Lead gains his objective (the happy ending).
2. The Lead loses his objective (unhappy ending).
3. The Lead gains his objective but loses something more valuable (classic tragedy).
4. The Lead sacrifices his objective for a greater good.
5. The ending is ambiguous or bittersweet (mostly for literary fiction).

A good discipline is to write as much detail about the ending as you can before you get there. How exhaustively you do this will depend on what kind of writer you are, but one of the benefits of this practice is that you can "marble" action into your story and it will pay off later. This will give readers the feeling that there's more going on beneath the surface—always a good thing.

Of course, you're free to change the details once you get there, maybe have a whole new ending. Then again, you may find that the ending works wonderfully, and all you have to do is fine-tune it.

And put in *resonance*.

The best endings of any type of novel have this. Resonance is "prolongation of sound." It's like the perfect last note in a symphony. It leaves the reader with something beyond the ending.

Resonance can come from dialogue, description, narration—virtually anything that feels just right for the story.

How do you get that?

You just keep trying stuff.

You keep writing.

Additionally:

1. **MAKE SURE THE OBJECTIVE IS STRONG AND CLEAR.** Our old friend from the LOCK System, objective, is essential for a solid ending. Your Lead has had an overall objective throughout the novel. Now he has come to the point where he must make a final choice, or fight a final battle, to regain the equilibrium he lost when he moved through that first doorway of no return.

2. **DREAM ABOUT IT. BEFORE TRYING TO CONSTRUCT AN ENDING, LET YOUR IMAGINATION SUGGEST SEVERAL POSSIBILITIES.** Play around. You have all this story material in your head now. Your writer's mind, the "boys in the basement," will help you if you let it.

KEY POINTS

- Your opening line, paragraph, and page must grab the reader.
- Give us an early disturbance to the Lead's ordinary world.
- A little backstory is good in the opening, but start the action first and don't overdo it.
- When writing the middle, keep referring to the LOCK elements to keep you focused.
- Take time with your endings. Dream and brood about them. Seek resonance on the last page.

Exercise 1

Go to the library or bookstore and pick several novels at random. Read the opening pages. If there's a prologue, does it work for you? Why or why not? Are you hooked by the openings? Do you want to read on? Analyze your reactions.

Exercise 2

Compare those openings to the opening of one of your own manuscripts. What's the difference?

Exercise 3

Next time you watch a movie, think about the middle section (Act II). If things drag, ask yourself why. How would you do it better? Simply by asking this question and thinking it through, you're working your writing muscles.

Exercise 4

Have you ever been dissatisfied with the ending to a novel or movie? I think you have. Choose one and analyze the ending. What did it fail to do?

CHAPTER 8

Show vs. Tell

If there is any bit of ironclad advice for fiction writers, it's "Show, don't tell." Yet confusion about this aspect of the craft is one of the most common failings in beginning writers. If you want your fiction to take off in the reader's mind, you must grasp the difference between showing and telling.

The distinction is simply this: Showing is like watching a scene in a movie. All you have is what's on the screen before you. What the characters *do* or *say* reveals who they are and what they're feeling.

Telling, on the other hand, is just like you're recounting the movie to a friend.

Which renders the more memorable experience?

Remember the scene in *Jurassic Park* the movie, where the newcomers catch their first glimpse of a dinosaur? With mouths open and eyes wide, they stand and look at this impossible creature before them before we, the audience, see it.

All we need to know about their emotions is written on their faces. We're not given a voice in their heads. We know just by watching what they're feeling.

In a story, you would describe it in just that fashion: "Mark's eyes widened and his jaw dropped. He tried to take a breath, but breath did not come. ..." The reader feels the emotions right along with the character.

That is so much better than telling it, like this, "Mark was stunned and frightened."

In the nineteenth century, telling was common. Authors like George Eliot would write passages like this one from *Middlemarch*:

> When Fred stated the circumstances of his debt, his wish to meet it without troubling his father, and the certainty that the money would be forthcoming so as to cause no one any inconvenience, Caleb pushed his spectacles upward, listened, looked into his favorite's clear young eyes, and believed him, not distinguishing confidence about the future from veracity about the past; but he felt that it was an occasion for a friendly hint as to conduct, and that before giving his signature he must give a rather strong admonition. Accordingly, he took the paper and lowered his spectacles, measured the space at his command, reached his pen and examined it, dipped it in the ink and examined it again, then pushed the paper a little way from him, lifted up his spectacles again, showed a deepened depression in the outer angle of his bushy eyebrows, which gave his face a peculiar mildness (pardon these details for once—you would have learned to love them if you had known Caleb Garth), and said in a comfortable tone,
>
> "It was a misfortune, eh, that breaking the horse's knees? And then, these exchanges, they don't answer when you have cute jockeys to deal with. You'll be wiser another time, my boy."

If George Eliot had written in the 1940s, it might have gone like this:

> "I kind of got into debt with this guy," Fred said. "He advanced me some dough and I can't pay it back. I don't want my father to find out, and if you could find your way to give me a loan I'm sure I can pay it back quick."
>
> Caleb pushed his spectacles upward. He picked up a pen, tapped it a couple of times on the desk. Then he furrowed his bushy eyebrows and said, "So it was bad luck, huh?"

This *shows* us the dialogue, whereas the original *tells* us what was said. Obviously, if we need more information in the dialogue, we just have the characters say more.

One of the best "show" novels ever written is the classic detective tale *The Maltese Falcon* by Dashiell Hammett. Hammett ushered in a whole new style, called "hard-boiled," with this book. The mark of that style is that everything occurs just as if it were happening before us on a movie screen (which is one reason why this book translated so well into a movie).

In one scene, the hero, Sam Spade, has to comfort the widow of his partner, Miles Archer, who was recently shot to death. She comes rushing into his office, and into his arms. Spade is put off by her crying because he knows it's mostly phony.

Now, Hammett could have written something like, "The woman threw herself, crying, into Spade's arms. He detested her crying. He detested her. He wanted to get out of there."

That's telling. But look at what the masterful Hammett does:

> "Did you send for Miles's brother?" he asked.
>
> "Yes, he came over this morning." The words were blurred by her sobbing and his coat against her mouth.
>
> He grimaced again and bent his head for a surreptitious look at the watch on his wrist. His left arm was around her, the hand on her left shoulder. His cuff was pulled back far enough to leave the watch uncovered. It showed ten-ten.

How much more effective this is! We *see* Spade glancing at his watch, which tells us just how unsympathetic he is to this display of emotion. It reaches us much more powerfully.

Just after this little episode, the widow asks, "Oh, Sam, did you kill him?" Instead of *telling* us how Spade feels, Hammett writes:

> Spade stared at her with bulging eyes. His bony jaw fell down. He took his arms from her and stepped back out of her arms. He scowled at her and cleared his throat. … Spade laughed a harsh syllable, "Ha!" and went to the buff-curtained window. He stood there with his back to her looking through the curtain into the court until she started toward him. Then he turned quickly and went to his desk. He sat down, put his elbows on the desk, his chin between his fists, and looked at her. His yellowish eyes glittered between narrowed lids.

TOO MUCH TELLING IS LAZY …

Here's an example of lazy telling from a best-selling writer. It comes in the second paragraph of the book:

> She cared, she loved, she worked hard at whatever she did, she was there for the people who meant something to her, she was artistic in ways that

> always amazed her friends, she was unconsciously beautiful, and fun to be with.

There are two major problems with this paragraph.

First, it is pure telling and therefore doesn't advance the character or story at all. Why not? Because we, as readers, are being asked to take the author's word for it, rather than having the author do the harder work of showing us the character in action.

Second, it's an exposition dump. There's no marbling of the essential information. It's poured out all at once and has no effect but dullness.

BUT YOU CAN'T SHOW EVERYTHING

A novel that tried to *show* every single thing would end up one thousand pages, most of it boring. The rule is, the more intense the moment, the more showing you do. Take this excerpt:

> Don felt the pressure of each step on the bottoms of his feet, heard the clickety-clack of his shoes on the tile floor, as he walked toward the bathroom. The doorknob was ice on his fingers. His guts stampeded like scared wildebeests as he turned the knob and pulled the door open. One step, then another and another, and he was in.

If this is a moment when Don walks into the bathroom, washes his face, and thinks about things, then gets a phone call, you probably don't need this much detail. The scene doesn't need it. Just write:

> Don walked into the bathroom.

On the other hand, if Don has just been beaten up by the bad guys, the excerpt may provide the intensity required.

Telling, or narrative summary, is best used for transitions. For example, when getting from one setting to another, we don't need to see all the steps necessary to get there.

> Don walked out of the bathroom, picked up his car keys, went out the door of his apartment and to the stairs. He went down the two flights of stairs and opened the door to the parking garage. He entered the parking garage and walked to his car. He unlocked the door with his key fob and got in the car. He put the key in the ignition, started the car, backed

out, then put the car in Drive and headed for the street. He turned right out of the driveway and got in the flow of traffic. The first traffic light was red, so he stopped. When it turned green, he continued on, finally reaching the front of the bar. He slowed the car, then came to a stop at the curb outside the front door.

We don't need this, unless something important happens at one of these stages. Instead, this would do:

Don grabbed his car keys. Ten minutes later he pulled to a stop at the bar.

When using narrative summary for transition, make it fast. Just get there. And get into the next scene.

LET YOUR EMOTION SHOW

Don't be afraid to pour out the emotion the first time out. Press your story and characters to their limits. You can always tone things down on the rewrite.

CHARACTER EMOTIONS AND FEELINGS

Showing character emotion and feeling when the heat is on helps readers enter the experience.

What I mean by the heat being on is that emotion and feeling is important to the moment. It's perfectly fine to write something like the following if you're just getting Mary to the store:

Mary was tired from the party and decided a double latte was just the ticket.

But suppose, after a long argument, Mary is just drained, and that's going to cause her to fall asleep at the wheel of her car? Then you're going to want to show more than tell.

Mary caught her lids drooping. She slapped herself. *Come on, only ten miles to go.*

A helpful tool for deciding when to show character emotions and feeling is the *intensity scale*. You analyze your scenes on a shifting scale from 0 to 10, with 0 meaning no intensity at all and 10 meaning over the top.

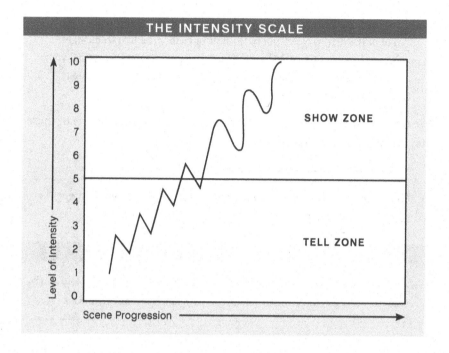

THE INTENSITY SCALE

A scene is going to vary in intensity as it proceeds. It might start low and build, or start high and drop back, or anything in between.

Don't ever have a scene that has 0 in it. Also, very rarely, maybe only once or twice per book, should you even think about going up to 10.

But cover all the ranges in between.

Rule of thumb is this: When the intensity level is above 5, you're going to want to err toward *showing*. That's the show zone. Below that is the tell zone.

As you gain more experience, you'll be able to judge the intensity of your scenes naturally.

To show character emotion in such instances, look to *actions, metaphors,* and *dialogue.*

A few examples:

ACTIONS

- Her chin began to quiver.
- He drove his fist through the wall.
- She threw the phone across the room.
- He put his hand on his stomach and doubled over.

METAPHORS

- He was trembling like the ground in an earthquake.
- Pins pricked her from the inside.
- A hot stitch ran up his body.
- A worm of fear turned in her stomach.
- Terror ballooned in her heart.
- White light exploded in her brain.
- Shock stole her breath.
- His spine felt like a column of ice.

You find these by trying things out, trying other things, and eventually settling on what works best. Don't expect to get something just right the first time out.

Character emotion can also be shown through dialogue. Consider the following excerpt from Hemingway's "Hills Like White Elephants":

> "I'll go with you and I'll stay with you all the time. They just let the air in and then it's all perfectly natural."
>
> "Then what will we do afterwards?"
>
> "We'll be fine afterwards. Just like we were before."
>
> "What makes you think so?"
>
> "That's the only thing that bothers us. It's the only thing that's made us unhappy."
>
> The girl looked at the bead curtain, put her hand out and took hold of two of the strings of beads.
>
> "And you think then we'll be all right and be happy."
>
> "I know we will. You don't have to be afraid. I've known lots of people that have done it."
>
> "So have I," said the girl. "And afterwards they were all so happy."

We know from the dialogue itself how the girl is feeling. We know she is anything but sanguine about their prospects for happiness.

KEY POINTS

- You must fully understand the difference between summary and scene.
- Telling is best for fast transitions and less intense beats.
- Showing is best for intense beats.
- Action metaphors are best for showing strong character emotion.

Exercise 1*

In the following segment, identify the parts that are *tell* and attempt to change them into *show*. Don't worry about a "correct" answer. There isn't one, as every approach is going to be slightly different (for one possible approach, see the appendix). The purpose of the exercise is to help you identify summary and start you thinking about how to make it "showier."

> Don walked into the bar. The smell in the place was terrible, and reminded him how depressed he was. A small dog barked at him, startling him. So he kicked it.
>
> *
>
> "How dare you!" a woman shouted. She was an imposing-looking woman, seated at a table holding the dog's leash.
>
> *
>
> Don told her what she could do with her dog, and she called for the bartender. The bartender came over and asked Don to leave.

Exercise 2*

Convert the following into action beats that show:

> John was angry.
>
> *
>
> John was sad.
>
> *
>
> Mary walked into the room, dog tired.
>
> *
>
> Mary read the riot act to John.

CHAPTER 9

Voice and Style

Of all aspects of the craft of fiction, voice and style are the two things it's virtually impossible to teach. That's because they are (or should be) unique to each writer. What comes out of you and your keyboard is a fictive alchemy, weaving a story where voice and style are largely hidden.

If they jump off the page, shouting *look at me*, you're removing the reader from the narrative experience.

That's why it's best to allow voice and style to emerge naturally in the telling of your tale. Attend to the fundamentals of the craft, and voice and style will seem organic. That's your goal.

So, while we can't give any hard-and-fast rules about voice and style, there are things you can do to expand your prose boundaries. That's what this chapter is about—to help you get a feel for voice and style, and to give you some techniques for developing these in your writing.

What is the difference between voice and style? I'd put it this way:

Voice is your basic approach, the sound of the words, the tone of the sentences, paragraphs, and pages.

Style is the application of voice on the whole. It's the overall feel the reader gets as the novel progresses.

The following tips and exercises will begin to pay off as you write your drafts. You won't have to think so hard about the words as you write them, which is always advisable, especially when putting them down for the first time.

FINDING YOUR VOICE AND STYLE

Mark Twain had a distinctive voice. It came with a twinkle in the eye and a satirical bent toward the human condition. Also, the ability to string words together that make us laugh, sometimes uncomfortably, at ourselves.

William Faulkner had a unique voice. So does Dean Koontz. In fact, Koontz's voice has consciously changed over the years as he has tried new things in his writing. There's hope here for everyone. You don't have to sing the same tune over and over again.

Authors' styles differ, too, of course. You're never going to mistake a Faulkner for a Koontz, or a Hemingway for a Danielle Steel.

So what's unique about you?

Let's start finding out.

Read

It seems obvious, but writers are readers. And not just of one type of fiction. All types.

Everything you read adds to your reservoir, gives you more options.

Some writers don't like to read when they're writing, afraid that somebody else's voice may creep into their manuscript.

Novelist Linda Hall disagrees:

> I can't understand people saying you might "lose your voice" if you read something while writing. To me that's like saying you might lose your personality or part of your character, something that can't be done. Or can't be done easily. I never worry about losing my voice, and when I'm writing, even after I've read something very different than my own style, it seems my "voice," whatever that is, always is there. I've had this very question come up in writers conferences on panels and my best advice is to always read, and not be ever afraid of losing your voice, and never stop reading.

As does novelist Athol Dickson:

> A voice that one could lose would not be their voice to begin with; it would be something else they've consciously invented, the way some people fake an accent because they think it makes them seem more interesting. One's true voice flows from writing the words that come, just as they come. That said, I do learn a lot about craftsmanship from other writers, by both positive and negative example. But craftsmanship is not about figuring out your

voice, it's just training the voice you already have. The way to figure out your voice is to stop trying and just write the words that come.

Let It Flow

Letting your voice flow the first time out, without writhing on the floor looking for the perfect word, is one way to develop a voice. When you click off that internal editor and let the words come out, you sometimes write things you never would have if you were more purposeful about it.

Some novelists write one page, then keep working and working that one page until it's just the way they want it. And then move on to the next page, and do the same thing. This also seems to be an apt description of madness, yet it works for some.

One thing you can do is print out your daily writing and carry those pages with you, reading them at odd moments during the day. Do this rather than surf the Internet on your iPhone. You want to be a writer, don't you?

The First to Third Flip

Want a radical suggestion? Turn your first-person point of view into third person. Or try it with a portion of your manuscript. You may even, when first drafting, start off in first and, once you've established a voice, switch to third, keeping the voice.

Here's what I mean. I once began a novel as first-person POV. Here's a short section:

> My cross of Officer Siebel was the last order of business on a hot August Friday. Monday we'd all come back for closing arguments. I had a whole weekend to come up with some verbal gold. Which I'd better if I hoped to get Carlos Mendez a fair shake.
>
> Actually, since he was guilty as sin, I could have been practically co-matose and it wouldn't make a difference to Carlos. But he had to think so. He had some nasty customers in his family tree that might take issue with a less than competent defense.
>
> I drove the Ark toward my Canoga Park office. The Ark is my vintage Cadillac, if by vintage you mean *has seen better days*. It dates from the Reagan administration and has been overhauled and redone and taped together many times. I got it at a police auction five years ago. The main advantage was it was big. I could sleep in it if I needed to. Even then, as I was sucking blow up my snout like some Hollywood brat, I suspected I might be homeless someday.

Hadn't happened yet. And with the help of the State Bar's Lawyer Assistance Program, maybe it wouldn't. The LAP is supposed to help lawyers with substance abuse problems. I'd managed to keep the coke monkey off my back for a year. Not that I wasn't close to falling, especially on those nights when I could not sleep.

For a couple of reasons I decided to switch the book to third-person POV. I had written about 10,000 words already in first, and had established a voice (first person is all about *attitude*), but I was able to keep the voice consistent, even in third:

Steve's cross of Officer Siebel was the last order of business on a hot August Friday. Monday they'd all come back for closing arguments, giving Steve a whole weekend to come up with some verbal gold. Which he knew he had to if he hoped to get Carlos Mendez a fair shake.

It would also give him time, he hoped, to get some sleep.

Steve pointed his Ark toward his Canoga Park office. The Ark was what he called his vintage Cadillac, and by vintage he meant *has seen better days*. It dated from the Reagan administration and has been overhauled and redone and taped together many times. Steve scored it at a police auction five years earlier. The main advantage was it was big. He could sleep in it if he needed to. Even back then, as he was sucking blow up his snout like some Hollywood brat, Steve suspected he might be homeless someday.

Hadn't happened yet. And with the help of the State Bar's Lawyer Assistance Program, maybe it wouldn't. The LAP is supposed to help lawyers with substance abuse problems. Steve had managed to keep the coke monkey off his back for a year. Not that he wasn't close to falling, especially on those nights when he couldn't sleep.

What happened for me was a much more intimate third-person narration. The first to third flip will do that for you. It makes the prose richly related to the character the story is about.

You only have to do this with a couple of chapters to get the feel for the style you're creating. Just be sure to change all the pronouns!

. . . .

In most branches of human endeavor there is said to be a right and a wrong way of doing things. In writing there can only be your way, whether you

pose as an aesthete, or whether you frankly admit
you write for money.
—JACK WOODFORD

Emulate Your Favorites

This may seem counterintuitive if you're trying to develop your own voice
and style. But really, our writing is the product of all the reading we've done
in our lives. We've been influenced already by writers we admire.

There's nothing wrong with *emulating* your favorite writers, so long as
you don't try to *imitate* them.

Whenever I read a favorite author of mine, I mark passages I like. It may
be a line of dialogue, an apt description, or a tense scene. If I look at my manuscript and find parts of it to be lacking in a certain area, I might reread relevant passages and let the style of the author wash over me.

This clicks my head into a different mode, so to speak, and I can return
to my work with a heightened awareness.

For example, I read John D. MacDonald to find what he described as a "bit
of magic in the prose style, a bit of unobtrusive poetry." So I'll mark passages
like the following one, from his Travis McGee mystery *Darker Than Amber*:

> She sat up slowly, looked in turn at each of us, and her dark eyes were
> like twin entrances to two deep caves. Nothing lived in those caves. May-
> be something had, once upon a time. There were piles of picked bones
> back in there, some scribbling on the walls, and some gray ash where
> the fires had been.

These few lines tell us more about the character than paragraphs of straight
description. That's what well-chosen word pictures can do for your fiction.

Start your own collection of favorite passages. Make copies of these pages
and put them in a notebook for personal study. Go through them periodically, letting the sound wash over you.

Read Poetry

Some writers, like Ray Bradbury, like to read poems before they begin the
day's work. As Bradbury said in *Zen in the Art of Writing*:

> Poetry is good because it flexes muscles you don't use often enough. Po-
> etry expands the senses and keeps them in prime condition.

Where to start?

Poetry is everywhere, and soon enough you'll find your favorites. A good introduction is Bill Moyers's *Fooling With Words,* his interviews with eleven contemporary poets about their craft.

As Moyers puts it, poetry is first about the music, the pleasure of listening to "the best words in the best order."

Do that with the poems you take in. Listen to the music.

You can read poetry before you revise a particular section, even paragraph, of your manuscript. The idea is not to copy the style of the poetry per se, but to let the words stretch your horizons.

Another thing you can do is write a section of description as a poem. It might turn out something like this:

> The conductor beats time for the band and all the performers follow him,
> The child is baptized, the convert is making his first professions,
> The regatta is spread on the bay, the race is begun, (how the white sails sparkle!)
> The drover watching his drove sings out to them that would stray,
> The peddler sweats with his pack on his back, (the purchaser higgling about the odd cent;)
> The bride unrumples her white dress, the minute hand of the clock moves slowly,
> The opium-eater reclines with rigid head and just-open'd lips,
> The prostitute draggles her shawl, her bonnet bobs on her tipsy and pimpled neck,
> The crowd laugh at her blackguard oaths, the men jeer and wink to each other,
> (Miserable! I do not laugh at your oaths nor jeer you;)
> The President holding a cabinet council is surrounded by the great Secretaries,
> On the piazza walk three matrons stately and friendly with twined arms ...
> —Song of Myself, by Walt Whitman

Then, as an exercise only—not for publication!—try to rewrite the poem as prose. For example, here are a couple of lines from Stanley Kunitz's *The Layers*:

> How shall the heart be reconciled
> to its feast of losses?
> In a rising wind

the manic dust of my friends,
those who fell along the way,
bitterly stings my face.

You can take the key words—*heart, feast of losses, manic dust of my friends*—and begin a narration, coming from you or a character you create. Work the words in as you will, change them if you like, but try to create a similar sound. Don't worry about the meaning. Just the practice of moving from poetry to prose will expand the horizons of your style.

• •

One day it dawned on me: writing is not recorded thought at all. Writing is recorded sound, and the melody the words create can enhance the thought they convey, or it can contradict it, or it can add another dimension that is entirely beyond the tethered confines of subject-verb-predicate. We all have a little person in our head who reads the words to us when we encounter good writing. With great writing, the sounds of the words work together, and that little person breaks forth into song.

—TOM MORRISEY

Write Long, Run-On Sentences

Another helpful exercise is to write long, run-on sentences—a page or more at a time. Let yourself go. The only rule is *don't edit yourself.*

William Saroyan wrote a book filled with run-on sentences, *Obituaries*, most of which is a reflection on life and death. A sample:

> I like being alive, but there were early times when I either didn't like it at all, or didn't like the kind of living I was doing, or thought I didn't, as at the orphanage in Oakland, and of course there are times when I do not feel any special pleasure in being alive but at the same time do not feel any special displeasure with it—certainly not for myself, for I have everything,

> and there is no reason at all for me to find any particular fault with the way
> I put up with time and the world and the human race ...

If you do this regularly, you'll find glittering nuggets of "unobtrusive poetry" popping out at you, phrases you can actually include in your work in progress. But the finding comes after. The first time out, let the words flow.

Here's a bit of run-on description from my writing journal. I didn't let my inner editor stop me, I just wrote:

> He had a hat the size of a Toyota on his head, a foam thing, red as blood
> and wobbly as a drunk at dinner, and as he walked down the street whist-
> ling like an old flute in a windstorm he would pause and look around,
> his jack-in-the-box head springy, his eyes a couple of water pistols, wet
> with tears of frustration ...

I may never use any of these images, but just the act of writing them exercises my voice and style muscles.

Similes, Metaphors, and Surprises

Dow Mossman, author of *The Stones of Summer* (the subject of a documentary, *Stone Reader*), says he considered each page of his massive novel to be its own poem. Naturally it's filled with metaphors and similes.

> He stood, leaning against the wooden jamb of the double glass doorway,
> looking back, and his eyes seemed almost dull, flatter than last year, mut-
> ed somehow like reptiles not swimming in open water anymore.

Dull eyes like reptiles not swimming surprises in a pleasing way, but also fits the overall tone of the novel. The best similes and metaphors do both.

So how do you find these images?

Make a list. At the top, write the subject. In the above example, it would be *dull eyes*. Dull like what?

List as many images as you can, absurd and farfetched as they may be. Push past your comfort zone. Force yourself to come up with twenty possibilities. One of them will surely work.

If not, make another list. That's how you find the word pictures.

Another stylistic technique is the *happy surprise*. This can be an unexpected word or a new spin on the familiar.

Robert Newton Peck uses nouns in place of adjectives to plant the unexpected in his novel *A Day No Pigs Would Die*:

> She was getting bigger than August.
> The whole sky was pink and peaches.

Like Peck, you should occasionally step outside the normal, grammatical box. You'll find some pleasant surprises when you do.

You can also take familiar expressions and glitz them up. Write out a description as it comes to you, as banal or cliché-ridden as that may be, and then find ways to make it fresh.

For example, you write, "She was beautiful." Now you start to play with it, adding or changing words along the way. You might jump immediately to the cliché, "She looked like a million dollars."

Harlan Ellison came to this point and ended up with, "She looked like a million bucks tax-free." That little addition at the end makes this a fresh expression. Hunt for the poetry, the music, the happy surprise. Come up with lots of possibilities, without judging, and only then sit back and pick the best ones. This added work will pay off as your prose reaches new stylistic heights.

Minimalism?

In the late twentieth century, *minimalism* became all the rage in most university writing programs. Mostly a reaction against commercial fiction, it seeks to strip away pretense and puffery in style. The use of modifiers—adjectives and adverbs—is largely discouraged.

On that score, minimalism is a good thing. Overuse of modifiers can make fiction too flabby.

But minimalist theory also preaches a certain ambiguity in style and theme. That's all right if you like that kind of fiction. But it's not the only kind, and minimalism isn't always successful.

In the hands of a Raymond Carver, and even a James M. Cain, it can work. But if you're not careful it can come off as pretentious, as having (to paraphrase Gertrude Stein) "no there there."

Take the good part of minimalism, the economical use of modifiers, and run with it. Also, when rewriting, look for places where you may have overcooked the emotion. Reading is an emotional experience, and you do need to have it in your story. But show it; don't shout it.

WRITE HOT, REVISE COOL

A good rule of thumb (and all the other typing fingers, too) is to write hot, revise cool. Don't try to make every sentence perfect before moving on to the next. Write hot, letting the emotion and passion for the story carry you.

Later, you sit back a bit and revise with a cool head. You can do this by looking at what you wrote the day before, editing that work, and then writing the current day's quota. Or you can do it by writing a first draft hot and then revising the whole thing cool.

When creating, try to be on fire. When editing, control the flames.

CLUTTER AND FLAB

What's wrong with this line?

> He nodded his head in agreement.

If you identified this as coming from the Dept. of Redundancy Department, well done. It is an example of flabby writing.

Cutting flab (what William Zinsser calls "clutter") is an ongoing process. There are no rules here, no one-size-fits-all technique. It's a matter of experience and willingness. Note that last word. A willingness to cut what you've written, to be ruthless, is one of the hallmarks of the professional writer.

Editing Example

Below are two versions of a section from my novel, *Sins of the Fathers*. The first is my original. The second shows a little of the thinking process that goes into self-editing.

ORIGINAL VERSION

First came the children.

In Lindy's dream they were running and screaming, dozens of them, in some sunlit field. A billowing surge of terrified kids, boys and girls, some in baseball garb, others in variegated ragtag clothes that gave the impression of a Dickens novel run amok.

What was behind them, what was causing the terror, was something dark, unseen. In the hovering over visions that only dreams afford, Lindy sought desperately the source of the fear.

There was a black forest behind the field, like you'd see in fairy tales. Or nightmares.

She moved toward the forest, knowing who it was, who was in there, and she'd meet him coming out. It would be Darren DiCinni, and he would have a gun, and in the dream she kept low to avoid being shot herself.

Moving closer and closer now, the screams of the scattering children fading behind her. Without having to look behind she knew that a raft of cops was pulling up to the scene.

She wondered if she was going to warn DiCinni, or was she just going to look at him?

Would he say anything to her, or she to him?

The dark forest had the kind of trees that come alive at night, with gnarly arms and knotted trunks. It was the place where the bad things lived.

Lindy didn't want to go in, but she couldn't stop herself.

That's when the dark figure started to materialize, from deep within the forest, and he was running toward her.

EDITED VERSION

First came the children.

In Lindy's dream they were running and screaming, dozens of them, in some sunlit field. A billowing surge of terrified kids, boys and girls, some in baseball garb, others in variegated ragtag clothes that gave the impression of a Dickens novel run amok.

~~What was behind them, what was causing the terror, was something dark, unseen.~~ [Weak sentence structure. Rethink. Check "dark." I use it a lot!] In the ~~hovering over visions~~ [Confusing.] that only dreams afford, Lindy sought desperately the source of the fear.

~~There was~~ [Sentences starting with "There" are generally weak. Rethink.] a black forest behind the field, ~~like you'd see~~ [Using "you" in this way can be effective in some places, but overuse is not good. Rethink.] in fairy tales. Or nightmares.

She moved toward the forest, ~~knowing who it was, who was in there,~~ [Awkward.] and she'd meet him coming out. ~~It would be Darren DiCinni, and he would have a gun, and in the dream she kept low to avoid being shot herself.~~ [See if I can strengthen this dramatic image.]

Moving closer and closer now, the screams of the scattering children fading behind her. Without having to look behind she knew that a raft of cops was pulling up to the scene.

~~She wondered if she was going to warn DiCinni, or was she just going to look at him?~~ [Tighten.]

Would he say anything to her, or she to him?

~~The dark forest had the kind of trees that come alive at night, with gnarly arms and knotted trunks. It was the place where the bad things lived.~~ [Rethink. There's "dark" again.]

Lindy didn't want to go in, but she couldn't stop herself.

~~That's when~~ [Unneeded verbiage.] the dark figure started to materialize, from deep within the forest, and ~~he~~ [How do we know it's he?] was running toward her.

KEY POINTS

- Voice and style should develop naturally as you attend to the telling of your story. Don't force it.
- Read a wide variety of literature and poetry to expand your stylistic possibilities.
- Less is usually more when writing emotion. The first time out, let it flow, but be ready to pull back when you edit. Write hot, revise cool.

Exercise 1

This is a suggestion from Natalie Goldberg. Take a portion of your writing, usually a descriptive passage (setting or character), and do a free-form exercise expanding it.

In your manuscript on the printed page or computer, jot a placeholder, like the letter (A) with a circle around it.

Then take a fresh page or open a new document, put the (A) at the top, and just go, letting your imagination run free. Don't censor yourself and don't try to make this good writing! You're going for images and insights. It's a total right-brain gabfest.

Here's what I mean. Below is a section from my writing journal:

It had an actual downtown, with rows of shops. Boutiques, hardware, shoes, antiques, books. The place hadn't been Wal-Marted yet, though it did have the obligatory Starbucks. He stopped in and treated himself to a Mocha Frap. The afternoon was warm and it was a long drive back to L.A.

He walked around a little. The town had a nice looking Mexican grill and a Carl's Jr. A bowling alley and a two-screen theater. Brad Pitt's latest, along with some teen horror flick.

For this exercise, I identify the places for a riff:

> It had an actual downtown, with rows of shops. Boutiques, hardware, shoes, antiques, books. The place hadn't been Wal-Marted yet, though it did have the **(A)** obligatory Starbucks. He stopped in and treated himself to a Mocha Frap. The afternoon was warm and it was a long drive back to L.A.
>
> He walked around a little. The town had a nice looking Mexican grill and a Carl's Jr. A bowling alley and a two-screen theater. Brad Pitt's latest, along with some **(B)** teen horror flick.

Now for the writing, just going:

> **A**
>
> Green monster, with tentacles all over the world, reaching into every town and city and home, the great Temple of need. Caffeine buzz, and wasn't that what the world needs now, buzz sweet buzz?

> **B**
>
> Ah yes, the teen horror movie, the kind that inevitably featured the latest TV hotties making their big-screen debuts in an entirely forgettable waste of celluloid with posters always featuring the ample bosom of the latest eye candy who will soon enough occupy the same dustbin of cultural irrelevancy as a Paris Hilton and what's-her-name, you know the one, or do you?

Strange, I know, but again this isn't for publication. And I would write more than the brief illustrative passage above. What I'm looking for is that one gem that can actually make the cut and please me stylistically.

Exercise 2

Read the following excerpts one at a time. Read each four or five times. Read them out loud once. Then write a page trying to capture the same voice. Make up your own story situation, and just go. Once you've done your page, pare it down to a single paragraph.

It may turn out to be some gold you'll want to keep.

> Know ye, now, Bulkington? Glimpses do ye seem to see of that mortally intolerable truth; that all deep, earnest thinking is but the intrepid effort of the soul to keep the open independence of her sea; while the wildest winds of heaven and earth conspire to cast her on the treacherous, slavish shore?
>
> —*Moby-Dick*, by Herman Melville

It was a pleasure to burn.

It was a special pleasure to see things eaten, to see things blackened and changed. With the brass nozzle in his fists, with this great python spitting its venomous kerosene upon the world, the blood pounded in his head, and his hands were the hands of some amazing conductor playing all the symphonies of blazing and burning to bring down the tatters and charcoal ruins of history.

—*Fahrenheit 451*, by Ray Bradbury

If you really want to hear about it, the first thing you'll probably want to know is where I was born, and what my lousy childhood was like, and how my parents were occupied and all before they had me, and all that David Copperfield kind of crap, but I don't feel like going into it, if you want to know the truth.

—*The Catcher in the Rye*, by J.D. Salinger

But then they danced down the streets like dingledodies, and I shambled after as I've been doing all my life after people who interest me, because the only people for me are the mad ones, the ones who are mad to live, mad to talk, mad to be saved, desirous of everything at the same time, the ones who never yawn or say a commonplace thing, but burn, burn, burn like fabulous yellow roman candles exploding like spiders across the stars and in the middle you see the blue centerlight pop and everybody goes "Awww!"

—*On the Road*, by Jack Kerouac

Eventually, all things merge into one, and a river runs through it. The river was cut by the world's great flood and runs over rocks from the basement of time. On some of the rocks are timeless raindrops. Under the rocks are the words, and some of the words are theirs.

I am haunted by waters.

—*A River Runs Through It*, by Norman Maclean

At two-thirty Saturday morning, in Los Angeles, Joe Carpenter woke, clutching a pillow to his chest, calling his lost wife's name in the darkness. The anguished and haunted quality of his own voice had shaken him from sleep. Dreams fell from him not all at once but in trembling veils, as attic dust falls off rafters when a house rolls with an earthquake.

—*Sole Survivor*, by Dean Koontz

CHAPTER 10

Setting and Description

Setting, of course, is where your story takes place.

Description is how you bring it, and the characters who populate it, to life.

You want to create the feeling in the reader that she is experiencing a real place right along with real characters.

That's what editors and readers are looking for. They'll ask, "Make the place come alive for me. I want to see it, smell it. I want to know the characters up close and personal. Think you can do that for me?"

Yes, you can.

SCOUTING A SETTING

Here's a major tip for setting: Think of it as another character in your book. Make it offer up possibilities of conflict and tension. Make it brood over the proceedings and exert influence.

Remember the Overlook Hotel in Stephen King's *The Shining*? The eerie place, closed up for the winter, is literally pulsating with ghostly life. And there's snow all over, which comes into play in a big way.

You need to get to know your setting intimately. If it's a place you've never been, you're going to need to do research.

Even if you write about a place you know well, that's not a license to take it easy. Most of my books take place in my native Los Angeles, but I still always try to walk through the actual locations, taking pictures, recording my impressions.

Use all your senses when researching a location. Take along a checklist and fill it out, with questions like:

- What is the weather like here?
- How does it affect the citizens?
- What are the most prominent buildings or features here?
- What does the place smell like?
- What sort of flora and fauna is present?
- What is everyday life like here?
- What do the homes tell me about the people inside?
- What does the place "sound" like? What do you hear at different locations in the area?
- What unique features are there?

These can become vivid details for your book. A great place to gather inside information on a locale is an independent bookstore. This can also serve the dual purpose of introducing yourself as a writer and starting a professional relationship with the store owner. Ask for stories about the town's history and recent past.

Pick up local newspapers and flyers. Stop by the Chamber of Commerce as well for visitor information. Collect e-mail contact information so you can follow up later with questions that may occur to you.

Use resources like Google Earth to remind yourself of layouts and features and roads. For his novel *Empire*, Orson Scott Card relied almost exclusively on Google Maps and Google Earth to give him the details of streets and locations, and even locales where he could construct imaginary reservoirs.

TELLING DETAILS

The *telling detail* is one that describes instantly and uniquely. It makes a place or character come to life immediately.

In *Description*, novelist Monica Wood writes that telling details come "suddenly, from your unconscious, to tell you what you need to know ... and deliberately, from your conscious writing self."

You can also go hunting for lots of details, make a list, and then choose the best ones.

Details, when woven into the narrative naturally, put the reader into a story world. This enables the weaving of the fictive dream, which is the goal of every novelist.

If details are scant, the story won't feel full. For the reader, even though he may not be able to articulate it, something will seem to be missing. The reading experience will be thin.

I once had a student present a historical novel with lots of action in the first chapter. The time was the sixteenth century. The place, the Netherlands. Yet for all the movement there were hardly any specific details. The time and place weren't nailed down. The story could have been happening almost anywhere, anytime.

The remedy for this is the well-placed, telling detail. In Part IV of my historical novel *Glimpses of Paradise*, the setting is 1921 Los Angeles, and Zee Miller is an aspiring actress:

> Zee Miller stopped by the light post and pretended to look in her handbag. She poked at the meager insides with her hand, feeling around as if in search of an item, but in reality keeping watch out of the corner of her eye.
>
> The grocer was finishing up his sidewalk display for the morning, whistling as he worked. Zee watched and listened. Her gaze from time to time fell upon the two oranges that sat especially succulent in the morning sun, atop a pile of freshly unloaded citrus.
>
> There were some window signs on the front of the grocery—*Carnation Milk, 11¢ per can; Roasted Coffee, 2-lb. pkg., 40¢; Ben Hur Soap, 5¢ per bar*. She couldn't afford any of it. Luxury items all. But oh, did the coffee sound nice.
>
> Zee made a pretense of looking ever more carefully in her bag, as if a loose dime might have fallen to the bottom. In truth she had not even a dime. But she made it seem so, telling herself that this is the way Mary Pickford would look for a dime were she a young wife with a hint of trouble at home. Wide eyes, furrowed brow, increasing the appearance of concern.
>
> The market on Ninth Street near Flower was, Zee had come to know, one of the busiest in the downtown district. A crossroads for the shopping traffic that would include a large sampling of the female population of Los Angeles—the upper crust from Angeleno Heights and Elysian Park; hardworking housewives from east of the Los Angeles River; domestic help from the mansions on Adams Street; unmarried women from Glendale and Hawthorne, who trollied in to their jobs at the phone company or stenographic pool.
>
> Even the occasional down-and-outer, the ones who defied classification because each had her own sad story, her tale of woe, one that occasionally turned up in the crime sheet of the paper when the inevitable

happened—caught stealing or skipping the rent, or occasionally rousted from a prostitutes' den. ... She wore a plain brown walking dress and brown leather shoes with fraying laces and a missing eyelet. Her brown shirtwaist had a hole just under the left arm, which necessitated turning her right side toward the grocer. She did not wish to arouse suspicion.

Turning now to a crate of apples, the grocer began whistling another tune entirely. This Zee recognized as "Ain't We Got Fun," a ubiquitous melody these days.

For a contemporary novel, the need for an immediate sense of place is equally important. Sol Stein opens his novel *The Magician* like this:

It had been snowing off and on since Christmas. For nearly a month now, while the men of the town were at work, boys would come out in twos or threes with shovels to clear a pathway on their neighbors' sidewalks. An occasional older man, impoverished or proud, could be seen daring death with a shovel in hand, clearing steps so that one could get in and out of the house, or using a snowblower on a driveway in the hope of getting his wife to the supermarket and back before the next snow fell.

At night mostly, when the traffic had thinned, the town's orange snow-plows would come scraping down the roads, their headlamps casting funnels of still-falling snow. Alongside these thoroughfares, the snow lay in hillocks, some ten or fifteen feet high, thawing a bit each day in bright sun, then refreezing, forming the crust on which it would soon snow again. It seemed impossible that spring might come, and that these humped gray masses would eventually vanish as water into the heel-hard ground.

Notice that Stein doesn't give us *snowplows*, but *orange snowplows*. That's called getting specific.

PUT DETAILS WITHIN ACTION

Details can be presented blandly:

There was a livery stable in town, at the end of the wooden sidewalk, where travelers stabled their horses. Today, the town was bustling with activity.

But here is how the Western writer Todhunter Ballard did it in *High Iron*:

Lonnigan stabled his horse at Chandler's Livery, asking the barn man to watch out for a buyer, then carrying his slicker-wrapped bedroll under one long arm, he moved out upon the slatted sidewalk, his eager gray eyes missing no detail of the town's busy main street.

Notice how specific, yet effortless, the details are. The livery stable is "Chandler's Livery," and the bedroll is "slicker-wrapped." The sidewalk is not just wood, but slatted. Ballard has painted a picture, but he did it *through the action and perspective of his main character*. Thus the details don't distract, but serve.

USE ALL THE SENSES

The use of specific colors seems to enliven a scene. Here's John D. MacDonald from a Travis McGee novel, *The Quick Red Fox*:

> She wore flat sandals with gold straps. She wore faun-colored pants in a fine weave. Around her slender throat was knotted a narrow loose kerchief of green silk, precisely matching the single jewel she wore, an emerald as big as a sugar cube ...

Sight and sound are easy. But what about smell and touch? Even taste? These are underutilized details. Watch for them in the fiction you read.

Remember to use the principle of *double duty*. Your words should do more than describe. They should add to the mood and tone.

The quintessential example of double duty in description comes from *Bleak House* by Charles Dickens. It opens:

> Smoke lowering down from chimney-pots, making a soft black drizzle, with flakes of soot in it as big as full-grown snow-flakes—gone into mourning, one might imagine, for the death of the sun. ...
>
> Fog everywhere. Fog up the river, where it flows among green aits and meadows; fog down the river, where it rolls defiled among the tiers of shipping and the waterside pollutions of a great (and dirty) city. Fog on the Essex marshes, fog on the Kentish heights. Fog creeping into the cabooses of collier-brigs; fog lying out on the yards, and hovering in the rigging of great ships; fog drooping on the gunwales of barges and small boats. Fog in the eyes and throats of ancient Greenwich pensioners, wheezing by the firesides of their wards. ...
>
> Never can there come fog too thick, never can there come mud and mire too deep, to assort with the groping and floundering condition which this High Court of Chancery, most pestilent of hoary sinners, holds this day in the sight of heaven and earth.

That brings up another tip: If you describe the weather, have the characters react to it. Don't just write:

> It was a hot day. Jack walked down the block to buy a newspaper.

Write:

> It was a hot day. Jack's sweat-soaked shirt stuck to him. He hated when that happened.

CREATING MOOD

Mood in your novel is like the score of a movie—it plays in the background, deepening the feelings in the reader. Illuminating details operate to both set up and pay off emotional moments.

In Raymond Carver's "A Small, Good Thing," the opening lines set up a mood that shatters later in the narrative.

> Saturday afternoon she drove to the bakery in the shopping center. After looking through a loose-leaf binder with photographs of cakes taped onto the pages, she ordered chocolate, the child's favorite. The cake she chose was decorated with a spaceship and launching pad under a sprinkling of white stars, and a planet made of red frosting at the other end. His name, SCOTTY, would be in green letters beneath the planet.

Notice that it's a *loose-leaf binder* with photographs *taped onto the pages.* These make the scene real. But it's the details of the cake that create a mood of childhood dreams and the hopes of a mother. Scotty's promise is infinite, like space.

So when he's hit by a car and dies, it jolts us all the more because so many hopes die with him.

Paying off with just the right details intensifies the final impact of a scene or an entire novel. Consider the ending of Don DeLillo's *White Noise*, which creates an ironic sadness as supermarket shoppers in a doomed world try to go on as normal:

> And this is where we wait together, regardless of age, our carts stocked with brightly colored goods. A slowly moving line, satisfying, giving us time to glance at the tabloids in the racks. Everything we need that is not food or love is here in the tabloid racks. The tales of the supernatural and the extraterrestrial. The miracle vitamins, the cures for cancer, the remedies for obesity. The cults of the famous and the dead.

A technique to help you capture mood details is the *eyes closed drill*. Close your eyes and let your imagination create detail-rich pictures for you. Don't rush this; experience it. Keep at it until you are emotionally charged by what you see.

Then start writing down the details as if you were a journalist describing a real place. Later, edit and shape the material to solidify the mood you're trying to create. Expand on images by using metaphor and simile.

Strive to come up with language as specific as this from Mary Karr's memoir *The Liars' Club*:

> Some firemen wearing canary-colored slickers started to move through the next room, and Dr. Boudreaux's thick fingers came again to rub the edge of my speckled nightgown the way old ladies at the five-and-dime tested yard goods.

DON'T DUMP

Beginning writers, especially those who write historical fiction, have a tendency to overdo their settings and descriptions. This is understandable, as they've usually spent a great deal of time in research. They want to pack every bit of information in, thinking this will grab the reader's interest and draw her into the story.

But the very opposite is the case. Readers are not interested in the setting or the details per se. They are, first and always, interested in the characters. As Sinclair Lewis used to say, "When I want to learn about the Azores, I'll read the *National Geographic*, not a novel!"

Avoid, then, the descriptive *dump*. That is when all the description is given at once, then the story picks up again. While on occasion, especially at the opening of scenes, you can put in a relatively full description, it's more often the better choice to "marble" the description in during the action.

The way to do this is to put the description in the character's point of view and use the details to add to the mood (double duty again).

For example, the opening of Dean Koontz's *Midnight* has a character, Janice Capshaw, who has gone running at night. She's not going to make it out alive. In fact, she's going to become a treat for a horrible thing that chases her. Here are a few passages that occur as she catches her first glimpse of the chaser. The descriptive details are italicized:

Someone stood on that *twenty-foot-high wall of boulders*, looking down at her. Janice glanced up just as a cloak of mist shifted and as *moonlight silhouetted* him. ...

For a moment, peering directly up at him, she was transfixed by his gaze. Backlit by the moon, looming above her, standing tall and motionless upon the ramparts of rock, with sea spray exploding to the right of him, he might have been a carved stone idol with luminous jewel eyes. ...

Janice broke her paralysis, turned back on her own tracks, and ran toward the entrance to the public beach—a full mile away. *Houses with lighted windows* stood atop the *steep-walled bluff* that overlooked the cove. ...

CHARACTER DESCRIPTION

Specific details about a character's background create the illusion that the story is about a real person. It aids in the suspension of disbelief. The fictive dream becomes so vivid it's very close to actual experience.

A clunky way of rendering essential background might go like this:

Maddie Pace sometimes had trouble sleeping. Things would worry her. She could fret over the littlest things, such as what visitors might have thought about her housekeeping. She'd often drive her fiancée crazy at restaurants when she couldn't make up her mind what to order.

Stephen King, who is a master at such characterization, did this much better in his story "Home Delivery":

Maddie Pace, who sometimes couldn't sleep if, after a visit from Reverend Johnson, she spied a single speck of dust under the dining-room table. Maddie Pace, who, as Maddie Sullivan, used to drive her fiancée, Jack, crazy when she froze over a menu, debating entrées sometimes for as long as half an hour.

"Maddie, why don't you just flip a coin?" he'd asked her once after she had managed to narrow it down to a choice between the braised veal and the lamb chops, and then could get no further.

Notice all the instances of specificity in these two small paragraphs:

- The visitor is named *Reverend Johnson*.
- The cause of her distress is *a single speck of dust*.
- The location is *under the dining-room table*.

- Her maiden name was *Sullivan*.
- Her fiancée's name was *Jack*.
- She would *freeze over a menu*.
- Sometimes for as long as *half an hour*.
- We get actual dialogue from Jack that reflects his frustration.
- We are told she was stuck between *braised veal* and *lamb chops*.

DESCRIBING KEY MOMENTS

A good novel always has key, or heightened, moments and scenes. They should be written for all they're worth. One way to do that is to write the moment in slow motion. Concentrate on each beat, as Dennis Lehane does in *Mystic River*:

> She took a deep breath, let it out. "At three in the morning on Sunday, Dave came back to our apartment covered in someone else's blood."
>
> It was out there now. The words had left her mouth and entered the atmosphere. They formed a wall in front of her and Jimmy and then that wall sprouted a ceiling and another wall behind them and they were suddenly cloistered within a tiny cell created by a single sentence. The noises along the avenue died and the breeze vanished, and all Celeste could smell was Jimmy's cologne and the bright May sun baked into the steps at their feet.

Celeste's admission is the crucial turning point in Lehane's novel. As such, it shouldn't pass without descriptive emphasis. Lehane gives a paragraph to draw it out. He does so with the following beats:

- Celeste thinks about the words being *out there now* in the *atmosphere*.
- The effect of the words is to form walls, isolating the characters.
- The space becomes more confining—*a tiny cell*.
- Other sensory details go away (*noises* and *breeze*).
- The sensory images left are immediate (*Jimmy's cologne* and the *sun baked into the steps*).

Look for key moments in your own work. By slowing down and focusing in on descriptive details and thoughts, let the moment stand out for the reader.

KEY POINTS

- Choose a location wisely, as if it is a character, and do your research.

- Use all the senses, and seek the *telling detail*.
- Create mood with your descriptions.
- Put scene descriptions within the actions and perceptions of a character.
- It's tempting to dump all your information in large chunks. Resist!
- When it comes to key moments, slow down and work to find just the right details. This is time well spent.

Exercise 1

Select a portion of your manuscript where you give a character background. Analyze it. Have you merely listed the details?

Make a list of *specific details* that would make the background seem like it comes from a real person's life. Take your time. Even do some research in obituaries and the like. Notice the examples of real life in these obits, then think up ways to render similar items for your character.

Come up with more details than you'll use. The writing exercise will do you good.

Look over your list and select one or two items to include in your character's background. If there are other details you like, find places to weave them into the story so you aren't giving us all the background at once.

Read the first five pages of your manuscript.

Now, underline all the details of description, and look at those pages again.

- Have you established a sense of setting?
- Have you used sensory details (sight, sound, smell, taste, touch)?
- Are the underlined words bunched up in one place? Or "marbled" throughout the text?

Try rewriting the pages, putting in as much description as you can. Go overboard. Wax poetic. Use all the senses.

Now read them again with your editor hat on. Keep some things, cut others. How does it read now?

Remember, it's not a matter of piling on details, but choosing the telling details that matters most.

Exercise 2

Keep a journal for description only. Take notes at various times in the day. Observe and record as much detail as you can, from the big things to the little.

Later, take these details and turn them into a descriptive scene. It doesn't matter what the scene is about. Just drop a character into the setting and set out the description in a poetic fashion.

Exercise 3

The following are some descriptions from best-selling novels:

> A worm of fear turned in his stomach.
>
> *
>
> The panic that lived beneath her skin burned through to the surface.
>
> *
>
> Her chin began to quiver.
>
> *
>
> Terror ballooned in her heart.
>
> *
>
> A ball of ice formed in his chest.
>
> *
>
> White light exploded in her brain.
>
> *
>
> Shock stole her breath.
>
> *
>
> His spine felt like a column of ice.

Take the following emotions and brainstorm some nouns that you can associate with each. If you want to add an adjective to the noun, go ahead. For example, *fear* may bring up the association of electric wires sparking around inside. So *frayed wires* might be one choice.

FEAR_____ _____ _____
JOY _____ _____ _____
ANGER _____ _____ _____
HATRED _____ _____ _____
LONGING _____ _____ _____
SHOCK_____ _____ _____

Now circle your favorite noun from each list. Write a sentence where you pair the noun and the emotion by way of a strong verb.

> Frayed wires of fear snaked around his insides.

Start a collection of your own creations for future use.

CHAPTER 11

Exposition

This is a short section on *exposition*, because the concept, while simple to understand, comes with a caveat: Too much of it in narrative form will bog your story down faster than anything else.

Exposition is *information* that's needed to explain something important about plot or character. For example, your story takes place in a town that hosts an annual rodeo. If you were writing nonfiction you could simply give the explanatory information straight, as Wikipedia does:

> Rodeo is an outgrowth of Mexican bullfighting. This Spanish word literally means "to surround." Rodeo often conjures up images of dusty cowboys scrounging up a living in out-of-the-way arenas, but in fact, modern professional rodeo is a very different sport. Its long season peaks on the July 4th weekend, but concludes with the world's richest rodeo, the Professional Rodeo Cowboys Association (PRCA) Wrangler National Finals Rodeo (NFR) in Las Vegas, Nevada, in December.

But when you're writing a novel, this sort of thing would bring the story to a dead stop. The skillful handling of exposition is one of the marks of a competent fiction writer.

So, how do you do it so it flows naturally?

DECIDE *WHAT* AND *WHO*

First, you decide what information is absolutely essential for the reader to know, and you get rid of all the rest.

That's right. It's never necessary to give the reader every datum of information. Part of the craft of writing is knowing what to leave out. It's not always necessary to know the complete history of the slave trade in order to do a Civil War novel. Selection is the key.

Next, always place the exposition in the context of a character's point of view. Otherwise, your voice will intrude in the proceedings and yank the reader out of the "fictive dream." Don't put in several paragraphs of exposition and then give us the point-of-view character. Instead, mix in the information as the character moves through the scene. Take a look at the difference:

> The Examiner building was on Main Street. It was one of the many buildings that made up the impressive skyline of downtown. That's why so many pedestrians could be found on the sidewalks on any given afternoon. A block from the Examiner was Frisbee Park. This land had been given to the city by Admiral Hyrum Frisbee in 1921 to commemorate the wedding of his daughter to the son of the King of Spain.
>
> Earl Jones saw all this as he walked down the street.

This is better:

> A little after noon, Earl Jones walked out of the Examiner building and turned right on Main Street. He loved downtown with its impressive skyline and bustling sidewalks. He loved walking by Frisbee Park and giving a wave to the statue of Hyrum Frisbee. It was the Admiral who had given the land to the city back in 1921, all because his daughter was marrying some Spanish prince.
>
> "Thanks, pal," Earl said as he walked by.

DIALOGUE IT

Another way to get in essential information is through dialogue. But you have to avoid one main mistake, and that is to merely put quotation marks around an "exposition dump" and think your work is done. As in:

> "Hey, Buck, what's going on here?"
>
> "It's a rodeo."
>
> "A real rodeo?"
>
> "Yep."
>
> "Gosh, I don't know much about rodeos."
>
> "Well, let me tell you," Buck said. "Rodeo is an outgrowth of Mexican bullfighting. This Spanish word literally means 'to surround.' Rodeo of-

ten conjures up images of dusty cowboys scrounging up a living in out-of-the-way arenas, but in fact ..."

No, that won't do. If you'll check chapter six, you'll note that one of the essentials of dialogue is that it truly goes from one character to another. It's not just a device to slip information to the reader. When it looks like that's what you're doing, the reader is immediately pulled out of the story.

So, to give exposition in dialogue, follow these steps:

1. Decide what information can be left out. Just because it can be explained doesn't mean it has to be.
2. Make sure there's a reason for the dialogue to include the information.
3. Drop in the information a little at a time, not all at once.

> "Hey, Buck, what's going on here?"
> "It's a rodeo."
> "A real rodeo?"
> "Yep."
> "Gosh, I don't know much about rodeos."
> "Ever hear of a bullfight?"
> "Sure."
> "That's what it's based on."
> "Yeah? I thought it was just a bunch of dusty cowboys hangin' around."
> Buck laughed. "Nope. It's a big time professional sport now ..."

You get the point. If you can work in some conflict, so much the better. An argument is often a good way to get information into the story:

> "Gosh, I don't know much about rodeos."
> "Ever hear of a bullfight?"
> "Sure."
> "That's what it's based on."
> "Yeah? I thought it was just a bunch of dusty cowboys hangin' around."
> Buck spat. "You don't know squat, do you?"
> "I—"
> "You know less than squat. If you and squat went to a rodeo, squat could wear a T-shirt that says *I'm with Stupid*. It's a *pro sport*, is what it is."

The Switcheroo Again

In chapter seven, I explained the chapter-two switcheroo. Apply this concept by considering tossing out your first chapter and starting with chapter two.

In the chapters that follow in your book, look at the opening paragraphs and see if you can move the exposition to a later point, perhaps sprinkling it in as you go along. I remind you of my rule: *Act first, explain later.*

KEY POINTS

- Exposition is information the reader needs. It will slow your story down if not handled well.
- Always cut what isn't necessary.
- Drop exposition in a little at a time.
- "Hide" exposition within dialogue.

Exercise 1

Here is an excerpt from Wikipedia's entry on firefighters. Create a character who is a volunteer firefighter (male or female) and create another character of the opposite sex who is ignorant about what firefighters do. Write a scene with dialogue where most of the following information comes through dialogue:

> The three main goals in firefighting are (in order) saving life, saving property, and protecting the environment. Firefighting is an inherently difficult occupation. As such, the skills required for safe operations are regularly practiced during training evolutions throughout a firefighter's career. Firefighters work closely with other emergency response agencies, most particularly local and state police departments. As every fire scene is technically a crime scene until deemed otherwise by a qualified investigator, there is often overlap between the responsibilities of responding firefighters and police officers, such as evidence and scene protection, initial observations of first respondents, and chain of evidence issues.

Put your scene aside for a few days, then come back to it and edit it. See how you can improve it by adding action beats, description, and other characters.

There is no one right answer for this. It's all up to your creativity. But you can repeat it by finding other information about professions (from places like Wikipedia) and doing more of the same.

Practice.

CHAPTER 12

Theme

"If you want to send a message," producer Sam Goldwyn once said, "try Western Union."

Which brings up the subject of *theme.*

Some writers hate it. Some ignore it. Some have theme firmly in mind as they write. Others wait until they've finished the novel to see what theme has emerged.

There is no one correct approach. There are, however, many pitfalls.

This chapter will help you avoid them.

WHAT A THEME IS

A theme is simply a *big idea.* It can be explicit or implicit, but there's always some feeling at the end that the story holds a message.

The noted writing teacher William Foster-Harris believed that all stories could be explained by way of a *moral formula,* the struggle between sets of values. A Foster-Harris formula might look like this: Value 1 vs. Value 2 = Outcome.

You plug in your values thus: Love vs. Ambition = Love. In other words, the value of love overcomes in the struggle against ambition. If one were writing a tragedy, the outcome would be the opposite, with ambition winning out. But in the end, we know which value prevails.

It is crucial, however, to realize that theme is played out through the characters in the story. Look to the characters, and what they're fighting for, and you'll find the theme of a story.

Understanding this concept—that theme is always wrapped up in the central conflict of the characters—will help you avoid:

- cardboard or one-dimensional characters
- a preachy tone
- lack of subtlety
- story clichés

These items commonly occur when a writer begins with a theme in mind, something he wants to "prove," and then forces all the action to be pressed through that filter.

So, always remember, *characters come before theme.*

Develop your characters first, your Lead and opposition, your supporting cast, and then set them in the story world where their values will conflict with each other. Write your story and watch your characters struggle. Make the story vivid and real.

If you have a theme in mind, keep it as wispy as a butterfly wing. Let the characters live and breathe. (And if you change your theme during the writing, guess what? You can.)

Or, like many writers, you can just follow the characters and plot and let the theme emerge. At first it may be like the faint glow of a miner's lamp as he enters the darkness of a shaft. You are in the darkness. Start following the light and see what happens.

Don't worry about theme. Worry about struggle. Give your characters humanity and passionate commitment to a set of values. Set them in conflict and as they fight, the theme will take care of itself.

In the movie *The Treasure of the Sierra Madre*, the old miner played by Walter Huston is telling his two younger companions—Humphrey Bogart and Tim Holt—the secret of panning for gold. "You gotta know how to tickle it so she comes out laughing."

Theme is like that, too. You don't want it to overwhelm your story.

MANY MESSAGES, OR JUST ONE

Think of theme as the "meta-message," the one big statement about the world that your work of fiction will convey. Your work will do this whether you're conscious of it or not.

A novel will have only one meta-message, though it may offer several sub-messages. For example, the theme of Dostoevsky's *The Brothers Karamazov* is "Kindness and justice are the highest values of human existence." But the novel propounds numerous messages, such as the futility of pure intellect and the burden of free will.

But you don't want characters who merely represent a thesis. They must be real people with passionate hearts.

Your job is to find out where that passion is. In your prewriting, allow time for your main characters to explain, in their own voices, a philosophy of life. Use the following exercise: Imagine your character sitting in a chair across from you. She seems angry. You, a trusted friend, ask her why she's upset.

Write down what she says, as quickly as it comes to you. Let this be a free-form, stream-of-consciousness exercise. Write for at least fifteen minutes. If you keep yourself from editing as you write, what your character says may actually begin to surprise you. Good. That's where real characters come from.

Later, come back and edit this voice journal to suit the needs of your character and story. Do this until you have a real person with real passions.

Once you've created well-rounded characters you'll have numerous opportunities to let them convey sub-messages in the actual story. But these must happen naturally, and that's a matter of learning the various "weaves" available to the fiction writer.

To that subject we now turn.

WEAVING THE THEME

Ever look at a beautiful tapestry? From afar it seems like a painting. Only up close can one see it is really a combination warp (the foundational weave) and woof (the decorative pattern). Put them together and you have art.

So it is with a great story, where plot and message combine to create a unified whole.

That's where weaving comes in. You must create the feeling of a tapestry, so the message emerges without fraying the rest of the story.

THE SPEECH WEAVE

Be wary of the straight speech—two or more paragraphs of one character speaking. Too often this becomes a thin substitute for the author's voice. If you come to a point in your story where a character wants to speechify, ask yourself some hard questions:

- Is the speech merely your voice in the character's mouth?
- Is there a dramatic need for the character to make a speech?
- Is the speech essential to the story? To character development?
- Are there alternatives (action, thoughts, dialogue) that could convey the information just as well?

Unless you can answer these questions satisfactorily, it's probably best not to give us a speech. But if you feel the speech is justified, make sure it is a window into the character's inner life. For example, in W. Somerset Maugham's *The Razor's Edge*, the spiritual pilgrim Larry Darrell tells about his search in a speech lasting several pages.

Here's some of the flavor:

> But that wasn't the chief thing that bothered me: I couldn't reconcile myself with that preoccupation with sin that, so far as I could tell, was never entirely absent from the monks' thoughts. I'd known a lot of fellows in the air corps. Of course they got drunk when they got a chance, and had a girl whenever they could and used foul language. ... If I'd been God I couldn't have brought myself to condemn one of them, not even the worst, to eternal damnation.

Here we have not only a glimpse of Darrell's struggle, but also some of his background (air corps). There is more going on than a mere conveyance of information. It is essential to Maugham's tale that we hear this speech. And it sounds like the character, Darrell, whom we have come to know.

In the film *On the Waterfront* (screenplay by Budd Schulberg), the theme is *humanity*—what does it mean to be a human being? Does it mean simply to survive? Or are we connected to each other?

Terry Malloy believes it's every man for himself. The ex-prizefighter, who has known nothing but "scrapping" all his life, wants to stay alive and make some money and be with the right people.

Edie Doyle is the very opposite. Educated in a religious school, she has a larger idea of what humanity is meant to be.

In this scene, Terry has taken Edie to a saloon for a little drink. Terry was unwittingly part of a scheme that ended in the killing of Edie's brother, Joey.

EDIE: Were you really a prizefighter?

TERRY: I used to be.

EDIE: How did you get interested in that?

TERRY: I don't know. I had to scrap all my life, I might as well get paid for it. When I was a kid my old man got bumped off. Never mind how. Then they stuck Charley and me in a dump they call a "children's home." Boy, that was some home. Anyhow, I ran away from there and fought in the club smokers and peddled papers and Johnny Friendly bought a piece of me.

EDIE: Bought a piece of you?

TERRY: Yes. I was going pretty good there for a while. And after that ... What do you really care, am I right?

EDIE: Shouldn't everybody care about everybody else?

TERRY: Boy, what a fruitcake you are.

EDIE: I mean, isn't everybody a part of everybody else?

TERRY: And you really believe that drool?

EDIE: Yes, I do.

[Drinks are served]

TERRY: Here we are. One for the lady and for the gent. Here's to the first one, I hope it ain't the last. Go ahead.

[Edie sips]

TERRY: No, not like that. One hook.

[Terry drinks his shot]

TERRY: Wham.

[Edie drinks hers, and is jolted]

EDIE: Wham.

TERRY: You wanna hear my philosophy of life? Do it to him before he does it to you.

EDIE: I never met anyone like you. There's not a spark of sentiment, or romance, or human kindness in your whole body.

TERRY: What good does it do you besides get you in trouble?

EDIE: And when things and people get in your way, you just knock them aside, get rid of them. Is that your idea?

TERRY: Don't look at me when you say that. It wasn't my fault what happened to Joey. Fixing him wasn't my idea.

EDIE: Who said it was?

TERRY: Everybody's putting the needle on me. You and them mugs in the church and Father Barry. I didn't like the way he was looking at me.

EDIE: He was looking at everybody the same way.

TERRY: Oh, yeah? What's with this Father Barry? What's his racket?

EDIE: His racket?

TERRY: Yeah, his racket. Everybody's got a racket.

EDIE: But he's a priest.

TERRY: Are you kidding? So what? That don't make no difference.

EDIE: You don't believe anybody, do you?

TERRY: Listen, down here it's every man for himself. It's keeping alive. It's standing in with the right people so you get a little bit of change jingling in your pocket.

EDIE: And if you don't?

TERRY: If you don't? Right down.

EDIE: It's living like an animal.

TERRY: All right. I'd rather live like an animal than end up like …

EDIE: Like Joey? Are you afraid to mention his name?

In this exchange, the theme has come out naturally. When using dialogue to weave in thoughts about theme, wrap it up in conflict.

Terry and Edie have natural conflict here. He inadvertently took part in the murder of her brother. And Edie has ideas which, if Terry ever bought into them, would lead to the shattering of the only world he knows.

Sometimes dialogue that carries theme can become ham-fisted, too obvious, maudlin. A deft touch with *humor* can allay some of that.

John Grisham uses humor to keep the conversion of a character from becoming maudlin. In *The Testament*, Nate O'Riley tells missionary Rachel Lane he tried to kill himself.

"I almost drank myself to death with cheap vodka."

"You poor man."

"I'm sick, okay. I have a disease. I've admitted it many times to many counselors."

"Have you ever confessed it to God?"

"I'm sure He knows."

"I'm sure He does. But He won't help unless you ask. He is omnipotent, but you have to go to Him, in prayer, in the spirit of forgiveness."

"What happens?"

"Your sins will be forgiven. Your slate will be wiped clean. Your addictions will be taken away. The Lord will forgive all of your transgressions, and you will become a new believer in Christ."

"What about the IRS?"

Instead of an easy pat answer to the religious presentation, Nate asks about the tax man. It's a light moment in a heavy exchange that works to strike the right balance.

And always remember that it must be the characters who speak, not the author. As Stephen King says in *On Writing*, the key to good dialogue is honesty. That is especially important for dialogue that carries theme.

INNER MONOLOGUE

What characters think reveals who they are. Thoughts, being secret, are honest witnesses to the soul of the character. But, like speeches, they're sometimes used by lazy writers to do all the heavy thematic lifting.

Inner monologue is best in short bursts within action. Give us brief glimpses of character thought while the character is under a condition of stress. In Alton Gansky's *A Ship Possessed*, a character in the midst of action has a quick reflection:

> It saddened him to think that his faith had atrophied over the years. He was still a believer and made no attempt to hide the fact. Still, he was not as active as he could be, nor did his faith occupy as much of his life as it once did. Now he wished he knew more.

That's all that's needed here. More details about his faith struggle, at this point, would have diverted attention from the scene.

Sometimes, however, a writer may want to get deep into the head of a character and let the thoughts go on. In that case the inner monologue will have to have a style and content that makes it compelling in and of itself.

Here's a short section of inner monologue from Walker Percy's *The Second Coming*:

> Everybody has given up. Everybody thinks that there are only two things: war which is a kind of death, and peace which is a kind of death in life. But what if there should be a third thing, life?
> Death in the guise of Christianity is not going to prevail over me. If Christ brought life, why do the churches smell of death?
> Death in the guise of old Christendom in Carolina is not going to prevail over me. The old churches are houses of death.
> Death in the form of the new Christendom in Carolina is not going to prevail over me. If the born-again are the twice born, I'm holding out for a third go-round.

The passage continues with the repeated phrase "Death in the guise of ..." and becomes, ultimately, quite poetic. It is perfectly in keeping with the style of the book.

How do you find the right style for a section like this? You really have to allow it to find you. It will if you let the writing flow the first time around. Step into the character's head and just let fly with his thoughts and words. Only later rewrite and refine. This right-brain, left-brain rumba is the best way to find a style that delivers.

METAPHORS, MOTIFS, AND SYMBOLS

Fiction that draws from the well of a religious tradition often uses metaphors to powerful effect. The emotional content of icons, rituals, sacred texts, and the like can be placed at well-chosen points in a story, giving it a richness of meaning.

Historical novelist Jack Cavanaugh uses this technique in *Glimpses of Truth*. The setting is fourteenth-century England, a time when it was against the law for Christians to read the Bible in English. In this scene, protagonist Thomas Torr, who is assisting the aged John Wycliffe to copy and distribute his rogue English translation of the Bible, has taught his guardian, an unschooled ploughman named Howel, how to write the letter T. Thomas then appended other letters to the Howel's letter to write a phrase from the Bible. The scene is witnessed by Howel's daughter, Felice.

> "These are words from the Bible?" Howel gasped.
>
> Thomas nodded, though he didn't understand Howel's reaction. "One of King David's psalms."
>
> "O my," Howel said, his voice quivering. His eyes glazed with tears. "And that's my letter."
>
> "Yes. That's the T you wrote."
>
> "My hand-printed Scripture?"
>
> "Yes."
>
> "Father, are you alright?" Felice asked.
>
> Howel didn't respond. His eyes were fixed in awe at the letters on the cloth strip. Tears spilled onto his cheeks. "Say the words again," he asked.
>
> Thomas read slowly, "The Lord is my shepherd."
>
> Softly, reverently, Howel repeated the words. ... "Oh! What a grand thought! And it begins with my T!"

> ... Thomas handed him the cloth strip. The ploughman took it in his oversized hands as though it was a splinter of the cross of Christ.

The last image is all we need to understand how the character feels.

A more extended use of this technique can be found in novels that are modern retellings of sacred stories. One of the most famous biblical parables is the tale of the Prodigal Son. When he finally returns home, after wasting his inheritance, his father welcomes him back with compassion. In her novel *The Note*, Angela Elwell Hunt gives us a prodigal *daughter*:

> King sat at the kitchen table while Peyton pulled glasses from the cabinet, then filled them with ice. She glanced over at him a couple of times, noticing how at home he seemed, and when she brought the glasses to the table she saw that he'd pulled two of her father's letters from the crowded napkin holder.
>
> "Thought you might like to read these," he said, deliberately dropping them to the table. "It's about time, don't you think?"
>
> Peyton stared at the letters as realization bloomed in her chest ...
>
> Picking up the phone, she punched in the number she hadn't dialed in years, then turned when a male voice answered. "Dad? This is Peyton."
>
> Glancing across the room, she saw King give her an enthusiastic thumbs-up. She returned his smile, then looked away, unable to hide a grimace as her heart twisted.
>
> Her father was weeping.

For an audience familiar with the biblical story, the scene takes on an added level of meaning.

Look to your own traditions, sacred or secular, for material that can deepen your stories.

A *motif* is something that recurs. It can be a setting, an object, words and phrases, character type—almost anything that's consciously used to convey meaning.

The land in *Gone With the Wind* is a motif, representing home and permanence interrupted by war and greed.

The ocean in *Moby-Dick* has several meanings, like dread and danger, as well as hope of reward.

A *symbol* is an object that comes to represent a thematic element. The green light on Daisy's dock in *The Great Gatsby* is a symbol for dreams and hopes that are, ultimately, unattainable.

In the film *Collateral*, Tom Cruise plays a hitman who forces cabdriver Jamie Foxx to drive him around to his appointed rounds. At one point the cab is stopped at a light on a city street at night, and a coyote runs across the road. The two men stare at it.

It is a symbol for what the hitman is: a predator in the city, alone and hunted. His fate is determined.

RESONANCE

The last chapter of your novel, indeed the last paragraph and sentence, is of crucial importance. They should leave the reader with a feeling of resonance—just the right tone. In Anton Chekhov's words, the end of a novel or story must "artfully concentrate for the reader an impression of the entire work."

Flannery O'Connor's story "A Temple of the Holy Ghost" does just that. It ends with the following imagery:

> Her mother let the conversation drop and the child's round face was lost in thought. She turned it toward the window and looked out over a stretch of pasture land that rose and fell with a gathering greenness until it touched the dark woods. The sun was a huge red ball like an elevated Host drenched in blood and when it sank out of sight, it left a line in the sky like a red clay road hanging over the trees.

This image resonates and makes the entire story seem somehow deeper.

Finding just the right ending is one of the great tasks of novel writing, especially when writing to inspire. A good exercise is to write several alternative endings. Try out different images, actions, and dialogue. Stretch yourself. The effort will be well worth it.

In New York's Metropolitan Museum of Art there hangs a Chinese silk tapestry from the Ch'ien-lung period. Royal birds soar among swirling clouds and exquisite flowers. It seems like a flawless painting, with all elements working in perfect harmony. Seamless fiction generates the same magic. Weave your messages into the fabric of your fiction and you will give your readers a deeply satisfying experience.

A FINAL THOUGHT ON THEME

What will your novels ultimately *mean*? What will they say about life beyond the confines of the plot? How will they illuminate your vision of life? Every story has a meaning. So does every author.

As Viktor Frankl puts it in *Man's Search for Meaning*, his classic book on the subject, "Man's search for meaning is the ultimate motivation in his life." It is a subconscious reason readers pick up books. In the fictional search, they're also exploring their own inner territory.

John Gardner, novelist and author of *On Moral Fiction*, says:

> I think that the difference right now between good art and bad art is that the good artists are the people who are, in one way or another, creating, out of deep and honest concern, a vision of life … that is worth pursuing.

So what are you writing for? If it's only for money or fame, you'll miss the spark that makes both of those things possible. Go further.

And I don't mean you have to change the whole world. Writing so readers will be transported is also a valid goal. Good, solid entertainment is a release, and goodness knows we need that today. But start by asking yourself what moves you. Put that into your novels, and the entertainment value will skyrocket.

Develop a vision for yourself as a writer. Make it something that excites you. Turn that into a mission statement—one paragraph that sums up your hopes and dreams as a writer. Read this regularly. Revise it from time to time to reflect your growth. But have something in writing that will inspire you.

Root that inspiration in the world—your observations of it, and what it does *to* you. "I honestly think in order to be a writer," says Anne Lamott, "you have to learn to be reverent. If not, why are you writing? Why are you here? Let's think of reverence as awe, as presence in and openness to the world."

If you stay true to your own awe, your books can't help but be charged with meaning.

But remember, your book has to be readable above all.

Albert I. "Buzz" Bezzerides was a novelist and screenwriter, perhaps best known for his script for the ultimate film noir, *Kiss Me Deadly*. The plot centers around a valise that has something, well, deadly in it.

For years, French film critics and other academics talked about the layer upon layer of thematic significance in the film.

Later in life, the cantankerous Bezzerides remarked:

> People ask me about the hidden meanings in the script, about the A-bomb, about McCarthyism, what does the poetry mean, and so on.

And I can only say that I didn't think about it when I wrote it ... I was having fun with it. I wanted to make every scene, every character, interesting ... I was having fun.

Write with meaning, but don't forget to make every scene, every character interesting. And try to have fun.

WATCH THE LECTURING

Beware the dreaded lecture.

A lecture is really the writer telling the reader what the story is all about. The writer may do this in narrative, which is the worst, because it is author intrusion.

This was done quite often in Victorian literature. *And so, gentle reader, Tom learned the hard lesson that crime pays, but only in small increments.*

Today, writers will more often try to stick the lecture into a character's mouth. Instead of a lecture on what youth is like, put the words into the mouth of a drunken doctor finally unloading his pain, as Paddy Chayefsky does in *The Hospital* (the character of Dr. Bock, played by George C. Scott):

I've got a son, twenty-three. I threw him out of the house last year. Pietistic little humbug. He preached universal love and despised everyone. He had a blanket contempt for the middle class, even its decencies.

KEY POINTS

- Often a theme only emerges for the writer after the first draft is done.
- Weave your theme using the various elements of the craft.
- Don't be preachy.
- Make sure the characters are real, that they believe in what they're doing, even the opposition characters. Justify all of their actions.

Exercise 1

Many of us hated "theme" exercises in literature class. Maybe this is because there's so much debate about themes. Critics often disagree about a book's meaning. It's the toughest part of fiction to nail.

Reread some favorite novels looking for thematic elements. Because you've read the book before, skim over the plot. See if you can identify where the author indicates a larger meaning, or view of the world.

Underline these sections and study the technique used.

Exercise 2

Have one of your characters make a speech about what's going on in the plot. Make it a long, run-on, stream-of-consciousness oration. Don't interrupt. Let her be preachy if she wants to.

This is only an exercise.

The speech can run as long as you want it to. Make it no less than 500 words. Have the character reflect on not only what's happening, but on what she *thinks* about what's happening.

When you're done, you may be surprised that you've actually learned something from the character. This may be your theme, or one that you want to incorporate.

While we discourage the use of long speeches in fiction these days, you may find a place in your book for this character to use some, if not all, of what she has just said.

Remember always to weave it in.

Exercise 3

Go through your manuscript and highlight, or make a list of, the prominent objects of the setting you mention.

Brainstorm ways in which those objects can become symbols for something your Lead character believes.

Choose one and heighten it slightly by:

- describing it more vividly in the scene
- repeating it later in the story, in a subtle way

PART TWO

Revision

. . . .

Keep working. Keep trying.
Keep believing. You still might not make it,
but at least you gave it your best shot.
If you don't have calluses on your soul,
this isn't for you.
Take up knitting instead.

—DAVID EDDINGS

CHAPTER 13

A Philosophy of Revision

It is said that Michelangelo, when asked how he had sculpted his masterpiece, *David*, replied, "I looked at the stone and removed all that was not *David*."

Not a bad description of the novel revision process. From the mass of words you have created, you'll take away all that is *not* your novel. You'll chisel and add, touch up, and cut, but in the end what you want is your story in its purest form.

And only you can decide what form that will be.

Depending on the writer, you'll get different answers to what rewriting is, such as:

Rewriting is hell.

Rewriting is fun.

Rewriting is dull, because all the delight was in the creation.

Rewriting is like getting to take a final exam again, only this time it's open book and with your old answer sheet for reference.

And so on. What all writers do agree on (or at least 99 percent of them) is that rewriting is essential to the production of a great novel.

Submitting a novel without rewriting is like playing ice hockey naked. You're just not equipped to put your best, um, face on things. And sooner rather than later a well-placed puck is going to hit you where it hurts most.

That puck is the editor's or agent's built-in prejudice against weak material. They are tuned to say *No*. That's why you rewrite. You want to take out all those *No* reasons.

HOW TO USE THIS SECTION

This section can be used in a number of ways.

If you've got a manuscript you want to revise right away, skip to chapter seventeen, "The Ultimate Revision Checklist," and dive right in.

If there's a specific part of your novel that isn't working, and you're not sure why, concentrate on that area.

Perhaps you're in the middle of a project and have come to one of those spots where you feel lost and unsure what to do next. Skimming through this section can lead you to a possible solution.

. . . .

Ernest Hemingway was absolutely correct when he said that every writer needs a "built-in, shock-proof, manure detector." Ernest actually used a pithier term, but his point is what matters: Writers need the ability to evaluate the quality of their own writing. Writers lacking such equipment make two kinds of mistakes—both equally destructive. On the one hand, they may conclude that their initial drafts are ready to be published. And so, they don't do the rewriting and fine-tuning that is an essential part of the writing process. On the other hand, they may never be happy with what they've written. They fall into the trap of endlessly rewriting their words, thus never finishing anything they begin. The best way I know to develop a well-balanced "quality detector" is to read lots of books with an eye toward understanding what each writer was trying to accomplish. In time, you become increasingly able to judge your own words.

—RON BENREY

HOW I LEARNED
TO BE A HAPPY REWRITER

Writing a novel is like falling in love. You begin with the chemistry, the spark of an idea. You ask it out and get acquainted. A kiss at the end of the evening fills you with hope and desire. You start whistling "Younger Than Springtime."

You jump in and write. The early pages appear quickly. You're discovering your novel as you write, caught up in the fragrance of creation.

At some point you pop the question and your novel says *Yes*. You're married to it now. The commitment has begun.

Then some problems surface. Bad breath in the morning. Crankiness. A shouting match. What happened to the bloom?

You begin to doubt. But you've made the commitment, so you are determined to work things out.

When you do, your marriage comes back stronger. So you start raising a family of future manuscripts.

Revision is like the counseling process that renders a better relationship.

THE LONG VIEW

Studies of successful people in various professions have identified several factors that top performers share. One of the most important of these is the *long view*.

It isn't the get-rich-quick artists who succeed, but those who know that ultimate success involves a long curve of learning, working, failure, trying again, patience, and perseverance.

Doctors train for years before they get to practice. They know going in that there's a long road ahead. But for the ultimate prize, they make the sacrifice. Those who build businesses, unless they're the latest dotcom darlings, must work long and hard in the early years. But the payoff is worth it.

As a serious novelist you need to approach your craft with the same view. If you want your book to be the best it can be, it's going to take work. And you won't get it right the first time.

I wrote my first screenplay like a puppy in a meat market. Excited, running as fast as I could, filled with wonder and hope. As I wrote, I thought, *This is so easy. I'm having so much fun it must be good.*

I showed it to a contact I had in the movie business. A week later she called me. Her first words were, "You don't have it."

My tail went between my legs. Did she mean I didn't have what it took? No talent? Fuggetaboutit?

No, that wasn't it. She explained that I didn't have it *on the page*. That I had a lot more learning to do.

Which reminded me of some advice I'd received from Darryl Ponicsan, author of *The Last Detail*. I wrote him when I was in college and asked him for advice on becoming a writer. "Guard your character," he wrote back. "If you've got nothing in you, you've got nothing to give. Be prepared for an apprenticeship of years."

That's right. Take the long view, and learn to see revision as a friend. Being a smart, disciplined reviser delivers a number of benefits:

- It makes you a better writer. With each revision session you learn more about your craft, and the next time you write you'll write stronger.
- It marks you as a professional. Editors and agents who see your work ethic will be more certain of your ability to produce good books.
- It builds confidence and encourages you to stretch your horizons.
- It is its own reward. When you've put in good, solid revision time, you rest easier at the end of the day. Like a gardener who has pulled an abundance of weeds, you can go to sleep knowing the garden is that much healthier.

So here are your gardening tools. Let's get dirty.

THE MENTAL GAME

Somebody once asked Robert Mitchum what he looked for in a script.

"Days off," he said.

I always thought that was funny, maybe half a cup full of truth. Mitchum never let on that he worked hard at acting or took the whole thing too seriously. He seemed to be bemused by his stardom. How could he get paid for doing this? And be world famous besides?

But I also suspect Mitchum did take his craft more seriously than he cared to admit. I know that because I've seen *Ryan's Daughter*.

That movie was a critical and commercial failure, a little story that David Lean tried to turn into an epic. It has some of the most beautiful cinematography ever put on film and a haunting score by Maurice Jarre.

But things just didn't click this time, and Lean only made one other film the rest of his career.

I saw it when it first came out and felt the same way as the critics. When it came out on DVD I decided to give it one more try. David Lean was one of the great directors—there will never be another *Lawrence of Arabia* because there will never be (1) another Peter O'Toole, and (2) all camels and exotic locations will be done via computer graphics in the future—and Lean deserved another look.

The movie was better this time, though still not great.

The great part was Robert Mitchum.

He played against type, a shy schoolteacher who somehow got a hunky body. The young Rose (Sarah Miles) has schoolgirl fantasies about him and gets him to marry her, only to find out he's not the physical pleasure center she thought he'd be.

Which leads to adultery, which leads to disaster, which leads to misery for Robert Mitchum.

Who was superb. Who should have been nominated for an Oscar.

So the actor who liked his days off was also truly committed to his craft.

That's how you should feel about writing. Enjoy the playfulness of creativity (and the occasional day off). But also take the craft seriously. Keep getting better at what you do.

So there's an element of play and an element of work that goes into this writing life.

A FEW TIPS AND REMINDERS

It's a great feeling to be confident in your ability to solve manuscript problems. You will, if you continue to study the craft all your life. I still read books on writing because I'll either learn something new or get a fresh angle on a useful technique.

Here are a few things I try to keep in mind when I'm about to revise.

It's Like Taking the Final Again ...
With the Answers and an Open Book

In my first semester of law school I took a philosophy of law class. I knew the material cold. So cold, I was approached by a struggling student who wanted me to help her study for the final.

The night before the exam I had a dream about how to approach the test. I wouldn't do it in the standard, boring fashion; I'd do it in storytelling form. It was a bold and risky move.

And it got me a seventy-seven.

Apparently the professor was not a storytelling fan.

And what of the woman I helped to study? She got the highest grade in the class.

Thank you very much. This is why writing is better than school finals. Because after you finish your first draft you don't have to turn it in. You get to go over it again, changing the answers you know are wrong, and using resources (like this book) to help.

Be thankful for small favors.

Don't Hold on Too Tight ...

Quite often you will find your novel changing slightly, or even significantly, as you revise. Don't let that spook you. During the revision process you need to give your novel room to breathe.

Be willing to let it.

But Don't Be Afraid to Work Through Your Plan

Resist the temptation to throw everything out unless it is the only conceivable thing to do. It's not the only conceivable thing to do if it's your first read through. You may think your manuscript stinks. Maybe it does. That's okay. Most writers understand that first drafts often stink to high heaven, or at least to a high ceiling.

It will get better.

Know Thyself

F. Scott Fitzgerald once said there are two kinds of writers: taker-outters and putter-inners. Some writers like to write a lean first draft, sometimes leaving out whole sections of description or the transition, and then add to the manuscript during the revision stage. These are putter-inners.

Other writers prefer to write and write and write that first draft, to put everything in they can think of and only worry about cutting back later.

Either approach will work, but usually the writer will feel more comfortable doing one or the other.

Are you the sort of writer who is anxious to get the manuscript finished as quickly as possible? You may be a putter-inner. Are you a writer who likes to discover the story as you go along, following different tangents as they arise? Then you are probably a taker-outter.

Think about it and prepare yourself accordingly for the task to follow.

Set Up a Reward System

If it's good enough for General Electric, it should be good enough for one measly writer. GE rose to prominence under Jack Welch, who loved to create little celebrations to energize his organization. He empowered his managers to look for creative ways to celebrate even the smallest victories.

"Business has to be fun," he says.

Writing has to be fun, too. So look for ways to celebrate the things you do. Revision is the tough, sleeves-rolled-up work of the professional writer. When you're done and the manuscript is finally ready to send off, you'll feel great. You deserve a reward. A deadline with a reward attached will get you closer to publication than almost anything else.

My favorite things to do after completing a project:

- Take my wife to an especially nice restaurant.
- Go to a movie matinee by myself and eat an entire box of Raisinets.
- Treat myself to a hardcover I've been salivating over.

Make a list of your favorite things and use them as incentives to get your work done.

Stay Healthy

The imagination is housed in the brain. The brain is housed in the body. The body is the temple of the soul. Treat it as such.

Your productivity and creativity improve with the care of your body. Take the long-term view.

The brisk walk is an easy way to start, and with a tape or MP3 player you can multitask. I listen to novels so I'm studying the craft as I walk. I make a little commitment to myself: I can't finish a tape unless I'm walking. That forces me to exercise because I want to know how the story turns out!

The history of literature is littered with geniuses who squandered their gifts through the bottle, drugs, or simple neglect. You've only got one writing life. Make the most of it.

George Bernard Shaw wrote more than fifty plays and was working on another when he died at age ninety-four. That's the way to go.

The Secret

My favorite actor of all time is Spencer Tracy. His performances were always so realistic and natural. You never catch him "acting." Humphrey Bogart agreed. He called Tracy the best, too, because you didn't see "the wheels turning."

He was the first truly natural actor in the movies. The silent era was marked by broad expression and gesture to overcome the lack of sound. When movies started talking, stage actors came in and played as if talking to a back row.

Tracy stepped in and blew people away with his simple, natural style. When asked what his secret was, he said it was nothing more than "Be yourself and listen to the other actor."

Once, in the 1950s, he was filming a scene with a young actor who was a disciple of the new "Method" school of acting (think Marlon Brando and James Dean). This type of acting involved lots of inner preparation, brooding about in order to discover character motivations and the like.

Also, holding up production. At one point the actor asked the director what his motivation was for coming through a door.

Tracy had had enough. "You come through the damn door," he shouted, "because it's the only way to get in the damn room!"

Which only goes to show that you can think this novel writing thing to death. Writers love to talk about art and theory and practice. I certainly do. But there comes a time when you just have to keep writing because it's the only way to finish the book.

You have to hang a little loose.

Lawrence Block, in his book *Spider, Spin Me a Web: A Handbook for Fiction Writers*, says that his best writing inevitably comes when he lets it flow without overthinking. Wise words.

You keep writing because it's the only way to finish the book.

And remember Tracy's big acting secret: Be yourself and listen.

Don't write for the critics.

The Boys in the Basement

Stephen King is a skilled novelist who just may break out one of these days. In his book *On Writing*, he talks about the *boys in the basement*, his metaphor for the subconscious writer's mind. When you write, and when you revise, you ought to get the boys working.

If you're a woman and don't like the idea of boys in your basement, feel free to come up with your own metaphor.

The trick is to get the subconscious on the job. ...

The Dream Game

Why not work while you sleep? The boys don't have to sleep, so keep them busy while you're in dreamland.

Here's a wonderful process that will yield some pleasant results.

You've been working on your manuscript. You've come across some problems, questions—basic things that just need changing. In other words, some problems that need to be solved.

Tackle them this way: On a pad of paper, just before you go to bed, write down your problem as a *question*. Be specific:

- How can I get Thelma out of the building in a more plausible way?
- What can John do that shows his courage?
- How can I make the doorman a more interesting minor character?

And so on. I recommend you write it down rather than just "think" it. For some reason, the physical act of writing the problem sends it more clearly to the basement.

Do this as close as possible to your head hitting the pillow. In the morning, *before you do anything else* (unless it's that first cup of coffee), sit down with a fresh piece of paper and write down as many answers to your problem as you can. Most of the time a thought will have bubbled up to the top.

But don't limit yourself. Make a list of possible answers, and push yourself in this great moment before your day begins.

Procrastination

On New Year's Day I made a resolution to procrastinate more, starting in February. Procrastination is something I wallow in before I start revising. Not everyone has that problem, but if you do, let me suggest a couple of things that have helped me.

1. **BREAK YOUR TASKS DOWN INTO DISTINCT SECTIONS, AND THEN *WRITE THEM DOWN*.** Working from an organized, written list helps you conceive of the rewrite as a more manageable project. You can start with general categories like:

   - read through
   - character fixes
   - plot points
   - polish

   Once you get into the rewrite, more specific items will present themselves. So, under "character fixes" you might have "Deepen Jenny" or "Make minor characters more colorful."

2. **ASSIGN TIME ESTIMATES TO YOUR TASKS.** These are flexible, but they work as "mini-deadlines" to keep you moving forward. For instance, you might decide it will take you four hours to go through your minor characters and see how you can spice them up.

3. **PRIORITIZE YOUR TASKS.** Put the most important things first on your list. You'll want to deal with major plot problems before you start polishing dialogue.

4. **THINK OF ONE TASK AT A TIME.** Don't look at the mountaintop. Look at the path in front of you. When you get around that bend, look at the next few steps. When you're working, keep thoughts of the whole project out of your mind.

5. **START YOUR REWRITE SESSION BY DOING THE HARDEST THINGS FIRST.** You'll be able to focus your best efforts on the more unpleasant tasks, feel good about getting them out of the way, and move on with confidence.

6. **SWISS CHEESE IT.** If you have some discretionary time but don't think you're up to a full rewrite session, take a bite out of the project by "Swiss cheesing" it. Put one little hole in the overall by taking on a minor problem.

Maybe it's that dialogue exchange at the end of chapter six. Take fifteen minutes to see what you can do with it. Maybe while the soup's heating up. Or if you're standing in a long line at Ticketmaster, take out a note card and write a list of possible fixes for Jenny. Set the boys in the basement to work.

Get creative the Swiss cheese way.

. . . .

Treat it as a job—not a mystical calling. Then you'll get up every morning and go "to work" instead of waiting for the muse to attend you.

—JEAN BRODY

The Writer in the Gray Flannel Suit Trick

Pretend you're at a job with a grumpy boss. John D. MacDonald, one of the best and most prolific novelists of the 1950s and 1960s, produced a massive amount of work doing this. For him, writing was a job. He had to put food on the table. So he worked on an eight-to-five schedule with one hour for lunch. At five, he knocked off for the day and had a martini, just like the man in the gray flannel suit.

When I was faced with two deadlines converging at about the same time, I had no choice but to become a working stiff. I imagined I was supposed to show up at work at eight and leave at five, with an hour lunch break. I really did this. I got to my office a little before eight. I conjured up a supervisor, and if it was a few minutes past eight, his look would be a little impatient.

I worked an hour, took a five-minute rest break, worked another hour, and so on. I took lunch, then got back to work at 1 p.m.

In this way I was able to meet my deadlines.

When you're unpublished or looking to be published, you have to impose your own deadlines. This is sometimes hard for creative types, who like to lie about in the fields of the imagination and let inspiration fly in, like a bluebird.

You may write this way, but don't rewrite this way. Revision is bare-knuckles time. Time to get tough with yourself.

It's a good thing, too. Imposing a deadline focuses your mind, makes you a little anxious. Gives you some butterflies in the tummy. Your job now is to make them fly in formation. Your mind will be forced to dig deep and come up with answers.

Let it.

If you *really* want to cook, set up a spreadsheet that keeps track of the time you spend working and aim to eliminate wasted time.

Work in fifty-five-minute chunks if you can, and count each as one hour.

When something happens to interrupt you, make a note of it. When it's your fault, as in a quick game of Internet backgammon, label the cell in red to show alarm.

You'll start to feel good about revision and your discipline as a writer.

Performance Review

Write up a performance review of yourself, as if you were your own supervisor. What are the problem areas? What are the places you could improve? What are the action items you are given?

Read the review and stew about it. Confront yourself and say it's unfair. Then be told that if you want to resign and not be the best writer you can be, fine, you're free to go. Accept the review and try to put it into practice.

Do all this in the privacy of your own office.

CHAPTER 14

Before You Revise

Robert Heinlein had two rules for writers:

1. You must write.
2. You must finish what you write.

Before you can revise your novel you've got to have ... your novel.

So finish it.

With a few revision principles in mind. Very few, because the object of the first draft is to get it done. Only then will you take a long pause to get it right.

REVISE AS YOU WRITE?

I don't recommend that you do major revision during the writing of your first draft. The temptation to stop and make major changes is constant, and it can drive you bats. And most of the time these changes aren't the best thing for the story that's trying to bubble up from your writer's mind.

You only truly get to know your novel when you've finished it. So consider your first draft an exploration into what's really happening in your story. Some of your best stuff will come into focus later as you look back at what you've written.

1. Revise Your Previous Pages

Look at what you wrote the day before (or during your last writing stint), and do a quick edit. This practice puts you back into the flow of your story and gets you ready to write the new material.

I like to print out a hard copy of pages and mark them up. Of course, you can do all this on the computer screen. I just find that the act of reading physical pages more closely mimics what a reader will be doing, and I catch more things this way.

Mostly I'm editing for style. The way the sentences flow. I want to make sure what I wanted to convey has actually happened on the page. If a major plot or character problem emerges, or I get an idea for something to add, I just make a note of it and get to my day's writing quota.

Write as fast as you comfortably can on your first draft.

. . . .

I edit as I go and I don't find myself making sweeping changes. So for me, there's not a first anything, just an only. When I'm done with the last page I am still working on the same Word document I started out with. I reread the previous day's work each day before beginning the next chapter or scene and I fix anything that needs fixing. If I do make a plot or characterization change midway through, I go back and fix anything written earlier that won't jive with the changes I've made.

—SUSAN MEISSNER

2. Try the 20,000-Word Step Back

Whether you're an NOP (No Outline Person) or an OP (Outline Person), the 20,000-word step back can be a tremendous tool.

After 20,000 words you stop, take a day off, then read what you have. By this time your story engine should be running. You've done enough of the novel to know pretty much what it's about. You then take some time to make sure you like the characters and the direction.

If you don't, make some changes now.

This is a good point to make your lead characters richer by adding background (whether you include this for the readers or not), behaviors, quirks, strengths, flaws, and tags (speech, dress, etc.).

You can also make a decision about the tone and feel of your novel. It may want to take on a different emphasis than what you had planned. A better novel may be asking to be released.

Here's what I mean.

I've been working on a novel with a premise I liked: A lawyer discovers his brother, whom he thought to be dead, is alive. They get together and learn how different their paths have been. Gradually, my lead character uncovers disquieting secrets about his brother and finds himself in danger.

I wrote the first 20,000 words with a plan in mind, to get the characters to a certain point and then begin a series of tense chases.

When I did my step back, I felt there was something missing from the book. It wasn't that I couldn't come up with suspenseful material—no problem there—but the feeling that I hadn't quite connected with the book persisted.

During this step-back period of a week or so, I thought about the book and wrote a free association letter to myself each day (see tip #3 listed below).

One day I woke up knowing what was wrong. The book was trying to tell me to get more deeply into my lead character's feelings about his brother and his childhood guilt over his loss. There would still be plenty of suspense, but it needed to pad up in soft socks, not steel-toed boots.

When I went back to the first draft, I felt the material and I were connected in a much better, fuller way. That's the value of the step back.

Now jump back in and finish your novel.

Then use this book to revise it, polish it, and send it out to agents and publishers.

3. Keep a Journal

The free-form journal is a great way to record notes for yourself as you go. Often, these notes will become fodder for your revision.

Remember, that first draft is also an act of discovery. Don't try to get it perfect the first go-around. Let it breathe. Then you'll begin the process of cutting out all that isn't your novel and adding more novel to it if you have to.

• •

Let the first version go as long as it has to.
—GINI KOPECKY

4. Take Advantage of All Your Tools

Writers today have a lot more tools available to them than ever before. It's not just blue pencils anymore.

Here are just a few that you can fine-tune for yourself.

Word Comments

Use the Comments feature in Word. When doing your first draft, you can use these to leave yourself notes about plot points that need to be filled in, research questions you have to answer, and anything else that comes to mind.

When you're ready to revise, you can refer to the Comments alone, or print them out.

Running Outline

As you write your first draft, keep a running summary—an ongoing outline—of your story.

I suggest you copy and paste your first couple of paragraphs from each chapter, and the last couple.

Then put a summary statement of the action at the top of each, in all caps.

Let's say your chapter begins like this:

CHAPTER ONE

Captain Lois Enloe walked through the front door of The Retreat at exactly eight-twenty-seven. This, according to her watch, was precisely seven minutes before the bomb would explode.

Then they would all know. They'd all know for sure.

And ends like this:

Somebody tapped her on the shoulder.

She turned.

It was the last man she wanted to see.

Your running outline entry might look like this:

1. LOIS ENTERS THE BAR BEFORE THE BOMB EXPLODES. SHE ENJOYS THE EXPLOSION AND ENSUING CONFUSION, BUT SHE'S DISCOVERED.

Captain Lois Enloe walked through the front door of The Retreat at exactly eight-twenty-seven. This, according to her watch, was precisely seven minutes before the bomb would explode.

> Then they would all know. They'd all know for sure.
> Somebody tapped her on the shoulder.
> She turned.
> It was the last man she wanted to see.

It only takes a minute or two to do this. At the end of the first draft you'll have a complete outline of your story as written.

Spreadsheets or Tables

Some writers, almost always outline people, like to put their outlines in a spreadsheet or table. Then, using color coding and other markers, they can see the outline of their story, the characters involved, and a summary of the action, at a glance.

Such a spreadsheet or table might look like this:

CHAPTER	1
SETTING	Starbucks
CHARACTERS	Pete vs. Mary
SUMMARY	Pete confronts Mary over her affair with Steve
OUTCOME	Mary throws coffee at Pete and storms out.

Paper

Yes, you're still allowed to use paper. You can actually write things down with implements like pens and pencils and crayons.

I know writers who like to lay out their stories on long rolls of butcher paper. They use different colored sticky notes and pens and make up a huge map. Then they roll this up and carry it around. (A couple of my writer friends actually use a map-carrying tube, with strap and all. Hey, whatever works, works.)

Critique Groups

Many writers have benefited from critique groups, reader networks, and paid critiques.

Almost as many writers have had negative experiences with the same. Are any of these for you?

Not necessarily. Most published novelists have gotten along just fine with a single editor. Thomas Wolfe had Maxwell Perkins. Ayn Rand had Bennett Cerf (who somehow survived).

But the days of the nurturing author/editor relationship are pretty much over. These days, a writer must look out for the quality of the manuscript with more responsibility.

So here are some guidelines to help you benefit from the input of others on your book.

The benefits of a small, dedicated group of writers are several. Novelist Jack Cavanaugh says:

> "Not until I joined a critique group did I begin writing for publication. The monthly meetings gave me a deadline, exposure to critique (which made me try harder to prove them wrong), and put me in contact with people who shared a common goal as well as information about publishers' guidelines and needs. If it had not been for the critique group I may never have started writing seriously."

The experience wasn't the same for Robin Lee Hatcher.

> "I participated in a critique group around books ten and eleven. It was a horrid experience for me. I don't do well writing by committee, and since I am an intuitive writer, I work best without other input during the creative process. With rare exceptions, my editor is the first person who sees the book. Occasionally I will ask a trusted writer friend to read a scene or a chapter if I'm struggling with something, just to make sure I'm conveying what I hope to convey."

If you need that extra push, especially early in your career, a critique group can help. But make sure the following factors apply:

- Look for people you have a rapport with. Previous relationships help.
- Keep the group small. Four to seven, give or take.
- Give as much as you get. Make sure you give adequate time to everyone else.
- Establish realistic deadlines and stick to them.
- Make sure the people in the group understand the genre you're writing in.

- Build trust. Check egos at the door.
- Be aware of the envy issue. It happens. If someone's writing takes off, it's going to cause some strain. Best to talk about this up front.

Any major drawbacks to being in a critique group?

- Sometimes you're crazy busy and you can't squeeze more into your already crammed schedule.
- If you don't trust each other, hurt feelings can result. That's why it's important to have a relationship already established.

Okay, you have the tools. Now get ready to use them. What follows is your systematic approach to revision. Roll up your sleeves (if you're wearing a shirt) and get ready to make your work the best it can be.

CHAPTER 15

The First Read-Through

Bobby Knight, one of college basketball's greatest (and most volatile) coaches, once said, "Practice doesn't make perfect. Perfect practice makes perfect."

Quite true. If you practice the *wrong* things, you're not going to be a better player or team.

So the old saw *Writing is rewriting!* needs a little tweak. *Good writing is rewriting with know-how.*

That's what this book is for: to give you both the tools and the strategies for approaching every aspect of revision.

And the first big moment is when you have a completed manuscript.

This is a crucial time, fraught with peril. Okay, perhaps *peril* is a bit much, but *fraught* is certainly applicable. What you must avoid is any temptation to stop and do wholesale revisions *before you have read the entire manuscript once.*

Think of this process as Google Earth. You want to get a complete overview of your "earth." Your novel. Your story as a whole. You can spin the earth a little here and there to get a better view, but stay up top. You'll tag a few places to visit later, to zoom in on. That'll be the nuts and bolts of revision.

But to start, you need the big picture. You want the *feel* of the story, to anticipate what the readers will pick up. Here are the steps to follow:

1. THE COOL-DOWN PHASE

It's essential to give yourself a break from the first draft. At least two weeks. Three is better, and if you can spare it, go for a month (but if you're like me that seems like an eternity. And if you have a deadline you may not have that luxury).

During this "cooling phase," try to forget about your book completely. Some writers use this time for a weeklong refresher and don't do any writing at all. Others, myself included, want to be working on something all the time.

If that's you, work on another project. Pour yourself into it. If it's another novel, get cracking. If not, write an essay or a blog post or do writing exercises (such as those you'll find in Brian Kiteley's *The 3 a.m. Epiphany*).

Or journal.

Or write opening chapters for novels you may never write. Just start with an intriguing opening line and write without any preplanning. Who knows? You may just get an idea you'll want to develop.

The main thing is to get all of your concentration focused on writing that is not your first draft.

2. THE PREPARATION PHASE

Try to work up a little excitement as you come to the first read-through. A good mental outlook helps generate insights. Make it fun.

One thing I like to do is create a cover for my manuscript. I do a simple design, and then I put a critic's blurb on it. Like this:

Try Dying

James Scott Bell

"Bell just keeps getting better. Yes indeed,
the suspense never rests!"

—*New York Herald Tribune*

The *New York Herald Tribune*, by the way, is long dead. But it was alive during my favorite period for crime fiction, the 1950s.

No one is going to see this, so lay it on thick.

The fun is about to begin.

If you're having some trepidation about the whole process of revision—which many writers do—you might want to write up a little list of positives you can refer to as you go:

- This rewrite is going to make the book stronger.
- I have the tools that will make the book better.
- Great writing is rewriting with know-how, which is what I've got.
- Rewriting with know-how is the mark of a pro, and I am a pro.

Add to the list as you desire, but give yourself every possible motivation to dig in and get to work.

3. PRINT OUT AND PREPARE A FRESH COPY

Get yourself a clean, crisp copy of your manuscript, with that cover on top. Should you print it out on one-sided pages? Double-spaced? Courier font?

All of these questions are up to you. Double spacing and one-sided printing allows for notes, but since I don't advocate copious notes for the first read-through, this isn't a major concern for me.

I like to use Times font, single-spaced, double-sided, because I want to create the feeling of an actual printed novel. I want to be like a reader looking at it for the first time.

I like to three-hole punch my manuscript and put it in a binder.

4. GET READY TO READ

Where do you like to read a brand-new book by your favorite author? I don't read for pleasure in my office. I have a nice soft chair by my living room window where I like to settle in with a nice cup of joe.

Whatever your ritual is, replicate it with your manuscript.

The only difference is you'll have a red felt-tip pen (or whatever you like to jot with) and notepad.

5. READ

Try to read the manuscript through in a couple of sittings—three or four at the most.

What you want to create is the feeling of being a fresh reader, getting into this book for the first time.

Don't stop to make changes at this point. You may jot a few things down, notes to yourself and the like, but keep going to get the overall impression of the book.

I do use some shorthand markings the first time through:

- a checkmark √ for pages where I feel the story is dragging
- parentheses ( ) around incomprehensible sentences
- a circle O in the margin where I think material needs to be added
- a question mark ? for material I think might need to be cut or changed, or that otherwise doesn't make sense

Using Outside Readers

Some writers like to give their drafts to trusted readers—people who know what they're doing and can offer an objective viewpoint. Readers like this are extremely valuable. Show them their value by treating them to an opulent meal (or something analogous) every time they help you.

You might want to include a simple response sheet along the following lines:

- What did you think of the overall plot?
- What did you like/dislike about the main characters?
- Were there places where you got bored? Please explain.
- Any suggestions for improvement?
- What did you like about the book? (Take as much time as you want with this section!)

6. ANALYZE

After the first read-through, begin to make notes. Answer these questions:

- Does my story make sense?

- Is the plot compelling?
- Does the story flow or does it seem choppy?
- Do my Lead characters "jump off the page"?
- Are the stakes high enough?
- Is there enough of a "worry factor" for readers?

Write a short essay about your book, as if you were a critic. How would you, objectively, rate your story? Don't be too hard on yourself.

Don't expect this first draft to be perfection, or anything close to it. All first drafts are lousy, many professional writers believe. That's part of the point. You need to get it down on the page before you can fix it.

At this point, go through your manuscript, making more detailed notes on those spots that need work.

The Summary Method

In *Writing a Novel*, noted British novelist John Braine suggested a technique to use following a first draft that many writers have found helpful. Braine advocated writing a first draft as quickly as possible, to stay in the flow. No looking back. No pause for major changes.

Write the maximum number of words you can at every session and push on until finished.

Then, after some cooling off, produce a summary of the novel—a synopsis, but one that's subject to change. Because you're going to try to make it better and deeper. You may even change it significantly.

The summary should be no more than 2,000 to 3,000 words, and you should produce several versions.

As described by Stephen Koch in *The Modern Library Writer's Workshop*:

> Tell yourself your emerging story again and again until you have, in capsule, a potent credible version that is propelling you into the new draft. If you like, summarize your first-draft version in the first. Then try some other ways of telling it. Change the beginning, change the ending, shift points of view and perspectives. Keep each summary short and try never to devote more than a day's work to any one of them. You are not rewriting. You are summarizing; you are testing possibilities. ... Don't talk to yourself *about* the story: Tell it to yourself in this concentrated form. Don't indulge in fancy meditations on the theme and do not theorize.

> But do include images and motifs and moments that you know drive
> the story forward ...

If you produce several of these summaries and finally fine-tune the best version, the method will give you a road map for an organic second draft.

Such is the John Braine method, and I'd advise you to give it a try sometime just to see if it works for you.

The Mess Factor

So, what do you do if your manuscript is a big fat mess? You have no idea where to go, where to begin. There are too many plot strands and characters and scenes that seem to go nowhere.

Perhaps you arrived here because you're an NOP (No Outline Person) who likes to write something new every day. I know several novelists who work this way, and they simply can't join the ranks of the OP (Outline People). They're willing to risk the "big mess."

How do you handle it?

Realize that there's nothing inherently wrong with this approach. If you roll right through a first draft this way, what you're doing in essence is writing a jumbo novel outline! Many OPs write 50-word, single-spaced "outlines." Maybe you've just done one that's 80,000 words.

Congratulations. Now find out what your novel is supposed to be and start over again. Don't rewrite, but, as Ray Bradbury said, *relive* it.

But what if you just can't escape the feeling that you're lost at sea? You don't even know which direction to run to begin swimming. You're flailing away with no land in sight.

Let me throw you a few life preservers:

1. Embrace Your Desperation

I know I sound like some yogi from the land of easy answers, but I do have a point. You can either be defeated by your desperation, or you can use it.

2. Practice Ping-Ponging

One the most prolific authors in history, Isaac Asimov, wrote an astounding array of books and articles and stories, on subjects as diverse as the Bible and robots. How did he do it?

He was obviously a smart man, conversant in a number of areas. But still, he had to physically write all those books. And he had to do it without his brain going on strike. Furthermore, he had to do it before the existence of the computer.

From reading about Asimov and his methods, here's what I discern were his secrets:

- First, he knew how to type. Fast.
- Second, he had several typewriters around his writing space.
- Third, he had a different project in each typewriter at various stages of production.
- Fourth, he roamed from project to project. If he ever got stuck on one thing, he would simply move to another unrelated project and work on that for a while.
- Fifth, he wrote every day and produced a quota. Day after day. Year after year.

Why was this method so successful? Asimov, either intuitively or by design, figured out that the brain, marvelous instrument that it is, works in curious ways. When it gives its attention fully to one thing, it gets tired of that thing after awhile. By switching to another focus, it begins again with fresh energy.

But even while occupied with that new item, the subconscious continues to work, effortlessly, on the previous project. When it comes time to concentrate again on the first thing, the brain is ready. It has new things to say.

Even when you're working on one primary project, I advise that you have others in the works. When you're hot and heavy in revision, you can still ping-pong between projects. This will spark a different part of your writer's brain, and when you come back to revise you'll have fresh insights.

This gives the mind a rest but keeps it active as a writer. So the boys in the basement will be on call, sweaty, warmed up, ready to work.

When I'm revising a manuscript, I'm either writing the first draft of another or, at the very least, doing some preplanning on my next project.

I will also have ancillary projects going, just to keep my writing muscles toned. A short story, an essay, an opinion, or a blog entry.

When I get a little tired of the revision, I find that my mind is fresh for one of these other projects.

After I've spent a little time away from the revision and come back to it, I'm primed again.

7. REVISE

Now you're just about ready to follow the Ultimate Revision Checklist, which is the subject of chapter seventeen.

But first we'll take one more look at how to make sure your story has the deepest impact possible on your readers.

. . . .

The beautiful part of writing is that you don't have to get it right the first time, unlike, say, a brain surgeon.

—ROBERT CORMIER

CHAPTER 16

Deepening

The kinds of stories that stay with us, that have us yearning for more from the same author, that leave us disappointed when they end because we want to stay in the book's fictive dream—these are stories that go *deep*.

It's not easy to define, this deepening. It's certainly easy to identify stories that don't have it. Even when we read an exciting, fast-paced novel, if it hasn't engaged us on a level that is more than surface experience, we forget about it soon after it's over.

Yeah, maybe it was a fun ride, a fine way to kill some time. But will we come running back for more?

On the other hand, when we are wrapped in a more complex emotional experience, that's when a story lingers, when characters stay with us long after the last page.

I think of novels like *To Kill a Mockingbird* and *The Catcher in the Rye*. Thrillers like *Lost Light* by Michael Connelly and *The Long Goodbye* by Raymond Chandler. Young adult fiction like *The Hunger Games* and the Harry Potter series.

There is more going on in these books than so many of their counterparts.

Again, as Gertrude Stein once said of Oakland, "There is no there there." We don't want that statement applied to our books.

In deep storytelling, there's not only a there there, but resonance. That's the pleasing last note that lingers. And keeps readers coming back for more.

None of this is easy, of course. If it were, first drafts would be all we needed to do. Typing would be the most important part of the craft.

Go deeper.

DEEPENING EXERCISES

In my Next Level workshops, I have writers go through various exercises to dig below their current surface level. So much of this deepening is simply a matter of *asking key questions and letting the imagination provide the answers.*

And always look for the *next* answer. So many times we settle for the first thing that pops into our minds, or the familiar. It's the unfamiliar we're looking for, the new insight or possibility.

Get in the habit of making lists of possibilities. Push yourself to list more than you're comfortable with. That's where you'll find the gold.

When you do these exercises you're going to come up with lots of surprises and things you'll want to keep or pursue.

What you do then is *justify* the new material. Often this means adding to your character's backstory and setting that new material somewhere in the novel.

Justification follows imagination, not the other way around. Imagination, creation, justification. This process will take you deeper.

One other note on these exercises. Sometimes I ask my students to do free writing on a subject. That means *writing without stopping for a set period of time.*

The object of the free writing exercise is to get material down without thinking about it, judging it, or editing any of the words. You give yourself permission to write badly and sloppily, and yet you do not reject anything that comes to your mind.

You follow any tangent that pops up. This is often where the real gold is.

Most of the time you will find a nugget or two buried somewhere in this mass of words. Usually in the middle or toward the end. That's because our minds jump to the obvious and familiar.

I then have the students look over what they've written and highlight the best parts. These become the basis of new material for the novel.

With all that in mind, here are the deepening exercises.

Chair Through the Window

We want to make sure the readers are taken on an emotional roller coaster, and the best ride happens when they are gripped by what's going on *inside* the main character.

So . . . imagine your lead character in a room with a bay window. In this room is a chair. Your character throws the chair out the window.

Why?

What sort of emotion would cause that to happen?

Anger?

Grief?

Frustration?

Now, justify that emotion. What in the character's past would have led to such a thing?

Finally, transfer that emotional intensity to a scene in your novel. The action doesn't have to be the same—chair through the window—but the feeling is replicated.

Spend any extra time writing a new justification for this feeling.

Lost Love

Write down the three things you love most in this world. They can be people, things you do, places, items. Just take a moment to make this list.

Choose the one thing you love most out of those three. If it's close, pick one at random.

Now put yourself in a scene. Yes, you. Create a movie in your mind where you have just lost the thing you love most. Watch this scene until you feel the emotion.

Write for two minutes without stopping, recording what your inner thoughts would be in that scene. You can think of yourself as an actor playing a role or as an author writing a journal entry for yourself.

Put that material away and come back to it an hour later. Read over what you've written and highlight the freshest thoughts, the surprising material, the turn of phrase that pops.

Transfer this material over to your lead character. Change the details of the lost love so they fit your character's situation—although you are perfectly free to hand your own experience over to the character.

Create and justify a scene where the character loses something he loves.

Fear Factor

Much of what makes page-turning fiction is based on fear.

Fear can cause anything from simple worry to the body shutting down because of extreme terror. This can be pictured on a continuum:

Apply this idea to your scene writing. Unless the viewpoint character in the scene is experiencing fear of some fashion, *nothing is at stake in that scene.* You either cut the scene or you put in a fear factor.
Do this:

1. What three things does your character fear? Write them down.
2. Justify each. *Why* does the character fear these things?
3. Choose the biggest fear.
4. Feel it yourself for a moment. Use the old actor's trick of sense memory to remember a time when you felt the same or similar fear.
5. Write a page-long sentence in the character's voice about the fear. Do not stop writing until you've done one page.
6. Revise that page down to a paragraph, and put that paragraph in the novel.

Do Tell

A *telling detail* is a single, descriptive element—a gesture, an image, an action—that contains a universe of meaning. Such details can instantly illuminate a character, setting, or theme.

Raymond Carver was a master at this. In his story "Will You Please Be Quiet, Please?" a husband and wife are having an intense conversation in the kitchen. The wife is reluctantly going over details of what happened at a party years ago, when another man took her for a ride in his car and kissed her. The husband's reaction as he listens:

> He moved all his attention into one of the tiny black coaches in the tablecloth. Four tiny white prancing horses pulled each one of the black coaches and the figure driving the horses had his arms up and wore a tall hat, and suitcases were strapped down atop the coach, and what looked like a kerosene lamp hung from the side, and if he were listening at all it was from inside the black coach.

The husband's interior thoughts and emotions are revealed completely in the images and in how he relates to the images. There is no need for Carver to tell us how the husband feels. The detail does the "telling."

1. Identify a highly charged moment in your book.
2. Make a list of possible actions, gestures, or setting descriptions that might reflect upon the scene.

3. List at least twenty to twenty-five possibilities, as fast as you can. Remember, the best way to get good ideas is to come up with lots of ideas and then choose the ones you want to use.
4. Write a long paragraph incorporating the detail, then edit the paragraph so that it is lean and potent. The telling detail works best when it is subtle and does all the work by itself.

The "That's Not Just Who I Am, That's Who the Hell I Am"

There's a line in the Broadway musical *How to Succeed in Business Without Really Trying*, where young go-getter J. Pierepont Finch meets the big boss himself—J.B. Biggley, president of World Wide Wickets.

Everyone in the office fears Biggley, for he holds all the power to hire and fire. When Finch asks him if he is indeed J.B. Biggley, Biggley replies, "That's not just who I am, that's who the hell I am."

He knows who he is and what he's about. He knows what he wants the world to think of him.

1. What three adjectives describe your main character?
2. Choose the one that your character thinks best describes her.
3. Now, voice journal for five minutes (see chapter 2 for a description of the Character Voice Journal). Have the character tell you why this is not just who he is but who the *hell* he is!

Now find a place in your novel where *another character* describes your character, either to her face or to another character in the book. Incorporate the material you generated in this exercise.

Next, go over every scene involving your main character. Yep, every scene. Freshen all actions, thoughts, and dialogue so they are consistent with what you have come up with.

The Ghost

When an event from the past haunts the character's present, we call this the Ghost. It causes the character to do things and say things that seem to other characters, and the reader, a little off, as if there's something going on beneath the surface.

Although we're all products of an infinitely complex web of experiences, in fiction you can simplify for a purpose. And the purpose is a deeper connection to the character.

Create an event in the past that wounded your Lead. Come up with several possibilities (remembering, again, that our minds jump to the familiar). Choose one and do a voice journal entry where the character describes this event *in detail*. Write it until you feel it right along with the character.

Next, write down five *nonverbal* ways the character can indicate he's haunted by the Ghost. Put those in your story without explaining them.

Finally, rewrite three dialogue exchanges where the Ghost is subtext, and not named, but influences how the character talks.

The Columbo

Last but not least is the Columbo. This is based on the TV character played by Peter Falk. He was, outwardly, a stumbling and bumbling police detective. He would annoy the suspects by showing up and pestering them with questions.

And just when the villain thought Columbo was through, the wily sleuth would pause, turn, and say, "Just one more thing . . ." That last question was always a corker.

So . . . what is the one question your Lead doesn't want anyone to ask?

Create an exchange in which someone insists on the answer. Note: Your Lead doesn't have to answer it! It's up to you.

Just like all deepening questions are up to you. But I believe you will find these exercises will result in the kind of material that takes books to the next level.

Which is always where you want to go when you revise.

Which is also the subject of the next chapter, "The Ultimate Revision Checklist."

CHAPTER 17

The Ultimate
Revision Checklist

Celebrate.

You have a completed manuscript. Most people who think they ought to write a novel someday never get to this point.

By finishing a draft, you learn things you can't learn any other way.

And if you apply the principles in this book every time you write, you'll learn even more.

The learning experience never stops. Or shouldn't. Don't let it.

Keep writing.

When it comes to revision, I've found that most writers need a more systematic approach. Too many writers just sit down and read a manuscript page by page, making changes as they come up. Big or small, each item is dealt with the moment it's seen.

Much better is to go from large to small. To start with the most crucial aspects and work your way down to the final step, which is The Polish.

Think of this chapter, then, as your ultimate revision checklist. Apply it to every manuscript you write.

Feel free to vary the order if you prefer, and add your own checklist areas.

And feel free to use this as is for the rest of your writing life.

It will serve you either way.

CHARACTER

KEY QUESTIONS ABOUT LEAD CHARACTERS

- Is my Lead worth following for a whole novel? Why?
- How can I make my Lead "jump off the page" more?
- Do my characters sufficiently contrast? Are they interesting enough on their own?
- Will readers bond to my Lead because he ...
    - ... cares for someone other than himself?
    - ... is funny, irreverent, or a rebel with a cause?
    - ... is competent at something?
    - ... is an underdog facing long odds without giving up?
    - ... has a dream or desire readers can relate to?
    - ... has undeserved misfortune, but doesn't whine about it?
    - ... is in jeopardy or danger?

COMMON FIXES

Use the Jump-Off

Lead characters must "jump off the page." The key to compelling fiction has always been characters that live, breathe, and have the capacity to surprise us.

If your main characters seem flat, try the "opposite exercise." Imagine they're the opposite sex. Close your eyes and replay some scenes in your mind. What's different about their behavior? What sorts of feelings do they show? What nuances suddenly emerge?

You're not going to change their sex in actuality (though you might!). You're trying to find different shades and colors.

A variation is "switch casting." First, cast your Lead. Who would you sign up for the movie role?

Next, cast someone else just for contrast. Watch some scenes in your movie-mind. Does the character click better as Tom Hanks or Robert De Niro? Does your lead sound more natural being played by Susan Sarandon or Sandra Bullock?

Color Passions

In her book *Getting Into Character*, Brandilyn Collins offers acting techniques for novelists. One of these is *coloring passions*. "Just as in acting," Collins writes, "three-dimensional characters in novels require three-dimensional emotions. ... When you focus not on the general passion of your character, but on its component parts, its opposite and its growth, your character will deepen in richness and represent human nature to its fullest."

To begin coloring the passions of your character, identify the overall emotion, the primary feeling at any point in your novel. This will usually be found in the character's desire in the scene (a character without desires is dull).

Push the desire to its limit. How far does it go?

Break the passion into parts. Revenge, for example, can come from anger, shock, resentment, embarrassment, shame. How can you explore each?

Now look at the opposite of that desire, which will give you the seeds of the character's inner conflict. How will you illustrate, in dramatic fashion, the character's emotional struggle?

. . . .

At every significant juncture in a story, consciously look at the situation from the viewpoint of every character involved—and let each of them make the best move they can from his or her own point of view.

—STANLEY SCHMIDT, *REVISE THE VOICE JOURNAL*

Revise the Voice Journal

After you've written your novel you should know your characters pretty well. But, as with people, there are lots of inner corners to explore and deepen.

If you did a voice journal for your main character (see chapter two), consider a revision. You want the characters to tell you, in their own voices, what the events of the story have done to them. How are they different now? What do they wish they'd done differently?

Who do they love (or hate) as a result of the story?

Are they mad at you, the author? Let them vent.

The number of areas your characters can give voice to is infinite. So just let them go and see what comes out.

Then you'll be in a position to deepen and expand your characters in the novel. And what they say will also direct you toward a possible theme (see chapter twelve).

Chart Character Change

Track the inner change in your character through the three acts. List the plot elements that are working on the character to instigate the change.

Make the change understandable and logical.

- Go through your manuscript and, with a highlighter, mark all the passages of inner life you've given us. These can be everything from one-line realizations to full-on reflections.
- Now, read through the highlighted sections only, in order. Is the flow of the interior life you're showing understandable and believable? Are there places that seem inconsistent? Are there gaps that need to be filled with other interior insights?

CHARACTER ARC TEMPLATE			
NAME:			
ACT I	ACT II A	ACT II B	ACT III

KEY QUESTIONS ABOUT OPPOSITION CHARACTERS

- Is he just as fully realized as the Lead?
- Is his behavior justified (in his own mind)?
- Are you being "fair" with the opposition?
- Is he as strong or (preferably) stronger than the Lead, in terms of ability to win the fight?

COMMON FIX

The Moustache Twirler

If your opposition character is a "villain" and you've made him too one-dimensionally evil (common flaw), do the following:

- Write a biography of this character from the point of view of his sympathetic mother. Force yourself.
- Then weave some of the material into a scene in your novel. It doesn't have to be huge. A little bit goes a long way.

Remember: The old moustache-twirling villain of melodrama and silent film is long gone.

PLOT

KEY QUESTIONS ABOUT PLOT

- Is there any point where a reader might feel like putting the book down?
- Does the novel feel like it's about people doing things?
- Does the plot feel forced or unnatural?
- Is the story out of balance? Too much action? Too much reaction?

COMMON FIXES

Keep Nabbing Ideas

All through the revision process your mind will be working on your plot. When you sleep, eat, shower, drive. The boys in the basement never stop.

So be able to nab any ideas that occur to you at odd moments. Have pens and paper handy in your home, car, office, backpack. Don't hesitate to jot down what occurs to you, without judgment. Later, you can sift through your notes and decide what to incorporate.

Create Two Trajectories

Create two trajectories for your main character: a personal problem and a plot problem.

- He's in his personal problem as the story begins, or it develops soon thereafter.
- The plot problem arises when the main conflict is engaged.

The two don't necessarily intersect as the story moves along, though they can. But the personal complicates how he deals with the plot.

In *Chasing the Dime* by Michael Connelly, Pierce, the Lead, is dealing with a divorce, then starts getting strange calls for "Lillie" over the phone. The divorce makes him a little more vulnerable to the plot twists.

Create a Calendar

If you haven't done this already, either when first drafting or afterward, print out a blank calendar covering the time of your novel. You can do this for historical novels as well as contemporary or futuristic ones.

The reason for this is you want to avoid having something happening on a Saturday that, according to what's taken place before, must be happening on a Monday. Or have the "next day" be for regular business, only to discover that it's really Sunday by the calendar.

I find it helpful to have a hard copy of this so I can pencil in the main events of each day. Almost always I have mistakes in the timing of the first draft that need to be corrected.

Revitalize Your Plot

Does your novel feel like a lazy uncle, overstaying his welcome, sitting on the couch and boring you with pointless anecdotes? Then get it up and moving.

Analyze the *stakes*. Ask yourself what the main character will lose if he doesn't achieve his objective. Unless it's something that threatens tremendous loss, either physically or emotionally, readers won't care what happens.

It's helpful to think of your plot as involving the threat of death. In a thriller, it's usually physical death. If the Lead doesn't get away from the bad guys, he will die (John Grisham's *The Firm*). But it can also be professional death—the FBI agent who doesn't catch the serial killer will be a failure (Thomas Harris's *The Silence of the Lambs*).

In a literary novel, psychological death often hangs over the character. This is the feeling that pervades *The Catcher in the Rye*. Holden Caulfield must find some reality that he can embrace, or he will die inside.

Another major area to explore is *adhesive*. What is it that bonds the Lead and the opposition together? If this adhesive isn't strong enough, the readers will wonder why the plot should continue at all.

Duty is often the key to adhesive. If the lead has a professional duty (e.g., a lawyer to his client, a cop to his case) then we accept that he can't resign. Duty may be moral, such as the duty to save a friend or loved one. *The Odd Couple* works only because Neil Simon planted a moral duty early: Oscar's best friend, Felix, is suicidal over his divorce. That is enough to remove the question *Why doesn't Oscar just kick his annoying roommate out?*

Next, see if you can add *another level of complication*. In Robert Crais's thriller *Hostage*, burned-out hostage negotiator Jeff Talley is suddenly faced with a tense standoff in an otherwise placid bedroom community.

Fine and dandy on its own, but Crais then adds another level: The hostage inside the house has in his possession incriminating financial evidence against the mob, because he's the mob's accountant! The mob needs to get that evidence before the cops.

To put pressure on Talley, the mob kidnaps his ex-wife and daughter and holds them hostage. This added level of complication supercharges the entire book.

Add a Character

Too few characters can result in a thin plot.

Too many can render it overweight.

But just the right character added at just the right time presents a whole universe of plot possibilities.

If your plot is plodding, consider adding a new, dynamic character to the proceedings. Give this character a stake in the plot. Give him plenty of reasons to be for or against the other characters. Search out possible backstory relationships between the new character and the existing cast.

BEWARE OF UNMOTIVATED ACTIONS

Do you have characters doing things that aren't justified in the story?

A character can't just show up. You need to give your characters a reason to act the way they do. Look to:

- desires
- yearnings
- duties
- psychological wounds
- passions

Add a "Pet the Dog" Beat

In screenwriting parlance, writers sometimes talk about the pet-the-dog beat. It's best to explain this with an illustration.

Let's say Clint Eastwood is playing a cop (I know—it's a bit of a stretch). He's got his .44 Magnum out and is chasing a killer through the dark streets. He's getting shot at. He has his back against the wall in an alley when he hears something crash. He spins around and points his gun at this scraggly old dog who has tipped over a trash can. The dog comes up to Clint's leg.

Clint looks down at the dog, out to the street, then back to the dog. He bends over and pets the dog and says, "Better be careful, little fella. It's dangerous out here." And then he takes charge of the dog. What he has done here is to take a moment from his own concerns to look out for something weaker and more vulnerable than he is. He has shown he cares just as much for this little dog at that moment as he does for his own safety.

A pet-the-dog beat, properly executed, creates great sympathy for the character, while at the same time may add to the suspense. It doesn't have to be a literal dog, but any other character who is vulnerable.

In the movie *The Fugitive*, there's a wonderful pet-the-dog beat.

Dr. Richard Kimble (Harrison Ford) has disguised himself as a maintenance worker for a busy Chicago hospital. His plan is to access the records of the prosthetics section so he can find the possible identity of the one-armed man who killed his wife. Meantime, he's being hunted by the police and the federal marshal played by Tommy Lee Jones.

As he's trying to leave the hospital without being noticed, Kimble comes to the emergency ward. It's a mass confusion of gunshot wounds and accident victims.

He waits for his opportunity, but as he does he hears a groan next to him. He looks down. There's a boy on a gurney. Kimble can't help wondering what's wrong with the boy. He's a doctor, after all, and healing is what he does.

An on-call doctor tells Kimble to wheel the boy down to an observation room. As he does, he asks the boy where it hurts and checks out the X-rays. In the elevator he figures out that the boy has been misdiagnosed and changes the chart. Kimble takes the boy to the emergency operating chamber so he can get immediate attention.

Kimble has taken time from his terrible trouble to care about someone. The movie makers use this moment masterfully, because it gets Kimble into more trouble. When he gets back to the emergency floor, the on-call doctor, who had seen him looking at the X-rays, stops him, takes his identification badge, and goes to call security.

And the fugitive is on the move again.

Look for a place where you can add a pet-the-dog beat.

Change a Setting

Usually the main setting of your plot is going to remain as is, because you have so much invested in it. You've done research, set up locations for scenes, and so on.

But if it's possible to change, give it some consideration. Will it add levels to your plot? More exciting possibilities?

Even if you can't change the main location, many of your scenes can be enlivened this way.

Look especially to these locations:

- restaurants
- kitchens
- living rooms
- offices
- cars

These are the places most of us are in most of the time. For that reason they're overly familiar.

Look at each instance of a location like the above and see if you can't find a fresher venue. For example, instead of a restaurant scene, what if the characters were outside eating hot dogs on a pier? Or at a carnival where there's too much noise?

You don't have to move every scene, of course, but this is one way to sharpen a plot.

DON'T HOLD BACK ON MAKING TROUBLE

Have you been resistant to making things as bad as possible for your Lead? Did you pull your punches when creating obstacles, challenges, points of conflict? Were you too nice to your characters?

Go through your manuscript and define what the point of conflict is for each scene.

- Are there two characters with opposing objectives? Can you rework it so this conflict is clearer?
- Can you ratchet up the conflict by making these objectives more important to each character?

- Can you show us, through inner thoughts, just how important it is to the viewpoint character?
- Can you make the conflict hotter, more intense?
- Think things through. Don't worry about going too far. You can always pull it back a little in your final polish.

THE OPENING

KEY QUESTIONS ABOUT THE OPENING

- Do I open with some part of the story engine running? Or am I spending too much time warming up?
- How do my opening pages conform to Hitchcock's axiom ("A good story is life with the dull parts taken out")?
- What is the *story world* I'm trying to present? What mood descriptions bring that story world to life for the reader?
- What is the tone of my novel going to be? Are the descriptions consistent with that mood?
- What happens in Act I that's going to compel the reader to keep reading? What danger will threaten the Lead?
- Who is the opposition to the Lead? Is he as strong, or preferably stronger, than the Lead? How do I show this?
- Is there enough conflict in the setup to run through the whole book?

COMMON FIXES

Rev Up a Flat Opening Line

Give us a character in motion. Something should be happening to a person from line one.

Make that a disturbing thing, or have it presage something disturbing. Remember, a disturbance is any sort of change or challenge. It doesn't have to be "big" to hold interest.

If you want to open more leisurely, at least give us these elements within the first paragraph or half page.

Weed Out Too Much Backstory, Exposition, or Cast

While some backstory is good in the opening, it should come only after action is established, and then dropped in sparingly.

Exposition (information) can also usually be put off until later.

Remember the rule *act first, explain later.*

Remember the chapter two switcheroo (see chapter two). Try opening with your second chapter and see how it feels.

Another error is the introduction of too many characters in the opening chapters. Readers want to know who the main character is and why he should care. If you bring on too many characters, that bond will be diluted. You can:

- Eliminate characters.
- Delay some character introductions until later.
- Make sure you are strongly in your Lead's point of view throughout.
- Combine characters to reduce the size of the cast.

MIDDLES

KEY QUESTIONS ABOUT MIDDLES

- Do I deepen character relationships?
- Why should the reader care about what's happening?
- Have I justified the final battle or final choice that will wrap things up at the end?
- Is there a sense of death (physical, professional, or psychological) that overhangs?
- Is there a strong adhesive keeping the characters together (such as moral or professional duty, physical location, or other reasons characters can't just walk away)?
- Do my scenes contain conflict or tension?

COMMON FIXES

Strengthen Your Opposition

Alfred Hitchcock always said the strength of his suspense lay in the strength of the villain. It makes sense. If your readers aren't worried about your Lead because the opponent or opposing circumstances are soft, the middle will seem a long slog indeed.

Look to the three aspects of death to give your opposition strength.

- Does the opposition have the power to kill your Lead, like a mafia don, for instance?
- Does the opposition have the power to crush your Lead's professional pursuits, like a crooked judge in a criminal trial?
- Does the opposition have the power to crush your Lead's spirit? Think of the awful mother played by Gladys Cooper in the 1942 film *Now, Voyager*. She has that power over her daughter, played by Bette Davis.

Once you decide on the type of power your opposition character can wield, you can go back and explain it. You can come up with any background material you choose to show us exactly how the opposition got to be the way she is.

Caveat: Don't make your opposition so strong that she becomes a caricature. Color your opposition. Make her complex. No one, with the possible exception of Dr. Evil, wakes each day thinking of new evil things to do. Characters feel justified in what they do. Show us the shades of gray in the opposition.

Add a Subplot

One sure way to prop up a sagging middle is to add a subplot. A good subplot can add thematic depth, provide additional outer and inner conflict, and power the book with another level of interest.

A few kinds of subplots are:

- **ROMANTIC:** The Lead has to deal with romance, which should threaten to complicate his life. Some of the types of romantic subplots are:
  a. The Lead falls in love with a character he can't connect with, due to class, family, or other considerations. The lovers want to be together but are prevented by circumstance. Think *Romeo and Juliet*.
  b. The Lead and another character hate each other at first but are forced into companionship. Think the classic movie *It Happened One Night*.
  c. The Lead is married or committed to another, but the love interest comes along to generate sexual or romantic tension.
  d. The love triangle.

- **PLOT COMPLICATION:** Another plotline comes along to mess up the Lead's pursuit of the objective. In Robert Crais's *Hostage*, police captain Jeff Talley thinks he's dealing with some thugs who have taken a family hostage. But then it turns out the father inside is the accountant for the mob, and the mob decides to take Talley's own family hostage until he can recover some important evidence.
- **PERSONAL:** Some crisis from the Lead's personal life is making his life more difficult. The detective on the hunt for a serial killer has a wife threatening to leave him.
- **THEMATIC:** This is a subplot that can have many permutations, but the main reason for its existence is to deepen the theme of the novel. Often, this is a personal story line that demands the Lead grow or learn some important lesson.

So what's the best way to come up with a subplot? There are two primary ways:

1. CHARACTER

- Take a character other than the Lead and bring her into more prominence. Is there something this character can do to complicate the life or goal of the Lead? Play with several possibilities.
- Create a new character to plug in. I did this in a recent book. I felt some sag and thought up a colorful minor character. Then I did some brainstorming where the character might fit. Eventually, I came up with a plotline for him.

2. PLOT

- Look for a plot need or plot hole and create a plotline to cover it. In my book I needed a transition to impart some important information coming to the Lead. I came up with a character to provide the information, then built a plotline around that, expanding this character's reach.

Raise the Stakes

Plot Stakes

Brainstorm a list of new events you can add that will bring more trouble to the Lead. Go wild. Don't throw anything out. You usually don't get gold until you're down past four or five possibilities. Keep going.

Some possibilities to get you started:

- An unexpected enemy shows up.
- A friend turns out to be an enemy.
- A minor character turns out to hold more deadly power than previously thought.
- Someone dies unexpectedly.
- Someone thought dead shows up alive.
- The Lead gets fired.
- The Lead gets in an accident or gets lost.
- A crucial message is lost.
- Ed Sullivan comes back from the dead (see, go wild).

Character Stakes

How can you raise the stakes for the Lead character?

Put him on the horns of a dilemma.

A dilemma presents two choices, both of which are bad.

Make a two-sided table, onscreen or on a piece of paper. Then brainstorm, on one side, all of the reasons the character cannot walk away from the conflict. Think up as many psychological, personal, familial, and any other type of reason the character can't just quit.

For example, why can't Dr. Richard Kimble quit in *The Fugitive*?

- He'll be executed for a crime he didn't commit.
- His wife's true killer will get away.
- He'll be haunted by memories (there's a dream sequence in the movie).
- The killer may strike again.
- The true villains (if they exist) would continue to operate.
- The justice system would be perverted.
- Loyal friends will think they've been saps.

And so on. Now, on the other side of the table, put in all the reasons the character *absolutely must walk away* ... in this case, go somewhere and hide out.

- The U.S. Marshals have all the resources.
- He's only one man and no one believes him.
- The conspiracy is too great.
- He's a *surgeon*, not a superhero.

Another way to raise the stakes for the character is to *make it personal*. In *The Big Heat*, tough cop Bannion is trying to get at the crime boss. He uses his usual hard tactics, but the brass (in the pocket of the boss) wants him to back off. He reluctantly does so, but then the thugs plant a car bomb. It blows up the wrong person—Bannion's wife.

Now it's personal.

Societal Stakes

Is there some larger issue at play? For the community at large?

What would be the consequences for the town where Will Kane is the marshal, should he be killed? Or walk away? The town has a lot of the killer's friends in it, and they like things the way they were before Will Kane.

What about Rick's antiheroism in *Casablanca*? If he goes his own way and keeps Ilsa, it will harm the efforts of Lazlo, the war hero. The world itself will be harmed. Talk about stakes!

Trim

Sometimes sag is caused by being overweight. There's simply too much flab. You can do some trimming here and there, and then strengthen the good stuff that remains.

Try the following:

Combine or Cut Characters

If a character is in your plot for no apparent purpose, shove him off the stage. Maybe this is a character who you thought was colorful enough to be carried along on charm alone.

Not. Each character must serve a purpose.

If it's a major character, ask what her stakes are in the story. How does she relate to the Lead character and the main area of conflict? If she wasn't in the story, and the plot would pretty much be the same, she doesn't need to be there.

Supporting characters should also be there as *allies* or *irritants*. If they aren't helping or hindering the Lead, they have no purpose.

Walk-on characters—those very minor characters—should appear only to make something happen that has to happen. Like a cab driver when a cab is taken, or the waiter when your Lead is in a restaurant.

It's also possible to combine two or more characters. Think about how all the characters relate to one another. Make a web diagram, like on the following page. Then see if you can combine two or more characters to fulfill the same function. For example, a grandmother and crazy aunt might be combined to provide the same pressure on the Lead as they would individually.

Absorb a Subplot

Did you begin a subplot strand that ran out of steam? Or takes off on a tangent that's too wild?

Take what's good and let the main plot absorb it. Take what's good in the subplot—maybe a character or an incident—and instead of giving it more attention, give it less.

CHARACTER WEB

CURLEY

MOE   BUD

MRS. BRADY   LOU

LEAD CHARACTER

SHIRLEY

DEAN

LAVERNE

JERRY

Add Research

Some writers like to do extensive research before they start writing. This seems advisable for writers of historical novels. It would be a fine how-do-you-do to finish a manuscript and find that several key plot devices couldn't possibly happen because of the time frame.

Other writers, like Stephen King, prefer to get a first draft down on paper and only then go back and fill in the holes.

Research done after the fact can only help you during the revision process. It not only plugs up some gaps, it can offer new plot insights that deepen the novel.

Ask an Expert

Ridley Pearson has a good method for interviewing. He does enough before-you-write research to be able to start his writing. Then he writes and makes the best guess as to how characters will react as issues arise. Then he checks it with experts. That way, he knows what questions to ask, thus following the first rule of expert interviews: *Don't waste their time.*

- Before going to a great resource, do your homework—again, don't waste his time. Know what you want to ask! Decide what materials you need before you contact him. Do as much on your own as you can, then go to the expert for the telling details.
- When visiting offices of public relations of police departments, etc., make sure they know you're *not* an investigative reporter! Ask them questions such as, "Can you put me in touch with someone who will spend time with me talking about X?" Tell them how much time you'll need. Thirty minutes is about the limit for a first-time interview.
- Use open-ended questions, as well as specifics. Allow for the serendipity of the talker. Encourage stories. But get to your *key questions* before you leave.
- Mid-interview questions (once your expert is "warmed up") that are always good to ask: (1) What's the *best* part of your job, what you love the most? (2) What do you *hate* most about your job?
- It's a show of bad manners to run more than your allotted time.
- If you need follow-up, ask for permission to call back. "Hi, it's me again. Is this a good time to talk or should I call back later?" Let him know you won't waste his time.
- Sources *can* turn into "buddies," which you can take to lunch, etc.
- Try to find out if your expert is a reader. Then you can connect that way. Listen for *visual* images.
- Take specialized classes (e.g., gun classes).
- Participate in ride alongs (police, or paramedics if cops won't let you).

Be on the lookout for sights, sounds, how people talk, etc. Note the catch-phrases they use.

Or Just Go Find It

A young Dean Koontz wrote a novel called *The Key to Midnight* under the pseudonym Leigh Nichols. It begins in Kyoto, Japan.

> At four o'clock in the morning, the city of Kyoto was quiet, even here in Gion, the entertainment quarter with its nightclubs and geisha houses. An incredible city, she thought ... a fascinating hodgepodge of neon signs and ancient temples, plastic gimcrackery and beautiful hand-carved stone, the worst of glossy modern architecture thrusting up next to pal-

aces and ornate shrines that were weathered by centuries of hot, damp summers and cold, damp winters.

A little later, the characters enter a restaurant:

> Mizutani was an *o-zashiki* restaurant, which meant that it was divided by rice-paper partitions into many private dining rooms where meals were served strictly Japanese-style. The ceiling was not high, less than eighteen inches above Alex's head, and the floor was of brilliantly polished pine that seemed transparent and as deep as a sea. In the vestibule, Alex and Joanna exchanged their street shoes for soft slippers, then followed a petite young hostess to a room where they sat on the floor, side by side on thin but comfortable cushions.

A writer friend who knew Kyoto well called Koontz to congratulate him, thinking Koontz must have been there. "I've never even been in the Pacific Ocean up to my neck," Koontz said.

So how did he accomplish this illusion of being there? Through travel books, photo guides, tourist tomes, language primers, maps, memoirs of those who'd been to Kyoto, restaurant guides, and anything else he could get his hands on. He absorbed a thousand facts, even down to the name of the largest taxicab company in Kyoto. Koontz also read cultural books, including the novel *Shogun*, to get a sense of the Japanese mind-set.

He had to do all this since he was setting a novel there and didn't want to get wet in the Pacific Ocean.

ENDINGS

KEY QUESTIONS ABOUT ENDINGS

- Are there loose threads left dangling? You must either resolve these in a way that doesn't distract from the main plotline or go back and snip them out. Readers have long memories.
- Does my ending provide a feeling of resonance? The best endings leave a sense of something beyond the confines of the book covers.
- Will the readers feel the way I want them to feel?

COMMON FIXES

Pull Threads Together

Go back through the manuscript and read only those portions relating to the particular thread in which there might be a problem.

You know where they are.

Read only these parts, skipping the rest.

Make notes on your observations. Make a list of all possible solutions, no matter how off the wall.

Brood about it for a day or two. Add any ideas that occur to you after sleeping on it.

Choose the solution that suits you best.

Another idea is to utilize a minor character to explain or embody a solution. It used to be a staple of mystery fiction that the detective would gather everyone in a room at the end and explain what happened. We're more subtle now, but it can still be done in small chunks.

In general, try to tie up your loose ends in the reverse order of their introduction.

The following chart may help:

INTRODUCTORY PROBLEM INTRODUCED → MAIN PROBLEM → ADDITIONAL PROBLEM #1 → ADDITIONAL PROBLEM #2 → ADDITIONAL PROBLEM #3

The solutions come this way:

ADDITIONAL PROBLEM #3 SOLVED ← ADDITIONAL PROBLEM #2 SOLVED ← ADDITIONAL PROBLEM #1 SOLVED ← MAIN PROBLEM SOLVED ← INTRODUCTORY PROBLEM SOLVED

Note that the introductory problem is not the big issue of the book. It's usually an opening disturbance of some kind. So at the end, to keep from anticlimax, make sure you wrap it up in one scene.

In *Midnight* by Dean Koontz, we learn that Sam Booker has a personal problem with his teenage son. The book unfolds from there. In the end, Booker has one scene with his son, where reconciliation begins.

Create Resonance

The perfect last page, last paragraph, and last line are crucial. There is no one way to accomplish this, as every novel is unique.

You can, however, approach it this way: Write several last pages. Try different lines and rhythms.

Look for a line of dialogue in the novel that could be repeated at the end. For example, I once wrote a novel where the male Lead, a bounty hunter, was asked by the female Lead (whom he was helping) what he expected them to do in the midst of trouble. "Improvise," he said.

At the end of the novel, when the two of them were about to become romantically involved, he was the one who asked what they should do next. "Improvise," she said.

That was the last line.

Or, come up with a line of dialogue that just sounds good. Create several of them. Pick the best one and find a way to plant a hint of that line earlier in the novel.

Final Twist

Come up with several alternative endings. If one of them seems better than what you've got, consider plugging it in.

But don't get rid of your old one. Consider using it as a twist ending. You'll have to tweak the details, but you might be able to use it.

Or use one of the other alternative endings you came up with.

The final twist should be short, to avoid anticlimax.

SCENES

KEY QUESTIONS ABOUT SCENES

- Is there conflict or tension in every scene?
- Do you establish a viewpoint character?
- If the scene is action, is the objective clear?
- If the scene is reaction, is the emotion clear?

COMMON FIXES

Relive Your Scenes

Not rewrite. *Relive.*

Have you ever imagined yourself to be the characters? Tried to feel what he or she is feeling?

Then try it now. It's not hard. Be an actor.

Often, after I've written a scene, I'll go back and try to live the emotions. I'll act out the parts I've created. Almost always what I feel "in character" will make me add to or change the scene.

You can also vividly imagine the scene, step-by-step, in your mind. Let it play like a movie. But instead of watching the movie from a seat in the theater, be *in* the scene. The other characters can't see you, but you can see and hear them.

Intensify the proceedings. Let things happen. Let the characters improvise. If you don't like what they come up with, rewind the scene and allow them do something else.

Look at the beginnings of your scenes. What do you do to grab the reader at the start? Have you spent too much time with description of setting? Often the better course is to start *in medias res* (in the middle of things) and drop in description a little later.

Examine scene endings. What have you provided that will make the reader want to read on? Some great places to stop a scene are:

- at the moment a major decision is to be made
- just as a terrible thing happens
- with a portent of something bad *about* to happen

- with a strong display of emotion
- raising a question that has no immediate answer

Keep improving your scenes and your novel will soon develop that can't-put-it-down feel.

Heat Up the Core

Ask yourself what the core of your scene is. What's the purpose? Why does it exist? How does it answer one of the four key questions about scenes?

If the core is weak or unclear, strengthen it.

Think of it as the "hot spot" and find ways to turn up the heat.

Adjust Your Pace

If you need to speed up a scene, dialogue is one way to do it. Short exchanges with few beats leave a lot of white space on the page and give a feeling of movement. In the Lawrence Block story "A Candle for the Bag Lady," a waitress tells P.I. Matt Scudder someone was looking for him, ending her descriptions by saying he looked "underslung."

> "Perfectly good word."
>> "I said you'd probably get here sooner or later."
>> "I always do. Sooner or later."
>> "Uh-huh. You okay, Matt?"
>> "The Mets lost a close one."
>> "I heard it was thirteen to four."
>> "That's close for them these days. Did he say what it was about?"

To slow the pace of a scene, you can add action beats, thoughts, and description as well as elongating speeches. In the Block story, a killer confesses to Scudder about killing a bag lady. Scudder asks why he did it.

> "Same as the bourbon and coffee. Had to *see*. Had to taste it and find out what it was like." His eyes met mine. His were very large, hollow, empty. I fancied I could see right through them to the blackness at the back of his skull. "I couldn't get my mind away from murder," he said. His voice was more sober now, the mocking playful quality gone from it. "I tried. I just couldn't do it. It was on my mind all the time and I was afraid of what I might do. I couldn't function, I couldn't think, I just saw blood and death all the time. I was afraid to close my eyes for fear of what I might see. I would just stay up, days it seemed, and then I'd be tired enough to

pass out the minute I closed my eyes. I stopped eating. I used to be fairly heavy and the weight just fell off of me."

Stretch the Tension

Don't waste any good tension beats. Stretch them. Make your prose the equivalent of slow motion in a movie.

Show every beat, using all the tools at your disposal: thoughts, actions, dialogue, description. Mix these up.

In a famous early scene in *Whispers*, Dean Koontz takes seventeen pages to describe the attempted rape of the Lead character. It all takes place in a house. Read it and learn.

AVOID MUDDY VIEWPOINTS

Each scene needs to have a clear point-of-view character. The rule is one POV per scene. No "head hopping."

The exception is when you're using omniscient POV, which has its own challenges.

Otherwise, stick with one POV.

Go over your scenes and see if, within the first couple of paragraphs, you have made the viewpoint clear. You can quickly remedy the situation. Instead of starting a scene this way:

The room was stuffy and packed with people.

Do it like this:

Steve walked into the stuffy room and tried to get past the mass of people.

Throughout the scene, you may need to remind us whose head we're in. You can do this with little clues, like *Steve knew that he had to ...* or *Steve felt the sweat under his arms ...*

Cut or Strengthen Weak Scenes

Identify the ten weakest scenes in your novel. You should have an idea of what these are. Use your gut instinct. When you read through the manuscript, you sensed a certain letdown in some of the scenes, or even outright disappointment.

To help you further, look for scenes where:

- Characters do a lot of talking to each other, without much conflict.
- The scene feels like a setup for some other scene.
- The character motivations seem undeveloped.
- There is too much introspection going on.
- There is not enough introspection, which would explain motivations in action.
- There is little tension or conflict between characters.
- There is little tension or conflict inside the character.

Make yourself identify ten weak scenes. Even if you think only five are really weak, rate another five.

List the scenes in order of their relative weakness. The weakest scene is number one, the next weakest is number two, and so on.

Write these numbers on sticky notes and mark each weak scene in the manuscript.

Now you're ready to go to work. Follow these steps:

1. **CUT SCENE NUMBER ONE FROM THE MANUSCRIPT.** It's gone. It is the weakest link. Good-bye.

2. **MOVE TO SCENE NUMBER TWO.** Answer the Three O Questions:

- What is the **OBJECTIVE** in the scene, and who holds it? In other words, who is the POV character and what is he after in the scene? If he's not after anything, give him something to go after or cut the scene. You must be able to state the character's objective clearly and unambiguously. You must also make this objective clear to the reader at the beginning of the scene. The character must either state it or show in action what he's after.

- Next, what is the **OBSTACLE** to his known objective? Why can't he have it? There are three primary obstacles you can use:

   a. Another character who opposes him, either consciously or unconsciously.

   b. The character himself is fighting an inner battle or lack that gets in his way.

   c. A physical circumstance makes it hard or impossible for him to gain his objective.

- Finally, what is the OUTCOME of the scene? A character can gain his objective or not. For the greatest tension, which do you think it should be? Not. Why? Because trouble is your game, and trouble is tension for the character, and that's what keeps readers reading. Most of the time, let the outcome be a negative, or at least an unrealized, objective.

3. **ANSWER THE THREE O QUESTIONS AND GO DEEPER.** For instance, consider your answers for scene number two:

- **OBJECTIVE**

    a. Brainstorm ways you can make the objective stronger, more intense, more important to the POV character. Rewrite the scene showing us this new intensity. OR—

    b. Brainstorm other possible objectives. Make a list of at least five others. Which one is the most original, yet still consistent with the character? Consider rewriting the scene with that as the new objective, made as intense as you can.

- **OBSTACLE**

    a. Brainstorm how you can make the opposition to the objective stronger, more intense, more important to the opposition character.

    b. Brainstorm ways to intensify the character's inner battle, and show us through thought and action just what that is in the scene.

    c. If it applies, make the physical obstacle more real, immediate, and dangerous.

- **OUTCOME**

    a. Brainstorm the worst possible outcome for this scene. Not merely that the character doesn't gain his objective, but that the loss makes his situation worse. Much worse. Consider making this the outcome.

    b. It's good to have an occasional victory, for variety. But don't let that victory move the character ahead too far. Instead, brainstorm ways the good outcome can actually lead to a situation that causes even greater trouble. You have now taken your second weakest scene and strengthened it considerably.

4. **REPEAT THE ABOVE PROCESS.** You should do this for the remaining eight scenes on your list.

5. **GET A LITTLE EXTRA CREDIT.** Do a quick take on ALL your scenes with the Three Os in mind. Sometimes just a line or two is all you need to ratchet things up.

• •

My first draft is not even recognizable by the time I get to the last draft. I change everything. I consider myself at Square Zero when I finish the first draft. It's almost like I use that draft to think through my plot. My hard copy of each draft will be dripping with ink by the time I finish, and I'll do that several times.

—TERRI BLACKSTOCK

EXPOSITION

KEY QUESTIONS ABOUT EXPOSITION

- Do you have large chunks of information dumped in one spot?
- Is your exposition doing double duty? Cut out any exposition that doesn't also add to the mood or tone of your novel.

COMMON FIXES

Hide Exposition

The best exposition doesn't stick out. It doesn't give the feeling that the story has suddenly stopped so the reader can be fed information.

A "chunk" of exposition is any information of two sentences or more.

The worst way to present this information is as straight narrative in the author's voice.

So, take every chunk of exposition and do the following:

First take out any exposition material that the reader does not absolutely need to know. If it is just filler, get rid of it.

This is a matter of experience. If, for example, you're writing about the history of a place, you'll want to create a feel of the place, and that requires exposition. The temptation, especially if you love research, is to put in everything you know.

Cut what you don't need for flavor or the understanding of the story.

Now, put the chunks you have left in dialogue or character thoughts.

Even better, put the chunks in confrontational dialogue or make them highly tense thoughts.

Chapter Beginnings

Be especially vigilant about exposition at the beginning of chapters. Act first, explain later.

Take out all information that isn't absolutely necessary for the reader to know, especially at the beginning of chapters. See if you can put exposition in later, not all at once, but sprinkled in after action has begun.

VOICE, STYLE, AND POINT OF VIEW

KEY QUESTIONS ABOUT VOICE, STYLE, AND POINT OF VIEW

- Are there sections where the style seems forced or stilted? Try reading it out loud or having the speech mode on the computer do it. Hearing it sounded out will often help identify places to be cut or modified.
- Is your POV consistent in every scene?
- If writing in first person, can the character see and feel what you're describing?
- If writing in third person, do you slip into the thoughts of characters other than the POV character in the scene? Do you describe something the character can't see or feel?

COMMON FIXES

Visualize

Put yourself in the head of the POV character and visualize the scene through her eyes. Run through the paragraphs one by one, "seeing" the scene through the POV character's eyes.

Look for any beats that can't be perceived by the character. They're slippery, but the more you practice, the better you'll become at nabbing them.

Attitudinize

Especially in first-person POV, but even in the others, can you increase the attitude quotient? Get the words more in the voice of the character by exploring his emotional reaction to the plot.

SETTING AND DESCRIPTION

KEY QUESTIONS ABOUT SETTING AND DESCRIPTION

- Have you brought your setting to life for the reader?
- Does the setting operate as a "character"?
- Are your descriptions of places and people too generic?
- Are your descriptions doing double duty by adding to the mood or tone?

COMMON FIX

Add Telling Details

Go through your setting descriptions and look for places where you can put in one good "telling" detail. One vivid detail is worth ten average ones.

Smell, taste, and touch are underused in fiction, so why not use them?

Make a list of words you associate with your novel, the things you're trying to get the readers to feel. For example:

- outrage
- sadness
- hope
- healing
- victory

Under each word you come up with, brainstorm several possible sensory observations that go with the word.

For *outrage* you might think of: *red, fire, noise, crashing, screams, bitterness.* Next, go to specific scenes where you are trying to establish the feeling of outrage, and plug in one of these sensory elements to your descriptions.

Think of these additions as "spice." They work best when applied sparingly and purposefully.

DIALOGUE

KEY QUESTIONS ABOUT DIALOGUE

- Slightly "off" responses are more suspenseful than on-the-nose responses. Can you put in non sequiturs, or answer a question with a question, and so on?
- Can you change some attributions—*he said, she said*—to action beats?
- Good dialogue surprises the reader and creates tension. View it like a game, where the players are trying to outfox each other. Are they using dialogue as a "weapon"?
- Your dialogue should have conflict or tension, even between allies. Does it?

COMMON FIXES

Read It Out Loud

Read your dialogue aloud. Or have your computer's voice read it back to you. Keep a red pen or flying fingers ready to change words.

Compress

See how much dialogue you can actually do without.

Try arbitrarily cutting a line of dialogue and replacing it with an action beat.

Try compressing dialogue that goes over two lines by cutting words.

Orchestrate

If much of the dialogue from different characters sounds the same, orchestrate it by making the individual lines more unique. For example:

- Give the characters their own pet words or phrases they can repeat from time to time.
- Look at cadence. Some people use more words than others.
- Make sure you can "hear" each character's voice.

THEME

KEY QUESTIONS ABOUT THEME

- Do I know what my theme is?
- Has a different theme emerged in the writing? Am I fighting it?
- Have I woven in thematic elements naturally?
- Have I avoided "the lecture"?

COMMON FIX

Write an Essay

Yes, just like in school.

I don't care what kind of novel this is. Even if it's pure action and all you care about is speed, write an essay about the theme of your book.

The good news is you don't have to turn this in. You can grade it yourself. But force yourself to explore your novel as a literary work that has something to say.

This exercise usually turns up at least one dominant thematic element. Then you're in a position to weave it into your novel.

THE POLISH

You've done good work to this point. Hard but rewarding. You're using both sides of your brain, back and forth, as you revise. Analyzing, targeting problems, brainstorming, trying new things.

This is how you become a real writer. Yes, you can play those novels-in-a-month games, and that's fun and good practice.

But cutting, shaping, adding, subtracting, working it, making it better—that's what real writing is all about.

Do this, and you increase your chances of getting published.

Or, if you publish it yourself, of having it read and liked.[1]

Now, before you send it off, give it one more going over. This won't take long in comparison. But it will add that extra sparkle that could make all the difference.

This is The Polish.

Chapter Openings

Go through your manuscript, reading all the chapter openings. Consider the following:

- Can you begin a little further in?
- Does the opening grab? Does it have a hint of conflict or action?
- If you open with description, does it do double duty? If not, put it in later.
- Do most of your chapters begin the same way? Vary them.

Chapter Endings

Look at every chapter ending.

See if you can find a place to end the chapter earlier. One, two, three, or more paragraphs earlier. How does it feel? It may be better, it may not.

If it is, use it.

If it isn't, ask if it would benefit by adding something that would make the chapter end with more of a portent or prompt, like:

- a line of moody description

---

[1] If you're thinking of self-publishing, this book is even more important to you. The danger in self-publishing is that you get to publish it yourself! You don't have an editor to chew your tail. Chew your own tail.

- an introspection of fear or worry
- a moment of decision or intention
- a line of dialogue that snaps or sings

Or your ending may be just fine the way it is.

If that's so, don't touch it!

Dialogue

- Is there plenty of white space in your dialogue exchanges?
- Is your default attribution *said*?
- Do you vary these with action beats?
- Do you have too many action beats? Remember, *said* is good because it doesn't make the reader work.
- Can you cut any words to make the dialogue tighter?
- Is there a line you can "curve" to make it slightly more memorable?

Word Search

Collect the words and phrases you tend to overuse. You'll find these in the revision process and when a good editor or reader alerts you to them. These tend to change with different projects. You'll find yourself repeating a different word each time, because it gets plugged into your head.

I'm talking about words that stand out. Verbs like *scuffle* and *scamper*. Bold adjectives. Actions like *cleared his throat*.

Do a word search of your manuscript for instances of those repeated words and phrases you tend to overuse. Then modify them accordingly.

In addition, look for:

- *Very*. This is almost always a useless adjective. Cut it.
- *Suddenly*. Again, mostly not needed.
- Adverbs. Cut them unless absolutely necessary (some writers insist they never are).

Big Moments

When polishing one of my novels I went to a key scene, one where the Lead confronts the villain head-on and is taken away to be murdered by the villain's followers.

In my original version, the Lead, being held, was slapped by the villain. The Lead said something defiant but was then dragged out of the room.

This wasn't big enough for me, so in the polish I had the Lead break free of the hold on him and punch the villain in the face. The villain, an old man, crumbled to the ground, and this gave me several more beats of tension before moving on to the next scene.

Identify five big moments in your manuscript. Read them over one at a time.

After each moment, make a list of ten ways you can heighten that moment, make it more intense, give it more juice.

Your first two or three ideas will come quickly. Force yourself to go beyond that. Come up with ten, even though you may think some of them absurd. Just do it.

Then sit back and decide which one feels best. Try rewriting that moment in just that way.

Repeat this for the other five big moments.

Final Reminders

- Conflict rules. If you can find any way to increase conflict in a scene, do it. Look at the characters in the scene. Even if they're on the same side, can you create unspoken tension between them? At least have the tension within one character be bubbling beneath the surface, making communication more difficult.
- Look at character relationships. Can you increase the web of relations? Can their lives have intersected in the past somehow?
- Give each major character a secret, even if it never comes out in the story. It will give emotional color.
- Don't let your Lead character be all good, or your opposition all bad.
- *Emotion!* That's what your readers want! Even more than technique or plot. You must be moved in order to move your readers. *Write with emotion!*
- Always write lists of possibilities. Search for originality.
- Use at least one sense impression (hear, taste, see, feel, smell, emotion) on every page.
- Don't ever let a coincidence *help* a main character get out of trouble.
- As Robert Newton Peck once said, "So much of successful fiction hinges on one simple ploy: discomfort."

- Keep a novel journal as you write, jotting down what you learn and what works. This will be invaluable to you as your career proceeds.
- Learn always about the craft, but when you write, write like Fast Eddie Felson played pool in *The Hustler*, fast and loose. When you revise, revise slow and cool.

The Trick That Cannot Be Explained

When I was in college I got into magic. Close-up magic to be precise, the best kind. Cards, coins, cups and balls. All done right there on a table in front of a few people.

I got to hang out at the Magic Castle in Hollywood and talk to some of the legends. People like Francis Carlyle and Charlie Miller.

But the greatest of these was Dai Vernon.

Vernon, by then an octogenarian, is considered by most insiders to be the greatest card magician of the twentieth century. After meeting him, I devoured his books and tried to emulate the master.

In one of his books, co-written with Lewis Ganson, Vernon expounded perhaps his best single trick. He called it "The Trick That Cannot Be Explained," and it's never performed the same way twice. Yet in skilled hands it always produces awe.

The reason this trick cannot be explained is that the magician takes advantage of every technique he knows and applies them to the circumstances as they arise.

For example, he may write a prediction on a sheet of paper, then invite someone from the audience to shuffle the deck and select the card.

Every once in a while the predicted card is chosen, and the magician milks the moment for all it's worth.

But most of the time he has to improvise. He has at his disposal the entire arsenal of magic technique. False shuffles, forces, passes, and so on.

As Vernon said, "The more one knows about card magic the better the effect. It's just quick thinking to decide how to obtain the greatest effect according to the circumstances."

This is the secret of great fiction writing, too. It is why you study the craft in books like this and others, and it is why you should never stop learning. Because the more you know, the more you are able to apply in the infinite range of circumstances that arise when writing a novel. You are a fiction writer. You are a magician. You deal in illusion.

When it works, you're making a happy reader who will exhale and think, *What an amazing story!*

Can this "trick" be explained?

Not entirely. It's a combination of talent and technique, art and skill.

You have all of these, to one degree or another. And you'll keep getting better if you work at it.

So work at it. And go create some magic.

Exercise Answers

CHAPTER FOUR

Exercise 1

Frank ran into the room, <u>hoping</u> Sarah was still there. [The underlined word tells us we are in Frank's head.]

She was, <u>waiting impatiently</u>. [How would Frank know she was impatient? While he could be reaching a conclusion based on observation, we don't have the observation. We have really switched to Sarah's interior life.] "Quick," he said, "we've got to get out of here!"

Sarah <u>sighed</u>. [This is something either character can perceive, so it would fit either POV.] "What is it this time?"

"The cops. They're coming." *<u>Why couldn't she just do what he said?</u>* [A thought, so we are in Frank's POV again.] He went to the window and looked down at the street, watching for cop cars.

<u>Sarah got up from the easy chair</u> [If Frank is looking out the window, how can he know Sarah got up from the chair?] and said, "You're paranoid, you fool. It's your meds." <u>It was always the meds with him, every time</u>. [This is Sarah's thought.]

Frank spun around <u>as the first black-and-white pulled up to the curb and stopped</u>. [How can Frank see this if he has spun away from the window?]

"It's not paranoia if everyone is after you!" he screamed. "Look at me when I talk to you."

I'll look at you when I'm good and ready, <u>Sarah thought</u>. [Obvious switch.] She walked into the kitchen. <u>She was a lovely woman of thirty, popular among her friends. Just not with her husband at the moment.</u> [Now who is thinking this? Sounds like the author! Sarah is probably not going to be thinking so self-consciously.]

<u>Another black-and-white pulled up in front of the apartment building</u>. [Who sees this? The author again, not either character.]

<u>Frank and Sarah heard the bullhorn</u>. [Now we have a simultaneous POV! Never, never do this.] "We know you're in there! Come out with your hands up."

<u>They freaked</u>. [Simultaneous.]

<u>Sarah knew this meant prison</u>. [Sarah's POV.]

<u>Frank knew</u> what Sarah knew, [Frank's POV.] <u>because he was omniscient</u>. [Author intrusion again!]

In this clip, we had the following POV switch:

Frank ran into the room, hoping Sarah was still there.
She was, waiting impatiently.

We saw that by using the word *impatiently*, we went from what Frank, the original POV character, could actually perceive into what Sarah could perceive.

So how can we convey the same sense but stay consistent? By staying in Frank's head and seeing only what he can see:

Frank ran into the room, hoping Sarah was still there.
She was, arms folded, tapping her foot.

That's *showing*. And it's preferred to the following:

Frank ran into the room, hoping Sarah was still there.
She was, looking impatient.

That's *telling*, but it's acceptable when it's a small beat like this.
We also had:

"The cops. They're coming." Why couldn't she just do what he said? He went to the window and looked down at the street, watching for cop cars.
Sarah got up from the easy chair ...

And note that Frank, if he's looking out the window, would not have been able to see Sarah getting out of the chair. How to remedy that? Get in Frank's head and know what he's seeing, then add some link that would alert him:

"The cops. They're coming." Why couldn't she just do what he said? He went to the window and looked down at the street, watching for cop cars.

He heard a scuffing sound and turned. Sarah was standing now, looking right at him.

Exercise 2

I walked into the deli, looking for her. The place was packed, the people busy with their own food and <u>own problems</u>. [Frank could see people busy with food, but not what they're thinking. Some of them could be happy. If this is just a conclusion he has reached about human beings in general, he'd have to explain that more clearly as the narrator.]

Then I saw her. She had her back to me, sitting in a booth by the wall.

<u>With a determined look</u> [Frank cannot see his own look.] I went to the booth and sat across from her.

<u>She was not pleased</u>. [This is a conclusion, not based on anything Frank has seen. We will sometimes accept this as a shorthand for something the character sees. Still, it's better to let the actions and dialogue do the work.]

"How you doing, Sarah?" I said.

"How do you think I'm doing?" She shook her head disgustedly. [This is clunky—the use of the adverb—but it is not strictly a violation. Frank is describing how she shook her head.]

<u>A waiter with a plate of scrambled eggs came up behind me</u>, said, [Frank couldn't see the plate or the eggs if the waiter came up from behind] "I see you've got a friend," and put the plate in front of Sarah.

"I'll have coffee," I said.

<u>Coffee is one of those products with a fascinating history. It was primarily known in the Muslim world, but gradually made its way to Europe by way of the Dutch. It was in the Dutch East Indies that European coffee was largely grown. Its health benefits have been debated, but current scholarship indicates that moderate use is beneficial</u>. [This is author intrusion, unless Frank has a very good story reason for including this information. Even then, this does not sound like the character.]

<u>Sarah didn't like having company</u>. [Again, this might be Frank's assessment, but better to let the scene show us.] "What are you doing here?"

"I came to find out what you know," I said, my <u>blue eyes flashing</u>. [Frank cannot see his own eyes flashing.]

Sarah reached in her purse and <u>fumbled for the key</u>. [Frank cannot see what she's fumbling for in her purse.] She tossed it on the glass table, where it clanked in front of me.

"That's all you need to know," she said.

CHAPTER FIVE

Exercise 1

When the sun came up, <u>Sam</u> [POV character, because he's named and the next word is *thought*.] thought about driving over to Roz's and getting Heather himself. His wife talked him out of it, and he knew she was right. This thing needed some natural flow.

Besides, with no sleep, he couldn't be sure he'd be rational or understanding. He might end up chasing a dog down the street, or biting a mailman.

So he went into the office. But working was like slogging up a muddy hill in ankle weights. Sam tried to clear out the brain cobwebs with a triple latte, but after the early morning run in with Heather, anything he tried to concentrate on was a boulder he could barely move. *Call me Sisyphus.*

There was one thing he decided, though, and there was no going back in his mind. He finished his coffee and went to Lew's office.

"Hey, what's up, pard?" Lew was twiddling a pencil in his right hand as he tapped at his keyboard with the other.

"<u>I can't do it, Lew</u>." [This is where we pick up the objective. He had decided to go into Lew's office. But why? Now we see it is to deliver the news that he can't give up on a lawsuit.]

"Do what?"

"Give up on Harper. I'm taking it all the way."

<u>Lew threw the pencil on the desk</u>. "That's disappointing." [The action and dialogue establish Lew as the opposition in this scene.]

"I'm sorry. That's just the way it's going to be."

"Just like that?"

"I've been thinking about this a long time."

"So we don't make decisions together anymore?"

"You wanted to take the decision away from me, Lew. You made the pronouncement that it was up to me, but you didn't really want me to stay on this case. But I took it on, and it's my obligation as a lawyer—"

"Will you stop with the law school ethics? You're not a One-L."

"I happen to believe in what I'm doing."

Lew shook his head. "I'm not pleased. But I think you already knew I wouldn't be." He was silent for a moment. "<u>All right. Do what you have to do. But we are not waiving our fee</u>. [The outcome is an OK from Lew, but not without a condition.] Now get out of here and go do some work, will you?"

Work. Yes. Sam would do what he always had in the past—work his tail off. He was never the smartest one in his class at law school, he knew that. But he made sure nobody would outwork him, and nobody did.

He was going to work at getting his daughter back, getting justice for Sarah Harper, and making life come out even again. Raw effort, that would do it.

Exercise 2

This is clunky writing to begin with—the overuse of the word *cold* and the inclusion of meaningless details. While you may want to start a scene this way sometime, for pacing purposes, use this as an opportunity to cut to the chase. What would you do to get things going a little faster? Here are three suggestions:

John felt the bump before he heard the scream. He stopped the car and jumped out.

The old man lay motionless on the driveway.

Snow was everywhere, and the wind ripped right through John's coat.

*

"No," John said. "Don't be dead. Please don't be dead."

He hadn't seen the old man, just felt the bump and heard the scream. He'd just been backing out of the driveway. What was the old man doing there? Didn't he see him?

Snow was everywhere, and the wind ripped right through John's coat.

*

Death came cold and in the snow.

John was only backing out. He'd tell the cops that. He wasn't doing anything but backing out into the bitter cold of morning.

CHAPTER SIX

Exercise 1

Note: This is only one way to do it. There are lots of possibilities.

"Good evening."

"What'd you just say?"

"I didn't know you were coming."

"I got an invitation."

"Wonderful. Nice night, isn't it?"

"What's nice about it?"

"Don't you just love it when the breeze holds the scent of honeysuckle?"

"Oh sure."

Exercise 3

Franklin turned to me and read from his page, "I am certain that my fellow Americans expect that on my induction into the Presidency I will address them with a candor and a decision—"

"Stop right there," I said.

"What's wrong, dear?" he said.

"It's pretentious, is what it is."

"Just listen, will you?"

I sat and folded my arms.

Franklin lit a cigarette, then said, "With a condor and a decision which the present situation of our people impel."

He looked at me over his glasses. "You like that? *Impel?*"

"Go on," I said.

"This is preeminently the time to speak the truth, the whole truth, frankly and boldly. Nor need we shrink from honestly facing conditions in our country today. This great Nation will endure as it has endured, will revive—"

"Am I bothering anyone?"

It was Hull, barging in as usual.

"Yes," Franklin said. "This is not the time."

"When would you suggest?" Hull pulled himself upright.

"After I reassure the nation." Franklin winked at me.

Shaking his head, Hull backed out of the office.

"That was good," I said. "Put a little of that in the speech."

"Yes, yes, now listen. Where was I. Oh yes. And will prosper. So, first of all, let me assert my firm belief that the only thing we have to fear is the year ahead."

"Ugh," I said.

"What?"

"The year ahead? That's what we have to fear?"

"It looks bleak."

I stood and went to the desk. Without waiting for reaction I grabbed the pages from his hand, took up a pen and started scratching.

"What on earth are you doing?" Franklin said.

"Quiet."

I finished and showed him the pages. He snatched them, harrumphed, and started reading. A slight smile curved his mouth. "Fear itself. That's good. That's very good."

Another knock. From behind the door, "Franklin?"

"It's Eleanor," Franklin said. "Quick. Behind the curtain."

CHAPTER EIGHT

Exercise 1

Don walked into the bar. The smell of stale beer and sweat assaulted his nostrils. Just kill me now, he thought.

Yip yip yip!

Don jumped back. A poodle the size of a jug bared its teeth at him.

He kicked the dog, sending it *yipping* back from whence it came.

"How dare you," a woman said. She sat at a table, holding the dog's leash. She must have weighed three hundred pounds. She might have been fifty, but the years had been packed on. The jowls on her face had their own jowls.

"Why don't you control that mutt?" Don said.

"I beg your pardon," the woman said.

"Take that thing outside before I use it to floss my teeth."

The woman gasped. "Joe! Joe, will you come over here please?"

From behind the bar stepped a young guy with shoulders as wide as the bar top. His steps sounded like Godzilla's.

"Problem, Mrs. Hennessy?" Joe said.

"This man kicked Fluffy," Mrs. Hennessy said.

Joe looked at Don and shook his head. "I'm afraid I'm gonna have to ask—"

"Me to leave," Don said. "Yeah, sure."

Exercise 2

John slammed his fist through the drywall.

*

John put his head in his hands.

*

Mary walked in and slumped in her favorite chair, an old recliner.

*

"You jerk!" Mary paced, waving her arms. "You have ruined any chance we had at happiness. You and your insistence on making everything a joke. Here's a clue, dude. Everything's not a joke. You're the joke. And if you don't grow up now, I'm out of here."

About the Author

 James Scott Bell is a best-selling novelist (*Try Dying*, *Presumed Guilty*) and the author of *Write Great Fiction: Plot & Structure* (Writer's Digest Books). He lives and writes in Los Angeles. For more information, visit his website at www.jamesscottbell.com.

Index